Dr Lawrence E. Shapiro, Ph.D. is considered one of America's leading child psychologists and parenting experts. A pioneer in teaching children emotional intelligence skills through play, Dr Shapiro's techniques are used by thousands of counsellors and therapists. His parenting books have been translated into more than fifteen languages.

How to Understand the Secret Language of Children

Dr Lawrence E. Shapiro

SIMON &
SCHUSTER

LONDON · NEW YORK · SYDNEY · TOKYO · SINGAPORE · TORONTO · DUBLIN

A VIACOM COMPANY

First published in Great Britain by Simon & Schuster UK Ltd, 2003
A Viacom Company

1 3 5 7 9 10 8 6 4 2

Simon & Schuster UK Ltd
Africa House
64–78 Kingsway
London WC2B 6AH

www.simonsays.co.uk

Simon & Schuster Australia
Sydney

A CIP catalogue record for this book is
available from the British Library

ISBN 0-7432-0764-5

Typeset by Palimpsest Book Production Limited,
Polmont, Stirlingshire
Printed and bound in Great Britain by
The Bath Press, Bath

The names and facts used as examples in this
book were fictionalised to protect the
confidentiality of the children and families.

To my wife, Beth Shapiro,
for her constant support and love

Acknowledgements

Let me begin by thanking the professionals who have helped bring this book to fruition. My agents Marilyn Allen and Bob DiForio have been supportive from the first time that they heard about the idea. My editor from the United States, Hillel Black, has been instrumental in helping me make the book both practical and readable. My editor from Simon & Schuster UK, Cassandra Campbell, has been unwavering in both her enthusiasm and her patience, and thanks also to Helen Gummer. I would also like to thank Robin Morris and Beth Shapiro for their illustrations.

Next I'd like to thank all of the many family, friends and colleagues who have given me much appreciated encouragement in writing this book and in all of my endeavours to help parents help children: Frances Shapiro, Jessica Lamb-Shapiro, Ed Werz, Karen Schaeder, Jeanne Mangels, Joan Rondano, Beth Ann Marcozzi, Mark Tracten, David Greenwald and many others.

Finally, I'd like to thank the countless parents and children who have inspired my work and enriched my life.

– Lawrence E. Shapiro, Ph.D.

Contents

Introduction

The Secret Is Out

Few people would argue that open communication between a parent and a child is one of the most important ingredients in building a bond of warmth and intimacy. When children feel that they are understood and are confidently guided by their parents through life's hills and valleys, they develop a sense of security and self-confidence that forms the basis of their self-worth. In our increasingly complex and stressful world, psychologists have begun to feel that parents who find a way to communicate effectively with their children at an early age are more likely to raise children who are well-adjusted and who are less likely to suffer from the vast array of emotional and relationship problems that affect so many adults.

This is hardly a new idea. Nearly every parenting book you read emphasizes the importance of open communication with children. Yet very few books will tell you that talking to your child is only a small part of emotional communication. According to the psychological research, only about 10 per cent of our emotional communication is expressed in our words, the other 90 per cent comes from the behaviours that accompany the words: gestures, eye contact, posture, voice tone and inflection, and so on. Ask any expert on communication – negotiators, barristers, politicians, sales people, customer service staff – about how they 'read' other people and they will tell you that we all communicate in this secret language. This secret language conveys our meaning much louder than our words.

A psychologist will tell you that this secret language can tell you not just what your child is really thinking, but also that it reveals your youngster's deepest fears and conflicts, as well as their hidden needs and wishes. The secret language is a language that unlocks the door to a child's emotional development and yet parents hardly know that it exists.

From the moment of his birth your child begins to speak to you through the secret language of non-verbal communication and without even thinking about it you respond. But even when your child begins to speak words and sentences, the secret language remains the basis of his or her communication. As you will see in the many examples throughout this book, parents who know the secret language are more confident about responding to their children and guiding their growth. They know when their child is telling the truth or when their youngster is being evasive. They know when their child is experiencing stress or emotional conflict that he or she does not have the words to explain. And they use the secret language to provide comfort and build a lasting bond with their child.

As you read on, you will also find that the secret language includes many ways of communicating with children. Like other professionals who help children with emotional problems, I know that children do not have the words to talk openly about their innermost feelings, nor do the words that we use with them provide a great deal of comfort. The language of emotions is not a language of words, so when I want to help children understand and cope with their problems, I speak to them through their art, through their stories and dreams, and particularly through their play. And this is surely something that you will want to learn, too.

What's the big secret?

Over twenty-five years ago, when I was training to be a child psychologist, I would have considered a book like this one heresy. As did most of my colleagues, I believed that helping children understand their emotional problems required years of training to learn very sophisticated and subtle techniques. Largely influenced by the psychoanalytic theory of the developing child, a theory which emphasized deep symbolic meanings and unconscious conflicts, it never occurred to me that parents could be taught to unravel the Gordian knot of their child's mind. I see now that I was wrong. Now I believe that no one can better understand their children than their parents. No one is more interested in their health and well-being. Certainly no one spends more time with them – except perhaps teachers, who also should be expert in the secret language. And according to statistics from the National Mental Association, USA, no one is likely to help children with their emotional problems if parents do not. Only about 20 per cent of children with serious problems ever see a professional counsellor or therapist. The rest go unaided.

The growing recognition of childhood emotional and behavioural problems, and the realization that these problems are occurring in younger and younger children, have led many professionals to abandon their conventional methods of seeing young people one at a time in their offices. For many of us, parent training programmes seem to be the most logical and viable way to help children with all kinds of problems. And there is no question that parents can be just as effective at using the secret language to help children as any therapist. Programmes like the Filial Therapy Project developed at Penn State University by Bernard and Louise Guerney have been in use for decades. This programme trains parents in the secret language of play, and within three months, meeting just once a week for coaching, parents can learn to be just as successful in helping their children as professionals who were trained for years.

The secret language is the key to emotional intelligence

Effective emotional communication is the most important characteristic of emotionally intelligent people. When we look at the leaders in business, in our communities and in politics we see people who are successful because they can communicate on an emotional level. They know that the secret language of emotional communication is the foundation of all human relationships. They know how to read it and they know how to speak it.

In 1995 Daniel Goleman's best-selling book *Emotional Intelligence* raised the public's awareness about the importance of emotional communication to success in school, at work and in our relationships. Goleman quoted study after study that showed that emotional intelligence, or EQ, is more important to success than intellectual ability, or what we normally refer to as IQ. When people learn to express their feelings and understand the feelings of others, they get better jobs, have more satisfying relationships, and they are even physically healthier. This is true of political leaders, business leaders and community leaders, as well as just ordinary people.

In recent years, the secret about the importance of emotional intelligence has spread like wildfire through the corporate world. In businesses throughout the world, managers and employees are learning how emotional communication can enhance job productivity, decrease absenteeism and help people find value in both their work and in their homes.

Thousands of schools have also heard about the importance of helping children understand their emotional development. They have begun teaching children and teenagers emotional intelligence skills (also called personal and social education or PSE) as part of their effort to reduce school violence, stem the rising tide of behaviour problems, and reduce high-risk behaviours like cigarette smoking and alcohol use.

But even with the growing awareness of the importance of emotional intelligence, you cannot rely on schools to do this job. Teaching and communicating through the secret language of emotions begin at birth and continue every day of your child's life. Obviously what is taught in school cannot approach the day-to-day influence of a parent.

The secret signs of trouble

Perhaps the most compelling reason for parents to learn the secret language is to detect early signs of emotional or behavioural

problems. Most psychological problems can be prevented or significantly diminished when they are addressed in their formative
stage, even before symptoms appear.

Many books have focused on helping parents recognize the symptoms of psychological problems, but as we shall see parents can
learn how to recognize signs of distress and conflict long before
symptoms appear by understanding children's non-verbal communication, their art, their stories, their play and their friendships.
There is no better argument that underscores the importance of
learning the secret language of children.

By learning the secret language of children, you will also increase
your own emotional intelligence and become much more intuitive
with your children. Knowing the secret language of children enables
parents to become more effective in teaching their children values,
in making them more cooperative and sensitive to others and in
helping them relate better to their peers.

For example, a single mother of a 14-year-old once complained
to me, 'My son looks at me like I'm from another planet. He says
that I have no idea who he is or what his life is about. But he won't
sit down and talk to me for even ten minutes! So how am I supposed to find out who he is?' In fact this boy was telling his mother
exactly who he was, all of the time, but it was apparent that she
had not yet learned how to listen. His choice of clothes, the way he
wore his hair, the music that he listened to, the way he curled himself into a ball on the couch, were all part of his emotional communication to her. These are the ways that all children communicate
their feelings, needs and troubles, yet his mother did not know how
to interpret these messages.

Another couple I know was called into school in the month of
February to learn that their 12-year-old son was about to be expelled.
'I had no idea that he was having trouble,' the father explained to
the headteacher who then took out a report that showed over the
past five months his son was absent from school more than he
attended. 'I had no idea,' the father repeated under his breath. We
can wonder how parents miss so many signs that their children and
teenagers are in trouble, but if we look at the statistics on the mental

health of children, we must assume that this happens in thousands of households every day.

We know that 9 per cent of 11–15-year-olds smoke regularly, 1 in 5 have consumed alcohol in the last week and last year 8,000 children were permanently excluded from school. And many of the parents of these children say to each other or to themselves, 'I had no idea.' In truth, the signs that children and teenagers are struggling are all around them. They are just part of a secret language that they have not yet learned.

The secret language is the best route to enrich your relationship with your child

Perhaps the most important aspect of the secret language is that it will deepen your relationship with your child and it will help you become a more effective parent. Communicating in the secret language of emotions with your child will help you at every age and every stage of your child's development. Parents of infants can feel that they are more attuned to their needs. They can be more responsive to their baby's cries and provide more appropriate stimulation. When parents learn the secret language of their baby, they will be able to speak the only language that their infant knows.

The toddler years can be a frustrating time for some parents. 'No' is usually one of the first ten words that any toddler learns, and it is one that they do not readily forget. But again the secret language can help, because that is really the most important language that your toddler speaks. The secret language will help you understand what your toddler really wants from you, even though he does not have the words to adequately express himself. The secret language will also give you a new way to talk to your toddler and teach him the values and the behaviours that will shape his social and academic success. You cannot do this through words, but through body language, through stories and through play.

For example, once a mother of a 3-year-old came into my office and with a sombre expression told me, 'My daughter needs help and so do I. She is completely taking control of my life! She tells *me* what we are going to eat every night. I tell her that it is her bedtime, and she sends *me* to bed! I have to do whatever she says!'

I looked at the 3-year-old and I looked at the mother (trying not to shake my head in disbelief), and wondered to myself, 'How can this be? How do parents let their little ones get so much power?'

But this mother did not know how to talk to her daughter in the secret language of authority. She did not know that words are not enough to get strong-willed children to respect our rules and behave. So I taught her the secret language that so many parents seem to have forgotten: the language of getting children to behave.

The importance of the secret language does not diminish as your children grow older. Although they increase their vocabulary and their ability to reason, words and logic are rarely enough. Even when your children become teenagers, you will find that knowing the secret language of emotions will help you understand their needs and give you new ways to support them in facing each new challenge.

The secret language is the language of emotional healing

When you learn the secret language of emotional communication you can not only spot the early signs of emotional trouble, but you can help your child learn to cope with and solve his problems. The techniques that psychologists use with children are much simpler than most parents realize. For example, a number of years ago, when I was working as a school psychologist in Castle Rock, Colorado, I received a call from a distraught mother who was concerned that her shy 7-year-old daughter, Amy, was about to have a horribly lonely summer. 'She has no friends because she is so shy,' Amy's mother explained. 'I can't bear to see her spend the entire summer sitting in front of the TV set, when all the other children are running around outside playing.'

Amy had only two more weeks of school, but I promised her mother that I would see Amy at least twice, and that I would try to find something for them both to do over the summer that would help Amy with her shyness. At the end of our second session, I gave Amy a game that I had made for her, which I called the 'Friend Making Game'. The game was a simple board game that I designed just for Amy. I drew a snake pattern of thirty squares with a Start and a Finish square at either end. I drew in ten question marks at random on the home-made board, and I added some pawns and dice to the game. Then I wrote fifty cards that asked game players how they could respond to different social situations. Some of the cards were:

'Abigail was never invited to parties. What should she do?'

'Darren had problems reading and he didn't want his friends to find out? What should he do?'

'Name three things that you think other people like about you.'

The game rules were simple. Players rolled the dice and when they landed on a square with a question mark, they took a question card and responded to it. For a good response a player received two points. The first player to get to the Finish received three extra points. The player with the most points at the end of the game was declared the winner.

Over the last twenty years, I have prescribed hundreds of games like this to help children or their parents learn specific aspects of the secret language (see Part II, The Secret Language of Your Child's Play). In this instance, the game I gave Amy was designed to help her learn basic social skills like inviting a friend over to play, paying a compliment, and selecting activities that she and her friends would enjoy. I asked Amy's mother to play the game with her two or three times a week, and if Amy wanted, to invite some other children over to play it, too.

That September, a few weeks after school began, Amy's mother called and with barely a word of introduction, she exclaimed, 'Your game worked like magic! I can't believe that this is the same child. At the beginning of the summer Amy had no friends. Now she has three or four. I've lost count. She is so much happier now. She couldn't wait to get back to school to spend more time with her new friends.'

I was delighted to hear that the game 'worked like magic'. I am not a magician, however I do believe that parents can be. When you use the right tools and techniques, the secret language of emotions will give you more magic than you will find in any Harry Potter novel. It will give you the ability to help your children overcome both common and serious emotional problems. In Part III, you will learn story techniques that can help you shape your child's moral development and behaviour. In Part IV of this book, you will learn art techniques that can help your child overcome a trauma and prevent it from becoming a determining force in his life. And you will learn how to help your child to use the secret language himself: to stop a bully right in his tracks; to deal with recurrent nightmares; even how to help your son or daughter deal with physical pain and recover from an illness.

But there are no wizard's tricks to learn. These common-sense techniques that I will teach you are as simple as anything you have ever done. And they are fun! All you have to remember is to do them and make them a part of your daily parenting.

In just fifteen minutes a day you can change the course of your child's emotional development

As I will note time and time again throughout this book, you are already aware the secret language exists, at least on a subconscious level. You already read your child's gestures, postures and facial expressions without necessarily being aware that you are doing this. You certainly already know how to play games with your child, and tell stories, and draw pictures, all of which are important parts of your child's secret language. Now you will learn how to use these simple pleasures of childhood in the same way that psychologists use them, to help children learn about their feelings and the feelings of others.

But getting you to do them on a regular daily basis is the hard part. Like any other language, the secret language of emotions takes practice; daily practice if it is to make a difference in your child's development. Helping your child with his emotional health is not a sometimes thing, any more than good nutrition, good oral hygiene, or having your child wash his or her hands before a meal is a sometimes thing. As I have said elsewhere (*An Ounce of Prevention*), communicating in the secret language of emotions with your child can prevent some of the most serious problems of childhood, from eating disorders to academic underachievement, *but only if you use the language every day*. Just fifteen minutes a day is all it takes, but that fifteen minutes is crucial to success.

So before you begin to use the secrets that you will learn in this book, make a commitment to practising emotional communication with your child or teenager everyday, just the way that you would commit yourself to helping your child learn multiplication tables or a new sport. Throughout the book, I will suggest many exercises and activities that you can use with your child and I urge you to try as many of them as you can.

You do not need to set a specific time of day to practise emotional communication, because as you will see the secret language can take many forms, from a bedtime story to a word game that you play in the car on your way to the supermarket. I assure you that this small amount of time that you give each day to communicating in the secret language will pay dividends throughout your child's lifetime.

Part I

The Secret Language of Babies

Chapter 1

Babies Really Can Talk

Parents are pre-programmed to understand what their baby wants and needs simply by watching him and listening to him. For example, a 6-month-old might turn his head and purse his lips in a certain way and his mother responds, 'Oh, you want your bottle?' The baby's look of delight and eager acceptance of the bottle tells his mother, 'You're right, Mummy, I'm dying of thirst! Thanks! You're the greatest!' The mother's accurate reading of her baby's body language is both confirmed and rewarded by his immediate pleasure.

Most parents have very good intuition about what their baby is trying to communicate to them, but some babies are more difficult to 'read' than others. Also parents vary in the amount of time that they spend with their baby. If you work and your baby is taken care of by someone else during the day, you may sometimes feel out of touch with your baby's needs. This is particularly true if you have a 'difficult' baby. Margaret, the mother of a 6-week-old, complained to her own mother, 'I don't think my baby likes me. He doesn't seem happy when I come into the room. He often cries when I pick him up. I feel like I'm always doing the wrong thing.'

There is no question that some babies are very easy and even-tempered and others are more fussy and easily irritated. Difficult babies do not sleep well and often have eating problems. They cry much more than other babies and their cries tend to be more shrill and discordant. Parents of difficult babies need to be more conscious of the secret language of their children. The bad news is that your baby's temperament is fairly stable as he develops. Difficult babies tend to be more difficult children and even more difficult adolescents. The good news is that this is not always the case. I tell parents that their baby's personality is about 49 per cent nature and 51 per cent nurture, which means that they have a better than even chance of changing their child's difficult nature. (No one really knows the percentage of nature vs. nurture in determining a child's personality, but I am a firm believer in the power of positive thinking.) If you have an 'easy' baby you will find that understanding his secret language will make him even more fun to be with and cherish. If you have a more difficult baby, then you will find that using the secret language is an essential part of making him more flexible and receptive to your efforts. We will begin by examining how you learn more about your baby just by being a careful observer.

You are on baby watch

It is hard not to look at a baby. In fact, it goes against our very nature. When we pass a baby (or even a baby animal) we almost always take a few more minutes to look at their face and expression.

Yet even though we love to look at babies, sometimes we do not see what they are trying to tell us. Cindy, the mother of a 3-month-old girl, complained to her husband: 'You have no idea what it's like keeping her entertained every waking moment. And when she starts to get cranky, nothing I do seems to help.' But Cindy did not see that her daughter was actually being over-stimulated. Cindy would play with her baby until her little one could not take it any more and then when the baby cried, Cindy would feel inadequate and play some more. But her baby did not want to play any more, she wanted to be left alone for a little time. Cindy was certainly trying to care for her baby in the best way that she knew how, but she was not seeing what her baby was trying to tell her.

To begin learning how to understand the secret language of your baby you must first learn how to be a careful observer. This probably seems like obvious advice, and yet many parents are so prone to action – eager to do things for and with their babies – that they do not take the time to really look at them. Objective observation is the first 'professional secret' that you must learn to communicate and interact on a deeper level with your baby. But be forewarned that this is a skill that may take a little time to learn. When I trained to be a psychologist, I spent hundreds of hours observing children of all ages, and it took me many months to feel that I was really a careful observer. It is even more difficult to learn to be objective about your own child. Sometimes we project our own feelings or anxieties on to our children and look for things that are not really there. I will never forget one woman who came to me for a consultation about her 6-month-old son. 'He reminds me so much of my father,' the young mother confided, 'and my father was an alcoholic. Is there any way I can tell if he is going to have a drinking problem too?' I assured this mother that at six months of age, the only drinking this baby had to worry about was drinking his milk and suggested that she might want some counselling about her relationship with her father.

Other parents may not be objective about their infants because they are simply too worried about them. When you are always concerned about your infant's safety and well-being, it is sometimes hard to think about the subtler aspects of your child's development.

Whatever the reasons that might make it difficult to see your baby objectively, careful observation is a skill well worth learning. Here are some simple guidelines to help you practise.

1. Pretend that you are watching something other than your baby; as if you were observing some creature from another planet. This will help you let go of any preconceptions that you have of how he or she should act.

2. Limit your observation to no more than three minutes. Objective observation is hard work and takes a great deal of concentration. You can learn a lot about your baby in just a few minutes.

3. Train yourself to observe in a methodical way. For example, start by observing him from the head down, noting what each part of the body (head, upper torso, arms, hands, lower torso, legs, feet) is 'saying', and whether the various parts are all saying the same thing.

4. Take note of the context when you observe your baby. When
    you observe your child you should look not just at your baby
    but everything that affects him: the time of day, the room tem-
    perature, the light, the sound. Your baby uses all of his senses
    to make sense of the world, and you should use all of yours.

The first thing that you will be looking for are what scientists refer
to as macro-signs. These are the obvious signs that include facial
expression, gestures, posture and movement. Parents do not really
think about the macro-signs they are constantly reading in their
infant, but they could describe them if asked. If a stranger asked,
'How did you know your son wanted milk?' a mother could explain,
'Well, he turned his head towards the table where I usually place
his bottle to cool, and then he raised his eyes and pursed his lips
and gave me the look I used to get when he was nursing.' It is easy
for this mother to describe the secret signal her baby gives when he
is hungry because she has received and responded correctly to it
hundreds of times. Macro-signs are obvious to parents, but they may
be a secret to the people who are not intimate with a baby, such as
a baby-sitter or a new caregiver at the child's nursery.

There is also another much more subtle form of non-verbal language that babies 'speak', but parents are not consciously aware of
it. This type of body language is called 'micro-signs'. Examples of
micro-signs are the colour of a baby's skin when she cries, how she
clenches her fist when she is in pain, or the way her eyes dilate when
she is confused. Micro-signs are very subtle, and take practice to see,
but you are probably already aware of them on some level. Micro-
signs are what we commonly refer to as intuition; the 'feeling' that
we have about people, that we can not always explain. Our emotional brain reacts to micro-signs, even when the thinking part of
our brain does not. As you learn to recognize even some of them in
your baby, you will be much more attuned to his day-to-day needs.

TRY IT

Using the chart below will give you a start on learning to understand the non-verbal language of your baby at six months and older. Continue the chart as you learn to recognize other macro- and micro-signs of your baby and what they mean.

What you see	What it means
Beating of baby's arms back and forth.	A sign of frustration or anger.
Pointing and gazing.	A desire or intention to go in a particular direction or to get something from a particular place.
Arms raised when your baby is otherwise motionless.	Uncertainty. Also a desire to be picked up.
Reaching out his hands with his palms turned up and with head tilted slightly.	A message of appeasement. Your baby wants to say, 'I'm sorry,' or 'Let's be friends.'
Arms held stiffly at his side.	Often a sign of anxiety or fear.
Hands clasped in front of him.	In babies over nine months, this can be a sign of submission. Watch for this sign when older children are around.
Hands over eyes.	This can be part of a game, or a way to get attention, but it can also be a sign of embarrassment or anxiety.
Massaging or rubbing her hands together.	This can be a sign of anxiety.
Chewing or sucking on fingers.	This is done for pleasure in younger babies, but after twelve months it can be a sign of anxiety.
Prolonged eye contact.	This is a 'welcome' sign. Your baby is inviting you to play.

Breaking eye contact after gazing at you.	When a baby breaks eye contact by moving his head to the side, he may just want to be left alone for a few minutes. When he breaks eye contact by gazing down, this can be a sign of submission or defeat.
Stroking or butting of the head.	This is a sign of frustration or anxiety.
Inclined head.	This is a friendship sign and is usually combined with a warm smile and direct gaze. It is the way that babies say 'please' or 'Do you want to play?'
Head lowered with chin tucked in.	This may be a sign of anger, when accompanied by clenched fists and other muscle tension.
Head tilted back.	Baby is relaxed, playful, friendly.
Stamping his foot.	In children over twelve months this is a sign to you that your baby needs attention or he is angry.
Clapping.	A sign of glee and joy.

Understanding your baby's cries

Nobody likes to hear a crying baby and that is the way that nature intended it to be. A baby's cry is his most potent way of speaking to his parents and insisting on their attention. When your baby cries, he demands a response.

The cries of a baby are stressful for anyone to hear. On hearing your baby cry, your heart rate will increase, your blood pressure will rise, and you may begin to have a sense of anxiety and foreboding. Every cell in your brain and body screams, 'Do something! Quick!' But how do you know just what that 'something' is?

Babies cry to tell you about their different needs, and they have different variations of crying for each one. Scientists who study the nature of baby cries use sophisticated sound equipment to record subtle differences in pitch, frequency and length of pauses. They have determined that a baby's cry contains not one sound, but a combination of several sounds made all at once. While basic baby cries that indicate hunger, rage or pain share certain characteristics, every baby has a unique cry, which can be distinguished from that of every other baby.

Most of the time parents know exactly what their infant wants when she cries. A few months ago we had a visit from some friends, Joan and her husband, Bob, and their 3-month-old son, Patrick. Patrick is a quiet baby, even-tempered and full of smiles. But about an hour into their visit, he started to cry. Within moments Joan said, 'He's hungry,' and almost before she had finished the sentence, Bob was reaching for the baby's bottle. Within three minutes Patrick was in his father's arms, happily slurping on a bottle of milk.

Parents of newborns typically figure out exactly what their babies want when they cry within a few weeks. They learn to distinguish the sound of one cry from another, but they also use visual cues to 'read their baby's mind', and, of course, they know their baby's schedule. Another couple, Frank and Sharon, were visiting with their 1-month-old baby, Amanda. Almost as soon as the family entered the living room, Amanda began to wail. Without pausing, Frank and Sharon turned to each other and went through a quick checklist of Amanda's needs.

Frank: 'When was she last fed?'

Sharon: 'Just an hour ago.'

Frank: 'When was she last changed?'

Sharon: [reaching inside Amanda's nappy] 'She's not wet.'

Frank: 'Is she tired?'

Sharon: 'She fell asleep for ten minutes in the car, but that probably wasn't enough.'

Both parents gazed for a moment at their unhappy daughter.

Sharon: 'I think she's tired. Let's try to put her down.'

Frank laid out a portable mattress in a quiet corner of the living room. Sharon placed Amanda on her side in the middle of it and began to rub her back. In less than a minute Amanda stopped crying. Five minutes later she was fast asleep.

Parents like Bob and Joan or Frank and Sharon will rarely think about how they learned to interpret their baby's cries. They just know what they mean. But some parents are not as in tune with their babies. And some babies are not as easy to soothe. Many infants spend a significant amount of the day with caregivers other than their parents, who will not have the same intuitive bond or who might not be as in tune with the infant. In these situations, adults must go beyond their intuition and take a more analytical approach to determine how to respond to a baby's cries.

Dr Barry Lester, Professor of Psychiatry and Human Behavior at Brown University, Rhode Island, has studied the cries of babies for more than twenty years and has found that an individual infant may have as many as twelve distinct cries. Although there will always be some variation from infant to infant, the following are characteristics of what different cries mean.

'I'm hungry'

This is the most common cry you will hear. It typically begins with a rhythmical cry or whine when your baby first starts to feel like he has an empty stomach. Within a few minutes, you may hear a short explosive cry, followed by a pause while your baby catches his breath. Then you will hear more cries, which will probably get louder and louder until your baby gets fed. Your knowledge of when your baby was last fed will probably be your best guide at determining whether you are hearing a cry of hunger, but sometimes parents are surprised to hear this cry just a short while after a feed. With young babies, it is recommended that you let your baby establish her own feeding schedule. If you are breastfeeding, and your child never seems to be fully satisfied, you should check with your doctor or health visitor. If you are feeding by a bottle and your baby does not finish it, first make sure that the hole in the teat is not too small, requiring too much sustained effort from your baby.

'I'm eating too much!' (when your baby is overfed)

Since hunger is the most common cry, feeding is often the first response that parents give to their baby's wails. It is important to remember that until a baby is six to eight weeks old, he does not know how to regulate drinking from a bottle and he will suck on it until it runs dry, even though he has had more than he needs. Sometimes older babies will also take the bottle or breast for comfort, even though hunger is not really what is making them unhappy. But babies have small stomachs and immature digestive systems, so if they overeat, then they are likely to be sick and start crying again. A baby that brings his food up and is niggly shortly after meals is telling you that more frequent and smaller feeding may be what is needed.

'I'm tired' (the cry of the tired baby)

When your baby is sleepy or overtired he may show signs of being fussy rather than just crying. His cries will more likely fluctuate in tone and volume and be arrythmical. Other non-verbal signs will also be consistent in your baby. He may bat his ears, suck his fingers, or rub his eyes. Since he wants to go to bed, he will likely resist being distracted by your efforts to play with him and will usually turn away. When you try other ways to comfort him, he may become more agitated, because all he really wants to do is to nod off. As your baby gets into a regular sleep schedule, you will recognize the way he communicates that he is tired, and when he just wants to be left alone. Most babies will cry themselves to sleep within five to ten minutes when nothing else is bothering them.

'Ouch!' (the cry of pain)

Babies cry pretty much the same way whether they are experiencing external or internal pain. This cry begins without warning and it is loud, long and shrill. Your baby will let out a good long wail of pain and then take a long pause, like he is holding his breath. When he cries again, his body will also tell you that something is really wrong. His body will be tense, and his hands and feet will be drawn up. His mouth will be wide open and you will see an expression of intense discomfort on his face.

The first thing you will want to do is to check for external causes of pain. Is a toe or finger caught in a zip? Does she have a rash? Is her clothing too tight? Often you will have to take off all your child's clothes to check and see that everything is all right.

A cry of internal pain, of course, is more difficult to determine. She may have an ear infection, a sore throat or a stomachache.

If this type of crying continues, you will certainly want to visit your GP, but you will also want to communicate to your doctor what your baby has told you. The physical signs that accompany your baby's pain include redness, swelling, sensitivity to touch, a fever, a change in her bowel movements (including a change in colour or smell), vomiting, noisy, fast or difficult breathing.

Make several copies of the information below to help you more systematically determine the secret meaning of your baby's cries. This may be particularly useful to share with baby-sitters, child minders or other caregivers who are not as intimate with your baby as you are. The more that you can tell a doctor, the more likely he or she will be able to prescribe a remedy that will alleviate your baby's discomfort. We will explore this more thoroughly in Chapter 3, How Babies Call for Help.

'Can't you see I've had enough' (the cry of irritation)

Babies get irritable when they are tired or over-stimulated, just the way that adults do. This cry is usually long and hard, and unresponsive to calming methods that usually work. This type of cry usually comes just before it is time for a nap or for bedtime. After a few attempts at trying to calm your baby down, just let him alone for a few minutes. His crying may be a form of tension release and after a while you should see him start to calm down. After he has quieted himself down, he may respond to a gentle massage or to the bottle or breast.

'I feel sick' (when a cry indicates a fever or illness)

This may be a whiny and nasal cry, similar to the cry of pain, but weaker. Your baby will look flushed and may be warm to the touch. Consult your GP if the fever continues or if other symptoms appear.

'Change me!' (your baby is wet or soiled)

With the increasing absorbency of disposable nappies many babies do not feel particularly uncomfortable when they are wet. Other babies will cry loudly and wail as if they are in pain. (Sometimes, of course, your baby is in pain, if the urine is irritating a rash.) Checking your baby's nappy is one of the first things that most parents do when they hear their baby cry.

'I'm afraid!' (the baby's cry of fear)

The cry of fear is typically sudden, loud and piercing, followed by gasping for breath. Some babies are much more sensitive to noise, temperature or being startled than others. Usually this cry subsides almost as suddenly as it begins.

'What do you think you are doing!' (the cry of anger or frustration)

Different babies have different frustration levels, just like different adults. Some babies get frustrated very easily and they let you know it. Different babies have different reasons for being angry (again, just like us). One baby gets furious if a shirt is pulled over his head. Another baby gets furious if her dummy drops out of her mouth. A third baby, just can not stand to wear a hat! Your baby's cry of frustration or anger will be revealed on his face and in his movements. His mouth may be drawn up into what is best described as a snarl. He may arch his back or turn his face to the side to show you that he does not like what you are doing. Usually these cries are short-lived when whatever is frustrating him is over.

'Pay attention to me' (cry of boredom or loneliness)

Patty put 9-month-old Elizabeth down for her nap while she prepared lunch for her neighbour. After five minutes, the neighbour was disconcerted at the baby's continual crying and hesitantly asked Patty. 'Don't you want to see if something is wrong?' 'Oh, no,' the mother replied, concerned more about pouring the coffee, 'Elizabeth is just faking it. She wants to be up with us at lunch, but it is really time for her nap.'

What Patty really means is that she feels that Elizabeth is trying to get her attention with her cry and that her baby's cry was manufactured and not a sincere sign of need. She believed that her baby was crying just to get attention, and she may have been right, but babies do not try to manipulate us, they just want what they want. A baby who is crying because she is bored or lonely is just trying to fill a need and when you understand what she is trying to tell you, you can choose the best way to respond to this need.

When you trust your own instincts, and with a little trial and error, you will figure out just the right things to do to respond to your baby's cries. The exception to this is when your baby cries too much, or when you do not feel that you know how to calm her down. The litmus test of whether you need to go beyond your intuition and analyse the communication behind your baby's cries is simple: you need to respond to your baby within a minute and a half and have him calmed down within ten minutes. Why do I say a minute and a half? Because research has shown that the quicker you respond to your young baby's cries (under six months), the quicker your baby will calm down. At least one study has shown that when adults take longer than a minute and a half to establish contact with the infant, it can take from two to four times longer to calm the baby down.

The ten-minute rule is based more on a gut feeling than on research. There is a wide variation in how much babies normally cry. Babies who cry up to three hours a day are still considered within the normal range. But to me, and I think to anyone who is holding a wailing baby, ten minutes is a lot of crying. Within ten minutes of reaching your baby, you should be able to provide some initial soothing to comfort him, and you should be able to relieve him from his distress. If you find that you or another caregiver cannot calm your baby down in ten minutes, then there is definitely a communication gap, and I would recommend taking a closer look at the meaning of your baby's cries.

Studying what your baby's cries mean will undoubtedly help you to be more connected to your baby. It will give him a sense of security and the sense that his needs are being met. And it will give you a sense of confidence that you are becoming more and more sensitive to the secret language of your baby every day. But do not expect too much of yourself. Studies tell us that at least four out of five babies cry for as much as fifteen minutes to an hour a day without any explainable reason. These crying periods typically occur in the evening, perhaps because baby is worn out from the stimulation of the day, or perhaps because this is just a more hectic time for most parents and your baby wants his share of your attention. Some babies cry themselves to sleep just because that is the way they react to fatigue and there is nothing you really need to do. For whatever reason your baby cries, or even if he cries for no reason at all, you can be assured that by seven or eight months your baby will find different ways to communicate with you.

Chapter 2

A New Way to Look at and Listen to Your Baby

Five-month-old Sara has just slurped down her bottle, had her bottom powdered and her nappy changed, and it is now time for her to get dressed. Her mother is in a hurry to get to the supermarket so that she can get home to start dinner. But instead of wiggling excitedly as she usually does when her mother slips on her coat, Sara whimpers forlornly, and then bursts into inconsolable wails. 'What's wrong?' her mother wonders, thinking that she may have to postpone her trip to the store. 'If only you could talk!'

If only babies could talk! All new parents have this thought at sometime and they eagerly anticipate when their children will begin to speak. They want their children to tell them where something hurts or what they like or do not like to eat. They long for their babies to utter the three words most dear to every parent's heart, 'I love you.'

Parents believe, mistakenly, that they will not really be able to communicate with their children until they can speak at least thirty or forty words at around eighteen months of age. But most parents do not realize that their babies are talking to them all of the time. They are just talking in a language without words. It is the language of touch, the language of cries, the language of facial expression, body position and body tension. It is the secret language of babies.

Although parents may not be consciously aware of it, they also speak the secret language back to their children. Parents and their babies are genetically pre-programmed to know what the other wants and to develop an intimate bond unlike any other. Yet in spite of the fact that communication comes naturally, most parents feel that they don't really understand the emotional needs of their young children. First-time parents are predictably insecure, especially when it comes to the emotional life of their children. According to a poll of more than 1,000 parents conducted by Peter Hart Research Associates, only about a third of parents felt sure that they could tell if their young child's emotional development was about right for his or her age.

When you know the secret language of your infant's facial expressions, posture, movements and cries, you will unlock a new way to understand your baby. The secret language will help you feel closer to your baby and to be more responsive to her needs. Studies suggest that as you communicate more effectively with your baby, you will also be able to provide her with an enriched environment which may in turn stimulate her intellectual growth.

Most importantly, understanding the secret language of your infant will help you in your child's emotional development. In this chapter we will look at three important milestones of your baby's emotional development: the bonding process, where he develops a sense of trust in you and himself; the stimulation process, where your baby learns *how* to learn in the give and take of human interaction; and self-calming, where he learns how to calm his own fears, his anxieties and his temper.

Bonding with your baby through the secret language

Pat and Jean Samuels were both lawyers and they both wanted to continue their careers while raising their family. They decided to hire a live-in nanny to take care of their first child, Lydia. But from the moment that Jean went back to work, when Lydia was just three weeks old, she began to worry if Lydia would love her. Most of the time it was the nanny that fed Lydia, it was the nanny that changed her and it was the nanny that sang her to sleep. Jean started worrying that little Lydia would think of the nanny as her mother and she began resenting the love that they shared. When she was not worrying that Lydia and the nanny would become too close, she worried that the nanny would leave. She thought that the baby might be traumatized to lose someone she depended on so much.

Jean's worries about bonding with her child were unfounded. Babies bond much more easily with adults than most people realize, and early loss is not an irreversible trauma as psychologists once thought. Some of Jean's worries were based on psychological research that just does not apply to most children. For example, just a few decades ago, many psychologists believed that there was a 'window of opportunity' for bonding with a baby that was relatively short. Their thinking was based on the work of Conrad Lorenz, who found that immediately after being hatched, baby geese would follow any moving object and then treat that object like their mother. Lorenz's geese followed a ball, a moving silhouette and him! At the time, Lorenz and others thought that bonding happened during a very brief 'critical time', and that once it happened it was irreversible. Psychologists believed that there was also a critical time that children bonded with their caregivers, and that after this period, they could never have quite the same attachment.

But we now know that infants and toddlers have a much greater capacity for bonding than once suspected. Although infants begin bonding with their parents or other caregivers in the first few hours after birth, their deeper attachment builds over a long period of time and children can have strong bonds with many people. As parents who have adopted older children know, you can develop an attachment with children that is equivalent to a biological parent, when children are eighteen months of age and even older.

The bonding process takes place between children and adults and through the secret language, which for infants is the language of the senses. One of the first ways that babies begin to know and recognize their parents is through their smell. Of the five senses, the sense of smell is the only one that is fully developed at birth, and it is a primary way that babies learn to recognize the first people in their lives. Although your baby will begin to recognize your smell in the first few days of life, you can help this process by not changing perfume, soap or your deodorant.

Another part of the bonding process is the way that you touch your baby. Most of all you just have to trust your instincts about how to hold and touch your baby. Nature has already pre-programmed you to interact with your infant in exactly the right way. For example, in one study of parents of newborns, it was found that nearly every mother caressed her newborn in exactly the same way: first stroking and exploring the baby's fingers and toes and then stroking his back and torso.

But as your baby gets older, you may not feel as comfortable in touching him. Cross-cultural studies of touching show that there is a wide variation of how much parents touch their young children, or indeed each other (people in the UK are generally considered to be 'low-touch' people). These studies also suggest that the more you touch and massage your baby the happier and more content she will be.

If you do not already massage your baby on a regular basis, you might consider making it a part of your daily ritual in speaking the secret language. This is particularly important if you are concerned about spending more intimate time with your baby, or if your child has a temperament that makes him more fractious and irritable. Every caress, nuzzle and kiss you give to your baby is important, but a five or ten minute massage covering every part of his body sends a very special message in the secret language. Infant massage not only fosters trust and confidence between you and your baby, it helps soothe tension, relieve pain and promote sleep. It also stimulates your baby's tactile awareness.

Baby massage is a very natural process, but you need to be aware of a few precautions. When you give your infant a massage, you should use massage oil rather than just your hands, since a lubricant will give your baby a gentler, smoother massage. Avoid using petroleum-based products like baby oil or talcum powder. Organic massage oils are better for babies (e.g., grape seed, sweet almond, coconut oils) because they are easily absorbed by the skin, and help clean the skin of its dead cells, giving your baby a healthy glow. Although these oils should not be ingested, if your baby puts an oily hand into her mouth, they will not be harmful. Few babies have an allergic reaction to these oils, but you should still always test for a skin reaction before using them. Apply the oil to a small area of your baby's skin and leave it for thirty minutes. An allergic reaction will show up as red blotches, which will then disappear within an hour or two. If your child already has known skin allergies, consult your GP or health visitor before trying any oils.

While almost all babies enjoy a massage, it is worth remembering that some babies are more sensitive to touch than others. These infants may enjoy a massage sometimes, but other times it can be annoying to them. Your baby probably will not like a massage if he does not feel well, or if he is overtired.

Before you begin, you should make sure that you are relaxed and your baby is in a good mood. The temperature of the room should be warm. From birth to two months, your baby will respond best to a light massage. With relaxed, well-oiled hands, begin by stroking down the side of your baby's body, from the shoulder over the arm, to the chest, hips and legs. Repeat this for about a minute.

Then with your baby laying on his side, in a clockwise movement, stroke your baby's back. Repeat this again for about a minute. If your baby is happy, you can lay her on her back and gently stroke the front of her body from the shoulders to the feet for a minute or two. If your baby continues to be happy, lay her on her tummy and gently stroke her back, from the shoulders to the spine for a minute or two.

Along with smell, and touch, the sound of your voice is also an important way that your baby learns to know and love you. The more you talk, sing and read to your baby, the more she will know your voice, and associate it with pleasure. Researchers tell us that even in the womb your baby reacts to your voice and your singing (her heart rate actually goes down rather than up), and within a week after birth she will show a marked preference to hearing her mother's voice to any others (this is measured by increased sucking).

Unconsciously, you also give your baby the exact kind of language stimulation that she needs. Have you ever wondered why adults use a silly, singsong and high-pitched voice when they are talking to babies? That is because this type of speech is exactly what babies want to hear. Babies hear the sounds of language most clearly when they hear this baby talk, and the more they hear the faster they will develop their communication skills. So above all, keep talking!

Teaching your baby about emotions through the secret language

You are your baby's first and best teacher, and you stimulate your baby's emotional development through the secret language that you share with your child. With every word, every look and every touch you teach your baby about something important. Babies are born with their brains wired to learn, forming millions of neural connections in the first year of life. Yet even though your baby soaks up knowledge throughout every moment of the day, developmental psychologists still recommend taking ten or fifteen minutes, once or twice a day, to stimulate your baby and teach him about his relationship with you and others and the feelings that he experiences.

Choose a time of day when both you and your baby are alert and ready to play. Sit your baby upright so that his face is in full view and you are both on the same eye level. Your baby should be able to see your hands, arms and upper body.

Now begin. Talk, sing a song, clap your hands, make a face, show your baby a toy, kiss her and tickle her. Just have fun and your baby will have fun and learn. There are many books suggesting ways to play with and entertain your baby, but most of all you can let your natural instincts be your guide. Although you may not realize it, the most common ways that we play with our babies are also the most important to their emotional development. Here are a few of my favourites.

Me and you

What to do: Take a baby-safe mirror and look at it with your baby. Point to your image in the mirror and then your baby's image. Make faces in the mirror and see how your baby responds. See if your baby imitates your face in the mirror, or your reaching towards the mirror.

The message: 'You and I are connected. Look at how much fun we can have together.'

Tick tock clock

What to do: Hold your baby under the arms and gently swing him back and forth like the pendulum of a clock.

The message: 'Let's have an adventure! I won't let you drop! You can trust me to take care of you.'

Where am I?

What to do: Walk around your child's seat, sometimes out of sight, and say 'Where am I?' waiting for your baby to turn and look for you.

The message: 'You can recognize my voice and find me when you need me!'

Peek a boo

What to do: Hide your face behind a handkerchief or other object.

The message: 'Even when I go away and you can't see me, I will always come back.'

Kick the pan

What to do: Hold a tin pie plate just a few inches from your baby's feet, while he lies on his back. Use it as a target for him to kick at. Make a noise and a face when he kicks it.

The message: 'When you act, I will respond. I like it when you concentrate and try hard.'

I'm going get you

What to do: When your baby starts to crawl, say 'I'm going to get you' with an excited voice. Let your baby get a few feet away, then grab her and nuzzle her (gently at first, more vigorously if she likes it).

The message: 'This is a little scary, but you can control your fears. You can handle different feelings at the same time.'

Let's do it together

What to do: Between ten and twelve months of age your baby will start imitating your everyday chores. Give her a spoon and bowl to imitate you mixing, a toy broom to sweep, a plastic hammer to pound. *The message*: 'I like it when you do what I do! I love to be your teacher!'

Your baby will tell you exactly what she likes you to do by smiling, wiggling her arms and legs, kicking and showing varying degrees of excitement.

This type of play is likely to be the favourite part of the secret language that you share with your baby, as you learn to take pleasure in the sheer joy of your interaction. But aside from having fun, and beyond the stimulation that you are giving your baby, you are also building a foundation for all of your baby's future relationships.

Let's spy for a moment on Joy and her play session with 3-month-old Rachel as they speak in the secret language below. As we watch them play, we see the many levels of emotional and social communication in the secret language. You may notice that each ten or 15 minutes of play has specific stages: preparation, greeting, interaction and disengagement. This structure is important in teaching a baby about human interaction. It provides a rhythm and order to the communication between you and your baby which will become the basis of her emotional communication.

What happens	What is communicated
Preparation Joy sits Rachel in a baby seat on the floor and spreads some toys out in front of her. Rachel watches her mummy spread out the toys and then smiles with pleasure as Joy lifts her head to begin.	Babies love a routine and recognize familiar rituals. Spreading out the toys is Joy's way of saying, 'Now it's time to play.' When the toys are spread out Rachel watches as Joy raises her head, and *continued*

	they instantly make contact. That is her way of saying, 'I'm ready to play!' This completes the orientation phase where Rachel and her mother silently agree on their activity.
Greeting 'Are you ready to play now Rachel?' Joy asks in the melodic 'baby voice' that we so naturally use when directly addressing an infant. Rachel responds by flapping her arms and legs and giving her mummy a broad smile.	This is called the greeting phase as Joy invites Rachel to the activity. Even by three months, babies begin to recognize their name and know that something special is coming when they hear it. The melodic, higher pitched 'baby voice' that Joy uses is common to every culture, so we must assume that we are pre-programmed to speak in a way which is most pleasing to an infant's ear. Rachel's body flapping is like a dog wagging his tail. It is an unmistakable symbol that we are doing the right thing.
Interaction 'Let's play "Noises", today, OK?' Joy asks. 'I'll pick some toys and make different noises and we'll see which one you like.' Rachel stares intently at her mother's face. Joy picks up a rattle and shakes it in front of Rachel. She waits for a response and says, 'Do you like that noise? Do you like that rattle?' Rachel reaches out for the rattle. Joy says, 'Good girl! You can do the rattle by yourself!'	Of course, Rachel does not really understand what her mother is saying, but she is learning about the language. Soon she will realize that when we ask a question our voice rises at the end of the sentence and then we expect a response. When Rachel reaches for the rattle, Joy responds. They are now synchronized in the dance of communication.
Teaching Joy takes a wooden spoon and bangs it on a plastic drum. She imitates the drum, 'Boom, boom,' but she begins to notice an expression of agitation on Rachel's face. 'Does that noise scare you?' she inquires. 'That's OK, we won't do that noise right now.'	This is the beginning of emotional learning. Babies have four basic emotions: disgust, sadness, happiness and fear, but from these they will build an infinite number of feelings. *continued*

Disengagement After ten minutes, Rachel begins to look bored. She turns away as her mother continues to play. 'Are you done playing this game?' Joy asks. 'Let's put these toys away and we'll get ready to go out.'	This is the disengagement phase. Babies tell us when they have had enough by turning away. Joy recognizes that this is not a rejection, just a signal that it is time to do something else.

You will probably notice that when you talk and play with your baby, you do this in a very special way. Your own body movements are slowed down and exaggerated. You may notice that you talk slowly and deliberately as if you were talking to a person who speaks a foreign language, repeating words and phrases many times. You will pause when your baby looks away. This gives her a chance to 'think about' what is happening and to organize what she has seen.

Teaching your baby to 'self-calm' in the secret language

Teaching your baby to calm himself when he is upset is the third most important part of the emotional communication. It is also the one that is most difficult for many babies and many parents to master.

In the first few months of life, parents are encouraged to respond to every one of their baby's cries, in order to foster their emotional bond. This is a time when your baby needs to know that you are there for every need and any reason. By the fourth month, however, your baby should have a pretty good sense of being secure in the world, and you should begin to be able to distinguish his different needs by the way he moves and the way he cries (we will explore this in detail in the next chapter).

Between three and nine months, you should experiment with different responses to your baby when he cries. As you learn to recognize the way he communicates that he is tired, or hungry, or bored, you will learn more about how to respond. You will want to rush to his side if you hear a cry of pain or fear, but not if it is a cry that just tells you: 'I'm tired and cranky.' In this case you will want him to learn how to calm himself down so that he can fall asleep. If you respond with an offer of comfort to every cry, day and night, your baby will not learn that he can comfort himself.

Self-calming is a critical emotional milestone because it sets the stage for later emotional control and self-discipline. Scientists believe that as a baby learns to control his emotions in the first years of life, his brain actually changes. They speculate that a part of the brain called the amygdala, which is the centre for our emotional control, acts differently in children who learn to self-calm. This part of the brain, in particular, seems to be able to help children 'put the brakes' on the biochemicals (adrenalin, noradrenalin, cortisol and others) that make them angry, anxious or fearful. When infants and toddlers learn to self-calm, scientists believe that their brains somehow learn to better control the biochemicals that are associated with emotional stress. When young children do not learn to calm themselves down, they continue to depend on their parents to do this for them. When they are older, they may be more at risk of a variety of emotional problems.

Consider the plight of Christine and Harvey, concerned parents of 11-month-old Emily. Emily was always a shy and sensitive baby. She did not like loud noises, she did not like to be held by anyone but her parents. She wailed every time that she was put in her cot. As a result, Christine and Harvey planned their lives around their daughter to a greater extent than was necessary or helpful to her. They always let her fall asleep in their arms. If she woke up during the night (which was common), they would take her into their bed. They never went out together without Emily. Once they tried to have a baby-sitter stay with Emily, but Emily burst into hysterical screams the moment they walked out of the door. Ten minutes went by and when they called from their cell phone, Emily was still crying. They turned around and went home, and that was the last time they tried to go out for the evening.

Over three years later, Emily was still a shy and fearful child. She still slept with her parents on most nights. She was hesitant and shy in her nursery school. Christine and Harvey had still not gone out for an evening without Emily.

Research done with shy babies and shy children tells us that this personality trait is extremely stable as children grow older. Shy babies usually turn into shy toddlers, who turn into shy older children, then shy teenagers, and eventually shy adults. (Angry and anxious babies are also likely to carry these personality traits with them as they grow, although not quite to the extent of shyness which seems to be tied to a specific 'shy gene'.)

But the fate of a shy, angry or anxious baby is not cast in stone; at least not if you teach infants how to calm themselves down using the secret language. Jerome Kagan of Harvard University has demonstrated that parents can be shown how to teach their shy children to calm themselves down, and that by the age of five, children who were once shy and timid no longer have these traits. In fact, they are indistinguishable from their braver, more confident peers.

Do you have a baby who is six months or older and depends on you too much? Are you afraid to leave him with a baby-sitter? Does he sleep in your bed, or do you have to stay in his room until he is asleep? Does he cry when you put him down, or if you leave the room for even a minute? If you have answered 'yes' to these questions, then you need to teach him self-calming skills. This is not just for your sanity, but for his emotional health as well. As paediatrician William Sammons writes in *The Self-Calmed Baby*: 'Self-calming creates greater self-assurance and self-sufficiency. Rather than being a helpless baby, your child can finally do something for herself. She feels a sense of accomplishment and is far less vulnerable, because she is less dependent on other people. [Self-calming] creates a level of comfort and flexibility that parents cannot create on their own.'

A baby's temperament is the best predictor we know of how he will behave as a toddler or an older child. If you begin to teach him self-control skills now, it will make a big difference as he reaches other emotional milestones later on.

So how do you teach your baby to calm himself down? How do you get him to go to sleep by himself and in particular, sleep through the night? Through the secret language, of course! The trick is to communicate your presence and comfort to your baby, without always picking him up and physically comforting him as you did when he was under six months. It is also important to point out that this is a gradual process. Psychologists call the process 'desensitization'. The desensitization process means that in small steps you respond less and less to your baby's *emotional* cries (as opposed to cries of hunger, discomfort or pain which are physically based), so that he gradually learns how to take care of his own emotional needs. Sammons recommends a five-step process for slowly teaching your baby to self-calm.

Step 1: When your baby cries, observe him to see if everything is all right. Read your baby's cries using non-verbal signals to determine what your child is really trying to tell you.

Step 2: Wait a minute or two and then say a few words softly to your baby. Your voice is very comforting to your baby, but does not provide complete comfort, as would picking him up. If your baby has trouble falling asleep at night, you might make a tape recording of yourself singing lullabies.

Step 3: Step into view and let your baby see you.
Just seeing you is the next level of comfort for your baby. It may also help to put pictures of yourself and your baby's other caregivers around the room, close to her cot. Your baby needs to learn to create a 'mental image' of you without you actually being there. Having something that smells like you can also help. Your smell is the first memory that your baby has of you and some parents have literally slept with a baby's blanket or plush toys in an effort to transfer their smell to these objects. Then the blanket or toy is placed in the baby's cot.

Step 4: If your baby still cries, check her nappy or rub her back for just a moment and continue talking softly. Do not pick her up.
This action communicates that you are present, but not really trying to comfort your baby. This is difficult to do, but an important part of the desensitization process.

Step 5: If nothing else helps, and your baby continues to cry, then pick her up and hold her for a few minutes. Soothe her, and then place her back in the cot in her favourite position.

Through your touch, voice and body language you convey to your baby that she is fine, and that it is time for her to sleep or play quietly. The message that you are trying to convey is: 'I love you, but I can't be with you all of the time. You are fine by yourself.' This is a message that you must also believe. It is hard to separate from a baby that wants you so badly. Every instinct may tell you to do everything you can to comfort your baby. But in this case your instinct may be wrong. Loving your children also consists of providing appropriate limits, not just now, but throughout their childhood.

If your baby continues to cry when it is time for her to sleep, repeat these five steps. Above all do not despair. As you will see there are many ways to help you raise a happy and healthy baby when you understand and speak the secret language.

Chapter 3

How Babies Call for Help

Understanding your child's pain

I am not sure if there is anything worse than seeing a young child in pain. Any parent I know would rather take ten times the pain on themselves, rather than see their child suffer. Of course, pain sometimes comes with the promise of better health, when, for example, your baby goes for her immunizations. Pain is also your child's fastest teacher. If your toddler touches a hot cup of coffee, or rocks in his high chair until it falls over and he bumps his head, it is much less likely that he will behave that way in the future.

But it is hard to find a rationalization for the pain of sickness or injury, no matter how hard we try. Chronic pain slows down a child's recovery from a serious illness. It interferes with her sleep and appetite. It affects the normal bonding between children and adults. It impedes your ability to stimulate your baby and as a result slows down her development.

There are those who think that babies do not feel pain to the same degree as adults, reasoning that their neurological system is not as developed as ours and therefore not as sensitive. But in fact there is reason to believe that the opposite is true: babies may feel pain more acutely than adults. Because of their immature nervous system and lack of cognitive development, infants do not have the same abilities we do to cope with pain. Even more disturbing, some recent studies suggest that the more pain children experience as infants, the more sensitive they may be to pain as they get older.

This is the theory of Dr M. A. Ruda, chief of the cellular

neuroscience section at the Institute of Dental and Craniofacial Research, Washington D.C. When Dr Ruda's team of researchers injected the paws of newborn rats with an irritating chemical, they found that, even after the animals were fully grown, and their paws long since healed, their paws were still ultrasensitive to pain and even touch. Ruda notes, 'We found that in animals that had experienced neonatal pain and injury, there were more pain fibers, and that the fibers covered more length in the spinal cord than they normally would.' Other studies suggest that premature babies with low birth weight, who we assume had significant and repeated painful procedures in prolonged hospital stays, complained more about pain and hurt as they got older than their full-term siblings.

If this hypothesis is true, the more you help your baby with pain now, the more you may be helping in the future. You can do this better when you understand the secret ways that babies communicate their pain and distress.

First, find the pain

Jane, a single parent of 8-month-old Lily, woke up one night to hear her daughter shrieking in bed. It was unusual for Lily to wake up at night and the piercing cry told Jane that something was seriously wrong. Jane rushed to her daughter's cot, picked her up and instinctively felt all over her body to see if something was jabbing or pinching her. As she held Lily, she noted that her baby's body was rigid and her back was arched. Her face was set in what could best be described as a grimace: eyes squeezed shut, brows contracted, and her tongue was taut with her mouth wide open. Lily's cry was louder than Jane had ever heard. After a few moments of her mother's rocking and soothing whisper, Lily's cries started to subside a little and became quieter and more rhythmical. At a visit to the GP the next day, Jane found that Lily had infections in both her ears.

An infant's cry of pain is hard to mistake. The rigid body, the grimace, the piercing cry that can not be ignored; these are the three 'signs' that your baby is in pain, although it is important to note that sometimes not all are present. For example, when my oldest daughter, Jessica, was five months old, she had a small cyst on her neck, which must have caused her a great deal of pain. During the day, Jessica refused to take a sip from her bottle of milk, even though usually she was a hearty eater. She made a face when she drank from the bottle, but she did not cry. By evening the cyst on her neck had grown to the size of a small ball and she was running a fever. She still did not cry, although she could hardly hold up her little head. We rushed her to the hospital and the cyst was lanced.

It is so frustrating for parents when they do not know just how to relieve their baby from pain, but fortunately there are only a finite number of things that will cause your baby to be in pain and if you are sensitive to the secret language of your child, you can likely find the cause of the pain quickly.

Like Jane in the above example, the first thing you should do is to try and locate the cause of pain to your infant. Since ear infections are such common problems, that might be the first place to look. If you rotate your finger around your baby's outer ears and she gets fractious or bats at your hand, then this may be the cause of the pain (although sometimes babies do not mind your touching an infected ear).

Next, you should examine your baby's body for redness and swelling. Nappy rash, of course, is a common reason for a baby's pain, although it is worth noting that there are at least eight different kinds of rashes that are common to babies. Some rashes look worse than others but do not really bother your baby. Other rashes may be quite painful to a baby, particularly when urine touches her sensitive skin.

When your baby is in pain, you will normally see a change in her sleeping or eating pattern within a day or two. Of course, if your baby runs a fever, has a change in her stool (smell or colour), vomits or spits up more frequently than usual, or has noisy, fast or difficult breathing, then you can immediately assume that she is sick.

If you suspect that your baby is in pain, you should immediately call your GP. The more that you can tell him on the phone, the more quickly he will be able to recommend help for your baby. Use the chart below to aid you or your baby's other caregivers in being a 'pain detective'. Note down everything that you see, hear, feel and smell. Remember that when you 'read' your baby's secret language, you must use all of your senses.

TRY IT

You may want to make several copies of this chart and make all of your infant's caregivers aware of how to use it. Put your GP's phone number and an emergency number on the chart as well.

Pain Chart	
GP's name and phone number _____	
Local hospital _____	
What to do	**Note what you see**
Make sure that the baby's fingers, toes or hair are not caught in anything.	
Look for rashes or other skin discolouration.	
Take the baby's temperature if he is at all warm to the touch.	
Examine the baby's stool.	
Note changes in eating or sleeping habits.	
Note the nature of your infant's cries.	
Note other physical symptoms (difficult breathing, stuffy nose, sensitivity to touch).	
Note any changes to your baby's environment or schedule (change in milk or food, a change in your schedule, new people or new pets in the house, etc.)	

Helping your baby with chronic pain

If your baby must have a prolonged hospital stay, it is inevitable that he will have both acute and chronic pain. With advances in neonatal medicine, more and more babies are being saved from defects and illnesses that would have killed them even a decade ago. But with these astounding medical advances also come procedures which cause prolonged pain and discomfort to your child. If your baby has a serious medical problem and requires an operation or a prolonged hospital stay, it may be comforting to know that the medical profession is also making great strides in understanding the secret language of your baby's pain.

There are several scales that professionals use to measure a baby's pain that typically involve both observation and medical measurements. Accurately measuring a baby's pain is important because the medical team will want your baby to have enough medication to keep him comfortable, while not over-medicating him. Too much pain medication may slow down his recovery, and in some circumstances it can be a risk in itself.

One example of such a scale is the CRIES post-operative pain scale which nurses and other medical practitioners use to measure five parameters: O = crying response; R = requires oxygen; I = increased vital signs (blood pressure, heart rate); E = expression; S = sleep. The baby's score is determined by a ten-point scale measured an hour before the rating, with a higher score equalling more pain.

You can measure three of the five parameters on the scale with your own observation.

For crying, give your child:
0 = No crying.
1 = High pitched cry, but baby is easily consoled.
2 = High pitched cry, but baby is inconsolable.

Noting his expression, give him:

0 = Your baby does not show any sign of pain on his face.

1 = Your baby grimaces by lowering his brow, squeezing his eyes shut and opening his mouth.

2 = Your baby grimaces and exhibits 'non-cry' vocalizatio such as a grunt.

In regards to sleep, give your baby:

0 = Your baby is continuously asleep an hour before observation.

1 = Your baby is awake at frequent intervals.

2 = Your baby is awake constantly.

A medical practitioner would also measure low oxygen saturation and increased blood pressure, but even without physical instruments or medical training you can have a good indication of your child's pain on a six-point scale. When your infant leaves the hospital after an operation or other procedure, make sure that you discuss how your baby communicates his pain and what you should do about it with your doctor.

Babies who cry too much

It was a typical start to a typical day for Michael, a 34-year-old accountant in a large Birmingham firm. His eyes were red and a little out of focus. He was showered and neatly dressed, but his demeanour was more like someone ending the day than starting it. He sipped his large mug of coffee as he waited for his computer to start up. He desperately wanted to put his head on his desk and to sleep for just one more hour before he started work, but he would have to wait until his lunch hour, when he would wolf down his sandwich and then head to his car for a forty-five-minute nap on the back seat.

This had been Michael's routine for five months, ever since his son Josh had been born. Although Michael loved his baby dearly, it had been 153 days since he or his wife Paula had had a full night's sleep. As Michael explained to a sympathetic colleague, 'Josh is a crier. He cries throughout the day and throughout the night, and nobody can tell us why. Our doctor says that he will eventually grow out of it, but I'm not sure I will live to see that day.'

Michael's sense of desperation is hardly unique. Many new parents face each day exhausted from the last, wondering how a baby that can bring parents so much joy can also bring them to a mental breaking point.

Crying is never pleasant, but some small babies have particularly loud and shrill cries. Conditions in pregnancy such as mild malnutrition or toxaemia can give a baby a cry of 700 to 800 cycles per second, as opposed to the normal 300 to 400. Cries of some babies are measured as high as 80 decibels (standing next to someone with a jack hammer is about 100 decibels). Premature babies or babies that are small for their age may have cries that are louder, more shrill, or more arrythmical than other babies and these cries are much more unpleasant to our ears. It is an unfortunate but true fact that babies with piercing loud cries are much more likely to be abused.

Excessive crying, frequently referred to as colic, occurs in 20 to 25 per cent of infants. Most paediatricians define excessive crying using the rule of 3:

- The infant cries for more than 3 hours a day.
- The infant has a period of excessive crying at least 3 days a week.
- This pattern continues for at least 3 consecutive weeks in otherwise healthy babies.

There are also other characteristics which define excessive crying. One is the onset of the cry. Excessive crying typically has a rapid and abrupt onset with little build up. More disturbing to parents, the baby does not seem to have an 'off-switch' to his crying. The crying just continues on and on without any sense of ebb or flow. Some parents describe these infants as having a 'fit'. Other parents say that their babies seem 'out of control' or constantly in pain.

Besides the crying, there are also distinct physical signs that a baby exhibits during these periods of intense crying. His stomach will tighten, his fists will clench, his legs and knees will be drawn up. Many infants look like they are holding their breath during these periods of crying. Their face becomes red, their feet become cold and they may become pale around the mouth.

But the most disturbing aspect of these crying periods is that the infant is inconsolable. The most dedicated and indefatigable parents report that nothing seems to work in getting their baby to calm down, and each crying period seems to just run its own course. With some babies the tried and tested calming techniques just seem to make things even worse.

Why me? Why my baby?

Parents naturally want to know why their baby has colic, but unfortunately science does not have a definitive answer. Certainly biological factors play a role in why some children develop colic and others do not. We assume that babies with colic have a difficult temperament and, in particular, they are more reactive to both their own bodily discomfort as well as to the outside world. Many paediatricians feel that colicky infants have an immature gastrointestinal tract, but this assumption has not led to any really helpful answers about what to do. Putting a baby on a soya-based formula is usually recommended as a first course of action, but doing so only helps with a small number of babies. Some people compare a baby's colic to an adult having a headache. Your head may hurt at your temples, around your eyes, in the back or the front, yet we describe all these different discomforts as just one ailment – a headache. Similarly, like colic, there are many things that can cause headaches – constant noise, hunger, lack of sleep, alcohol. Finally, we know that some people are much more prone to headaches than others, although again we do not know why. But unlike headaches, which are usually relieved quickly by various painkillers, colic does not respond well to medical intervention, and drugs are rarely prescribed for this condition.

One of the most distressing things about colic is the effect that it has on parents. The baby with colic can cause a wide range of adverse reactions in his parents – from depression, to inappropriate handling, to over- or underfeeding. The parents' irritable moods or behaviours can then make things even worse for their baby. The fact that every infant will outgrow this period of excessive crying, probably by four months and almost always by six months, is of little consolation to most parents.

What helps

The best treatment for a baby who cries too much is a combination of techniques to help reduce the baby's discomfort and to increase the parents' ability to cope. There are dozens of ways to calm a baby and even the most difficult infant usually responds to one or two. Here are some of the most popular.

- *Rhythmic rocking:* Most babies respond well to being rocked in your arms, a pram or a cradle. Immediately you will notice that your baby has his own preferred tempo – some infants like to be rocked very slowly, others more quickly (but never rock or shake your baby too vigorously, babies can get whiplash just like adults). Some mothers have observed that their babies seem to be stimulated by side to side rocking and calmed down by up and down rocking, but each baby and each parent has to find out what feels right.

- *Swaddling:* Wrapping your baby tightly in blankets is very comforting to some infants. Presumably this gives them the sense of being back in the cosy warmth of the womb.

- *A warm bath* helps some babies, but not others. Some infants become more agitated when put in a bath and you will find this out quickly. Remember to gradually introduce your baby to the warm bath, first wetting him with water from your hand, then gradually putting in his feet and legs and then his torso. Your calm and steady voice and hand will help your baby learn that this is a comforting experience.

- Certain *smells* are said to be comforting to a baby particularly the smell of lavender and camomile. A baby's sense of smell is fully developed at birth and babies react to strong smells in a similar fashion as adults. In some European countries mothers regularly place lavender potpourri in babies' rooms to foster sleep. In the last few years several cosmetic companies have made specially scented oil for a baby's bath which is also supposed to be soothing. I have not heard whether these are particularly helpful or not, but they might help *you* calm down.

    I do know that the most comforting smell to an infant is the smell of his parents or caregivers. If you have an infant under three months, take care to use the same soap, shampoo, perfume or cologne every day. These smells, combined with your natural body smells, are what your baby recognizes and will find pleasing.

- *Take a ride:* I have heard many parents tell me that their babies only calm down when going for a pushchair ride or a car ride.

- *Sing a song:* Although you may not be in a singing mood when you are holding a screaming baby in your arms, try it anyway. There is a reason that virtually every culture sings soft melodic songs to their babies – they like it! Find a song that your baby seems to respond to and sing it over and over again. Remember that babies love repetition.

- *Rhythmic sounds*: Some babies also seem to be calmed by machine noises such as a vacuum cleaner or a washing machine. If you do not feel like running these machines all of the time you can buy recordings of favourite baby noises or make a recording yourself.

- As mentioned in Chapter 2, baby massage is a wonderful way to communicate with your baby, and also a way to calm her down. But like other calming techniques, it does not seem to help all babies. Some infants are overly sensitive to touch and actually cry more when you massage them.

Above all keep trying. Don't let your subjective sense of whether your baby is responding to your efforts get in the way of what he is telling you in the secret language. Research tells us that parents of babies who cry a lot often overestimate the amount of time their babies cry and underestimate their own ability to calm their babies down. As we shall see, accurately observing and recording your baby's cries will help you see what works and what does not.

How much does your baby really cry?

An important part of helping a baby that cries too much is to first pin down the baby's crying habits. Psychologists call this a baseline measurement, and it is an essential starting point for reducing your baby's crying. This measurement will tell you whether or not your baby really cries as much as you think. It will also help you determine what times your baby is most likely to cry, making what may now seem like an unpredictable event more understandable. Generally babies cry most at meal times, particularly the dinner hour between six and seven. They tend to cry more in the evening and during the night. Knowing when your baby is more likely to cry will help you be more prepared for these periods of the day.

TRY IT

How much does your baby really cry? Keep a careful log of your baby's cries for three or four days and how he reacts to your response. Look for patterns of when he is most likely to cry and what he is most likely to respond to.

Many parents also find that it is helpful to review their baby's daily schedule. Sometimes babies cry less with more frequent feeding. Sometimes they need different sleep schedules. Be a detective in trying to understand the secret behind your baby's excessive cries. Does he respond to a different bedtime routine? Does he sleep better in one place or another? Does your mood affect him?

Time of day	Duration of crying	What do you see?	What does the crying mean?	What did you do?	What helps the baby?

Above all, consider whether you and your partner are getting the support that you need. Programmes that are successful in helping parents with their crying babies stress the need for support for both parents in order to avoid depression, anxiety and sleep deprivation, all of which will only make matters worse.

If you are the parent of a crying baby, ask trusted friends and family to help you look after your baby on a regular basis or to prepare meals and help with household chores. If you are with your baby during the day, make sure that you have at least thirty minutes to an hour each day to get out of the home by yourself and renew your energy. Take time at least once a week as a couple to help you get some perspective on your new family.

Above all, remember that your baby is just going through a difficult stage. Very soon he will have many more ways to communicate with you. He will grow and thrive and shower you with love and affection. This is his way of saying: 'Thanks for being so patient.'

Chapter 4

Hand Talk: Talking With Your Baby Before She Can Talk

Babies are smarter than we think

With every decade that goes by, we find out that babies are smarter than we think. In one study which investigated when babies start to recognize their parents, the researchers found that within an hour after birth, babies could distinguish pictures of human faces from drawings of random lines. Within a week, babies start to smile when they see a human face, and shortly thereafter realize that their smile will get a predictable reaction from their parents or caregivers. They realize that when they smile, the nice people with the big heads (almost any adults will do, but parents are preferred) will make funny faces and funny noises. Babies begin to understand that when they smile adults will give them attention, and when they turn away, adults will usually leave them alone. This is a baby's first dialogue.

Babies continue to try to talk to us in their own language and most parents listen. Take 10½-month-old Ella, who was having dinner alone with her father, while her mother stayed at work for a meeting.

Ella's father: 'Boy this looks good. Do you want to try some scrambled eggs, Ella?'
Ella looks away.
Ella's father: 'It's yummy.'
Ella looks curiously at her father.

Ella's father: 'Do you want some?'

Ella does not turn away. She lifts her head slightly. Her lips part a little.

Ella's father: [becoming more enthusiastic as a response to her interest]: 'Yum yum' [smacking his lips].

Ella smacks her lips in response.

Ella's father: 'Scrambled eggs. They're from a chicken! [He flaps his arms and makes a chicken noise.] Want some?'

Ella keeps eye contact with him (she would turn away if she was not interested in the new food) so her father feeds her a spoonful of egg.

She smacks her lips as a sign that she is ready for more.

In the above example, Ella never says a word, but that does not deter her father. To a casual observer, the conversations like the one between Ella and her dad might seem to be one-sided, but they are not. They are filled with meaning. Thinking that a conversation has to consist of words is a mistake. Too many parents of young children think that speaking only refers to vocal communication. They anxiously await their child's first words at around twelve months or his first sentences at eighteen to twenty-four months, not realizing that they have been talking with their children for months!

As important as words will eventually be, there are many other ways that infants communicate. For example, when Ella saw that her scrambled eggs were too hot, she pursed her lips and blew air out of her mouth at her dad. She knew that this is what he did to cool them off and this is how she made her request. When she wanted a drink from her juice cup, she simply reached towards it and stared at it. That usually did the trick. By the time that babies are seven or eight months old, they use gestures like this all of the time to tell us what they want. Now parents everywhere are learning that they can use these same gestures to actually engage their babies in a conversation.

In 1982 Linda Acredelo and Susan Goodwyn, both psychologists at the University of California at Los Angeles, noticed that young children were using gestures to stand for words that they could not yet vocalize. Over the last twenty years they have conducted hundreds of workshops to train parents how to understand their babies by the natural gestures that they use, and to use these same gestures to communicate with them. They call their method of enhancing communication through the baby's gestures 'Baby Signs'.

The Baby Signs programme does not involve teaching children a formal sign language (although this method of gestural language has some benefits of its own as we shall see in a later part of the chapter). Instead, it helps parents be more sensitive to the natural signs that their children are already using and to encourage the use of these signs by repeating them and pairing them with the spoken word.

Many times a baby's gestures are obvious to us, but other times a baby gives us signals whose meanings are not readily apparent. For example, Danielle's parents noticed that their 11-month-old daughter pulled on her ear whenever the family dog Ginger came into the room. Danielle always beamed with delight to see the big sheep dog, and she gave Ginger a broad smile while she pulled on her own ear. Her parents wondered why Danielle used this particular sign to 'name' the dog, until her mother suddenly remembered a time when Ginger was licking crumbs off Danielle's high chair and lap and Danielle grabbed one of Ginger's ears and gave it a sharp pull. 'No!' Danielle's mother remembers saying sharply, and pulling her own ear, she said, 'It hurts when you pull on Ginger's ears. She doesn't like that.' And so Danielle's 'sign' for Ginger, pulling on her own ear, began.

Danielle's parents had read about the Baby Signs programme and knew the value of speaking to Danielle in her own secret language. They began to use their daughter's sign for the family dog at every opportunity. When Ginger was not in the room, Danielle's father might say to her: 'Where's Ginger?' pulling on his ear at the same time. Danielle would look around, pulling on her own ear. Then her dad would whistle for the family dog and Danielle would smile and clap when Ginger bound in the room. This is true communication.

When Danielle's father used the sign for Ginger he also spoke directly to his daughter as well. It is important to point out that adding gestures to the way that you talk with your baby does not mean that you are entering into a silent world. In fact, when parents use gestural communication with their children they naturally talk more.

Most parents who begin to consciously use gestures to talk with their children also engage in more conversations with them. For example, Marcia saw that her son John used a 'petting' sign when their cat came into view. He would take his right hand and stroke the back of his other hand, just as if he were stroking the cat. On a walk in his pushchair, Marcia saw John using this sign. She exclaimed: 'Oh! You see a kitty! (looking around for it). There it is over there. (Marcia makes the sign herself.) That's right! That *is* a kitty! That kitty looks just like our kitty, doesn't it!'

Not surprisingly, when babies see that their parents are using more gestures, they use them more, too. As a result, adults talk more, babies gesture more, and the baby's language acquisition takes a leap. Using gestures, parents find a new way to 'converse' with their babies, as much as six months before this would normally happen using only the spoken language.

How to begin using gestures with your baby

If your baby is eight or nine months old, she has already begun communicating to you in a gestural language. Now, you just have to pay a little more attention.

Your 9- to 14-month-old baby already uses many signs. Some of these may be unique gestures that he has made up himself, while other signs are common to most children and more easily recognizable. I call these *imitative* signs because they are simple imitations of a movement associated with the word or phrase. Some common imitative signs that babies use are listed below. Look for these gestures, and keep note of other gestures that your baby may be using.

Word or Phrase	Gesture
Drink	Points to mouth; smacks lips
More	Fingers tapping table or other surface
Monkey	Scratches armpits
Hat	Pats top of head
Fish	Smacks lips together
Book	Holds palms together and opens and closes hands
Camera	Makes a circle with index finger and thumb and holds to eye
Gentle	Pets back of one hand as if stroking a pet
Smelly	Pinches nose with index finger and thumb and wrinkles nose
I don't know	Palms up, shoulder shrug, raised eyebrows
Where?	Palms up, arms outstretched

Just as learning to crawl is so exciting that it inspires babies to learn to walk, when your baby learns that he can communicate with gestures he will try to find even better ways to communicate. Researchers tell us that when parents make a point of using gestures with their infants and toddlers, children typically learn to communicate with words at an earlier age.

TRY IT

Look for other gestures that your child is using. Write them and their meaning in the box below. Test whether you are really sure what your baby's gesture means by asking him questions like 'Is this what you want?' Babies will nod their head 'yes' or 'no' or show you another sign of agreement.

Gestures	Meaning

As you learn to observe your baby's gestures, it is important to note that the signs that your baby uses do not always make sense. Tanya, an 11-month-old, made a hand-washing sign when she wanted her stuffed bear. She would go over to her parents and rub her hands together, and when they found the bear she would hug it with glee. Tanya's parents wondered why she made this particular sign to indicate that she wanted her bear. Had she associated hand washing with the bear when they washed it in the machine? Did she notice her mother washing her hands one day, while playing with the bear? Most of the times we can put together how babies associate a gesture with a particular meaning, but this is not always the case. Sometimes we just have to let the baby use her own made-up language to communicate her thoughts. The important thing is that when Tanya made her 'sign' for her bear, her parents knew just what she wanted.

The final step in using a gestural language with your baby is for you to start using your baby's own gestures to talk to him. For example, Derrick at fourteen months old still had not begun to speak. He said a version of 'mummy' and 'daddy', but not much else. On the advice of a speech therapist, Derrick's parents began to use gestures to talk with him. When they seemed worried that this might make matters worse and that Derrick might only speak in gestures, the speech therapist assured them that this does not happen. Derrick showed no signs of any hearing impairment or physical abnormality which would hinder him learning to speak. Some children, particularly boys, are simply delayed in their vocal language. Learning gestures typically accelerates a toddler's spoken language, it does not inhibit it.

Derrick's parents made a list of nearly fifty gestures that he was using. (It is not uncommon for children to use up to seventy different gestures to communicate their needs even before they can say seven words.) Then they began to use them as well. Derrick had three different signs for things he liked to drink. He pursed his lips for orange juice. He held up his hands as though he was drinking from a bottle when he wanted milk. He squeezed his hand into a fist when he wanted apple juice (he drank his juice from a cardboard juice box which he squeezed when it was done). Now when his mother said, 'Are you thirsty, Derrick? Do you want a drink?' she would add, 'How about milk?' and she would make Derrick's sign for milk. 'How about orange juice?' and she would purse her lips. 'How about apple juice?' and she squeezed her hand in a fist. Derrick beamed at this new game. He squeezed his hand into a fist. 'Apple juice it is,' his mother said enthusiastically and also made her hand into a fist. Now they were really communicating.

Teaching your baby new 'signs'

The elegance of the Baby Signs programme is that it is so natural. You do not need any special toys, books or equipment. Your baby leads the way, and all you have to do is follow. But there is also some benefit to teaching your baby new signs that he does not already use.

Joseph Garcia, author of *Sign with Your Baby*, takes a slightly different approach to communicating with babies through gestures. He advocates teaching children at eight months and older to use standard sign language, the same sign language used by children who are deaf. Like Acredelo and Goodwyn, through his research, Garcia found that hearing children have cognitive and language abilities which are much more advanced than their vocal abilities and that teaching children to speak with signs helped them have a better grasp of grammar and syntax, of past and present tenses and of language in general.

Garcia and other advocates of using sign language with hearing children note that teaching children signs should be a natural experience. If your baby is looking at children dance, just say the word 'dance' and show him the sign for 'dance' (one hand is held with the palm facing up and the index and middle finger of the other hand move on the palm as if they were dancing). Babies are quick to associate the meaning to a sign if it is shown to them at the same time as a shared experience.

When choosing which signs to teach your child, you should certainly start with ones that are important to you and your child. You can borrow a sign language dictionary from your local library, but you may just want to start with the twenty-five signs shown below that are commonly used by parents of young children.

Begin by picking one or two signs that are important to you and your baby, and use them frequently and consistently. For example, Donna and Eric started using signs with their son Seth when he had a bad earache just before his first birthday. Their baby had been

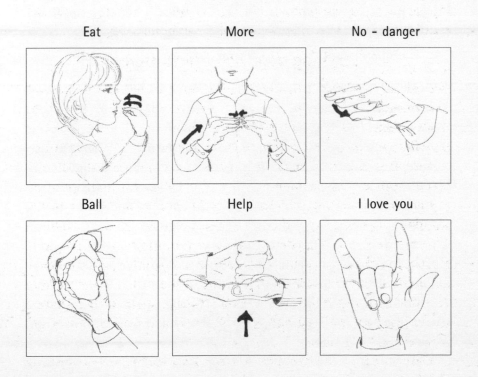

Eat   More   No – danger

Ball   Help   I love you

Yes

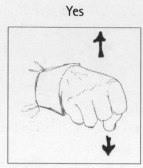

Toilet

Danger

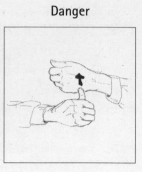

Hot

Cold

Pain – where?

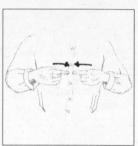

Bedtime

Where?

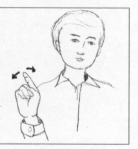

Cat

Dirty

Biscuit

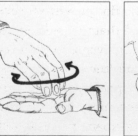

Tired

Cross

Happy

Stop

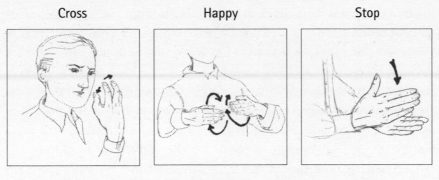

Go

Hurry

Come

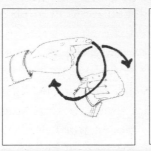

Great!

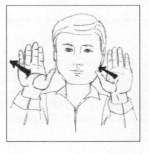

uncharacteristically unhappy and irritable for several days before they took him to the doctor, who discovered the ear infection. They immediately decided that they needed to teach Seth how to tell them when something hurt, even though he could not speak. They taught him the sign for pain (the index fingers of both hands tap together at the location of the pain) saying the words 'Ouch, that hurts!' Every time Seth fell or had a minor hurt, they would say 'Ouch, that hurts!' and show the sign for pain, pointing to the place that was obviously hurt. Within a few weeks Seth was using the sign for pain whenever he got a bump or bruise. But the 'breakthrough' really came when Seth was thirteen months old. That was when Seth gave the sign for 'pain' and pointed to his stomach. This was a hurt that his parents could not have seen, but in the secret language of signs, they now knew just what was wrong, and they knew just what to do. They gave him water instead of milk, they let him lie down and did not worry about him missing a meal. By the next day, Seth felt fine. When Seth got out of bed, his father pointed to Seth's stomach and made the sign for 'good', at the same time saying, 'Does your stomach feel good now?' Seth made the sign for 'good' and went off to play.

When you teach your baby a new sign, hold your hands close to your child's eyes and keep your face at his eye level. Say the word when you show him the sign and make an expressive face to go along with it. Do not expect your child to learn the sign the first time, but look for recognition on his face that shows he is making the association between the gesture and the spoken word. If your child shows interest, you may want to shape his hand to make the sign (but never force a child to do this). This will help him see that this particular gesture has meaning for him and you.

If you really want your child to learn sign language quickly, ask everyone in the household, adults as well as older children, to use the sign every time the word or phrase is spoken. Everyone should use the signs the same way, trying to say the same spoken phrase as well.

You might also consider teaching important signs to other care-givers, including baby-sitters and child minders. Teachers often use gestures or signals to get the attention of toddlers as well as older children. They might flick the room lights as a signal to 'be quiet' or ring a bell when it is time to line up. Teachers can also use sign language to talk to a class of toddlers, helping them communicate long before they can speak.

TRY IT

Give your baby's child minder a 'mini-dictionary' of the signs that you are working on. Perhaps she will make a wall chart for other caregivers and parents to see. The more ways we find to communicate with young children, the better off they will be.

Part summary

Babies speak and understand a secret language from the moment of birth. Their first language is the language of the senses, and whether they realize it or not, parents speak this language too, communicating to their babies through their touch, their voice and even their smell. Although you are genetically pre-programmed to give your child just what he needs to nurture his development, learning to speak the secret language of your baby can enhance your awareness of your infant's emotional and social development. Through observation and by paying attention to his different cries, you can heighten your intuition about your baby's wants and needs and this is particularly important if your child has a difficult temperament and if he is ill.

There is also growing evidence that you can speak to your baby through the language of gestures and open a new world of communication months before he utters his first word. Whether you choose to simply imitate your child's own natural gestures, or whether you teach him formal sign language, you can give him a head start in his language development which will also foster a closer relationship with you and his other caregivers.

Learning the secret language of your baby is just the beginning. As we shall see, you can learn to speak the secret language of emotions to your child at any age, and when you do you will open up a new world of communication for you and your child.

Part II

The Secret Language of Your Child's Play

Chapter 5

Play – the Work of Children

It is Saturday morning around 7 a.m. I am sitting on the couch sipping my morning coffee. My daughter Tess, still in her pyjamas, walks over to the couch. She begins her day of play.

Tess: 'You be the baby and I'll be the big sister.'

Me: 'Okay, I'm the baby. Waa, waa, waa.'

Tess: 'Oh, baby! Did Kelly hit you?' [Kelly is her favourite doll.]

Me: 'Yes, big sister. Kelly hit me and she was mean to me. Make her stop.'

Tess: 'I'm going to put her in the time-out corner right now! [Tess throws Kelly on to a chair.] There, there, baby. [Tess climbs on the couch next to me and pats my head.] Did you make a poopy in your nappy? Are you hungry?'

Me: [trying to get out of character] 'Hey Tess, do you want to go out to the playground this morning?'

Tess: 'Yay! Yay! Yay! Let's go to the playground and swing and swing and swing!'

Me: 'That's a good idea, isn't it?'

Tess: 'Yeah, that's a great idea! Now, I'm the beauty parlour lady and you're going to get a hair cut so we can go to the playground. Okay? [Tess climbs on the couch and pretends to cut my hair.] Cut, cut, cut. Cut, cut, cut. [She examines my pretend haircut.] Ohhh, you look a beautiful baby! I think I'll give you a ponytail today!'

As I spent time with Tess on this fairly typical Saturday morning – in the house, in the playground, and in doing a few errands – she made the following suggestions:

'You be the baby and I'll be the mummy.'

'Let's play Dunkin' Donuts! You be the shopper and I'll be the doughnut lady.'

'Let's play hide-and-seek. You be the hider and I'll be the finder.'

'Let's play cook out. You be the daddy and I'll make you oaty moatmeal (her word for oatmeal).'

'Let's play bookstore. I'll buy the books and you be the checker outer.'

We also played two games of the Candy Land board game and one game of hide the duck (I hide plastic ducks around the house and Tess finds them). During the rest of the day, Tess played in similar activities with my wife, and had a three-hour play period in the evening with her baby-sitter, who went home at 9 p.m. looking exhausted.

If you have a pre-school child in your home, you know that their energy for playing is bounded only by their naps and bedtime. Awake time is playtime. Anna Freud, the daughter of Sigmund, and a famous psychologist in her own right, is often quoted as saying: 'Play is the work of children.' But play is also the work of the adults who care for children and it is sometimes exhausting work at that.

Play is the most important part of your child's secret language. It is how she learns about her world. Through play she develops much of her language and intelligence. She also uses play to explore her emotions. With play she expresses her worries, her conflicts, her hopes and her fears. It is an essential part of the way that she learns to relate to others. Because play is such an important part of a child's emotional development, it is the primary medium in which counsellors and other mental health professionals treat the emotional and behavioural problems of children under twelve.

Through play, counsellors can teach children with ADHD (Attention Deficit Hyperactivity Disorder) self-control, and they can teach depressed children to find renewed joy in their lives. Using play they can teach anxious and fearful children to overcome their worries and strive towards the challenges of new situations and people. Through play, counsellors can help children with any emotional or behavioural problem you can name, but the secret of using play to help children with their emotional problems is certainly not limited to a mental health setting. A variety of programmes, some in existence for over four decades, have found that parents can be just as effective at helping their children through play as trained professionals.

One such programme, designed by Drs Bernard and Louise Guerney at Penn State University, teaches parents how to do play therapy with their children. Parents share their progress with other parents in group meetings, watching videotapes of their play sessions and inviting comments on how they can improve the quality of their play. The Guerneys' research suggests that trained parents are typically just as effective as professional therapists in helping their children through play.

In another programme called Parent–Child Interaction Therapy, developed by Sheila Eyberg and her colleagues, parents of children with extreme behaviour problems are taught how to bond with their children through play as a precondition to teaching them better behaviour. These researchers and many other clinicians believe that non-directive play, where parents participate in their child's play but let the youngster become the leader, is the best way to establish a deep and caring relationship between children and adults. This type of play, which I will describe in Chapter 18, is based on giving children unconditional positive attention while they express their innermost wishes, concerns and fears.

In my own work with children over the last thirty years, I have taught hundreds of parents to help their children through another play technique called *emotional learning games*. Most of these games are simple derivations of games that children already enjoy, but I give each game a slight twist to teach children (and their parents) a new emotional or behavioural skill.

For example, I gave a game of 'Feelings Checkers' to a family when I wanted them to communicate their emotions to each other more openly. Mr and Mrs Paul had complained that their 10-year-old daughter Anna no longer wanted to talk to them. Mr Paul complained, 'Anna talks to her friends on the phone for hours. I understand that she has a good relationship with her teacher and talks to her everyday. She's on her computer e-mailing God-knows-who for hours each day. But she doesn't seem to have anything important to say to her mother and me. If she says "pass the salt" at dinner time, that's a major conversation.'

So I decided to prescribe a game of 'Feelings Checkers' for Mr Paul to play with his daughter. To prepare the game, I taped different feelings words to the top of each checker; words such as angry, hate, fear, brave, surprised, proud, joyous and so on. The rules were: Play the standard game of checkers, except that when you 'jump' another player's checker you must say a time that you experienced the feeling on your checker. When you get a King, then you are the King of Feelings. When a King jumps, he can talk about any feeling that he likes. Although you win the game just like when you play the standard game of checkers, by getting all the other person's checkers off the board, the real objective, of course, is to get people talking about their feelings.

Mr Paul was sceptical at first. 'She won't play it the way you want her to,' he explained to me.

'I think that she will play if *you* want her to,' I suggested. 'Children like to play games with their parents at any age. And believe it or not, they like to confide in their parents, too. You just have to give them the opportunity to talk more openly. If you make the rules of the game clear, and you are enthusiastic in your own play, I can guarantee she will start talking about her feelings.'

On another occasion, I assigned a family a game I call 'Cooperative Robot'. The parents of 8-year-old Brian complained that he 'never cleans his room, never helps around the house, never thinks about anyone but himself.' When parents complain to me that their child does not cooperate, I explain to them that some children seem to be naturally cooperative, but others may have a temperament that makes them more wilful and stubborn. But all children can learn to be more cooperative, through the secret language of play. As we shall see in Chapter 8, you can teach children any behaviour that is important to their development through emotional learning games. Emotional and behavioural skills like cooperativeness, self-control, empathy, emotional communication or even just being polite are taught through simple and fun games.

To play the Cooperative Robot game, I asked Brian to stand between his parents and hold their hands. I explained to the family: 'In this game you have to function as a single unit – a cooperative robot. Brian, you are in the middle so you are the "brain". Mum and Dad you are on the outside, so you each have one hand to use. OK, Robot [talking now to the family unit], I want you to make yourself a peanut butter sandwich.' And I gave them a jar of peanut butter, a knife and two pieces of bread.

Making a peanut butter sandwich is not as easy as you might think when three people are holding hands. But the object of the game is to learn to cooperate without bickering or blaming and have fun at the same time, and this is not hard at all. In this game, as in other cooperative games, you either work together or you lose. Brian's family, as with other families who have played this game, smiled and giggled throughout the task, and succeeded in making a sandwich.

But this was just the first step in helping Brian and his family. Games by their nature are most enjoyable when they are played over and over again, which is exactly why they are well-suited towards emotional learning. I next wrote down three tasks for the Cooperative Robot (Brian and his parents) to perform in the next week: (1) clean Brian's room; (2) make pudding; (3) vacuum the living-room carpet. I added a further rule that each task must be accomplished in less than ten minutes. The next week at their family session, Mum reported to me that all three tasks had been completed by playing the Cooperative Robot game and, for once, there had been no arguing about what was to be done. But Brian had the last word: 'Give us three more things to do for next week, and I bet we can do them even faster!'

Creating a more playful home

To begin using the secret language of play you should first take a look at the current play habits in your family. Children have a natural drive to play and today's parents are more inclined than ever to play with them. Still, many times children do not get enough of the right kind of play. I place some of the blame on the predominance of television and video games in most homes, and on the reluctance of many parents to limit these activities. As a friend of mine in the toy business recently commented: 'The window of time in which children play creatively with toys is getting smaller. Children who played with dolls or action figures at age seven or eight are now asking their parents for video games. Of course, this is changing the nature of the toy business, but it is also changing the nature of childhood.'

Another part of the problem is that so many adults these days do not take the time to be playful even when they have young children at home. Advances in technology have made it easier for us to work virtually anytime and anywhere, and as a result, the lines between work and leisure family time have been blurred. For example, nearly every time I go to a particular playground with my 3-year-old daughter, I see at least one father or mother pushing a toddler on a swing while talking on their cell phone. Invariably that parent is talking about some business deal in the making, or some errand that needs to be done, even though they are there to play with their child.

If you want to speak the secret language of play with your children then you must begin by making play and fun a priority in your home, no matter how old your children are. There are many different forms of play – imaginative play, word play, board and card games, sports and more – so I am sure that you can find at least one that you can enjoy with your children on a regular basis.

From a mental health viewpoint, playing with your children is a critical part of parenting, because it is essential to your child's emotional development. Every day your child needs healthy food, adequate sleep, vigorous exercise, time to learn . . . and time to play.

Consider just some of the things listed below that make play such an important part of your child's life.

Play is the antidote to stress

Work causes stress, play helps reduce it. Play actually reduces the stress chemicals in the brain, which affect a child's mental and physical health. When children (or adults) experience stress, the brain produces a biochemical called cortisol, one of about 100 neurotransmitters that control our emotions and behaviour. In small amounts, cortisol stimulates our attention and awareness, but in large or moderate amounts over an extended period of time, cortisol will act as a slow poison. Excessive cortisol can cause mental health problems and physical health problems as well. High cortisol levels have been associated with many forms of disease, and can literally take years off of a person's life. When we play, however, our cortisol levels are automatically lowered, and there is evidence that the immune system might actually be strengthened as well.

Play teaches children social awareness

Research studies tell us that children who do more creative role-playing in their play tend to be more popular with their peers. Dramatic play, using dolls, small figures or puppets, helps children rehearse different forms of social communication which then translate into real life situations. Listen, for example, to 5-year-old Sally and her friend Amanda.

Sally: [holding a mummy figure in the kitchen of her doll's house] 'Kids, the dinner is ready. I made your favourites, pizza and ice cream!'

Amanda: [holding up a figure of a boy] 'We had that last night, Mummy, and the night before! Can't we have something good for us, like spinach and green beans?'

Sally: [again as the mummy] 'No, you've had too many

vegetables this week already. You can have pizza or ice cream or just go hungry!'

Amanda: 'Mummy, I think you have things mixed up. Vegetables are good for you. Pizza and ice cream are bad for you.'

Sally: 'Oh, I guess you're right. Let's have vegetables tonight for dinner. We'll have carrots and broccoli.'

Amanda: 'Yay! I love vegetables.'

Sally: 'OK, dear, now help me set the table.'

Now let us look at the social exchange that happened in these few moments of play. Sally started off with a humorous idea: a mother who thinks that ice cream and pizza are good for you. Amanda responded as the 'voice of reality', accepting this role reversal and reflecting the real life values she had been taught. Amanda also shows that she can be assertive in this exchange. Even though she is playing the 'child', in this little drama Amanda stands up to the 'adult' who is telling her something contrary to her beliefs.

When confronted, Sally shows her flexibility and willingness to get along. She could have argued with Amanda in this pretend world, and insisted, like the White Rabbit in *Alice in Wonderland*, that up was down and down was up, but instead she chose to acquiesce. The ability of these girls to try out different roles, to communicate their desires, to take both active and passive positions, and then resolve a potential conflict, shows a very sophisticated sense of social awareness.

If your children do not show this kind of social awareness in their play, then you should consider playing with them and modelling these important social skills. Studies have shown that even when children are playing with army men and other 'aggressive' action figures, they will demonstrate roles of nurturing and conflict resolution, when adults model them for them.

Of course, you can also model important social skills in other forms of play, including board games and sports. Use your child's playtime to teach the importance of respecting rules and limits, playing fair, taking turns and being a good winner or a good loser. This is how to communicate in the secret language of play.

Play provides physical exercise

Hardly a week goes by that we do not hear about the increasing problem of child and teenage obesity. A recent study suggested that nearly 10 per cent of children in the UK are obese and many more are out of shape. Active play can help. Children need at least an hour of vigorous activity a day and another half hour of moderate activity. Usually this routine does not pose a problem for younger children, but by age eight or nine, the average child in the United Kingdom participates in less activity than he needs, and this decline continues through adolescence. Although giving your child a balanced diet is the most important factor in keeping him at a healthy weight, exercise comes in as a close second. Make sure that your youngster spends as least as much time in active play as he does in sedentary activities like video games or watching television. As he gets older, regular participation in an active sport is the most effective way for teenagers to get the exercise essential to their well-being.

Play stimulates creativity and problem solving

Thirteen-month-old Connor was playing with his wooden blocks when he encountered the classic problem of putting a square peg into a round hole. He pounded the peg with another block, but it did not give way. He twisted and turned it to no avail. He tried to sit on the peg, which did not work at all, and did not feel too good either. Then he came upon the solution. He threw the square peg over his shoulder and tried a round peg instead. Such small victories occur constantly as children play. The world of play is a world where adult rules are secondary to the rules of children, and yet it is also an opportunity for children to discover about the adult world of logic and creative problem solving. From simple puzzles to advanced hobbies, play gives children unlimited opportunities to explore new ways of thinking about problems.

Imaginative play is particularly helpful for children trying to work out emotional conflicts. Children often use toys, dolls and puppets to re-enact problems that are confusing or troubling to them. By miniaturizing the problems that they experience in the larger world, they are able to gain a sense of control and resolution. For example, I remember getting a call from a distraught grandmother who was concerned about the repetitive play of her grandson, Alan, age seven. Alan's father had had a heart attack on a Sunday morning a few months before the call, and Alan had witnessed his father lying on the ground and then being taken away in an ambulance. His father had died after only a few hours in hospital. Alan did not attend the funeral, but from that day onward he played for hours with a toy ambulance, picking up one toy figure after another, and delivering each one to a box behind the couch. His grandmother was naturally concerned that her grandson was traumatized by this unfortunate event.

While I assured Alan's grandmother that this type of play was a normal part of his grieving process, I also felt that it was time for him to move on to the next stage in grieving his loss. Repetitive play can be an appropriate way for children to cope with their anxiety, but when the play lasts for too long, it is a sign that their anxiety is not being reduced, just kept away. I suggested that Alan's grandmother or his mother join in his play, but that they take it to the next logical stage. They should set up a play hospital for the ambulance to go to, and then a play cemetery for the patients that die in the hospital. I recommended that they tell Alan the story of what happened to his father using the small figures. Alan's grandmother said that she had told him what happened before, and that he had not asked any questions. I explained to her that children need to process this information in their own way, and the best way for young children is through play.

I suggested that after she told Alan the story of his father's death that she simply watch him play for the next few days, sitting with him on the floor and being ready for questions. As you might expect, when given the suggestion, Alan played out the whole story to its conclusion; his toy men were taken to hospital where the doctors tried to save them, sometimes successfully, sometimes not. Some of his men were buried in the cemetery after prayers and goodbyes from the other toys. This type of play went on for only a few days and then it seemed that Alan had said his goodbyes, at least for now. We knew this was true, because when his grandmother said, 'Do you want me to play with you today?' Alan replied, 'Yes, Grandma, but can we play something else?'

TRY IT

There are many types of play and children benefit most from a varied menu of play activities. Give your child the following Play Test to make sure that he or she is benefiting from all that the secret language of play has to offer. Take a week and put a tick by each type of play that your child does that day. Put a second tick if you (or another adult) joins in the play.

Remember that you cannot speak the language of your child's play by standing still and you cannot speak the language of your child's play in clothes that you are afraid to get wrinkled or stained. Loosen up! Put on something old and casual. Shake out your hands and your feet and your hips and your bottom. Mess up your hair, roll your eyes around five times and try to touch your nose with your tongue. OK? Now you are ready to talk the secret language of play.

Play Test							
	Mon	Tues	Wed	Thurs	Fri	Sat	Sun
Small motor activities (using scissors, drawing and painting, puzzles, crafts and other art projects)							
Building activities (using wooden blocks, Lego™ cars, small people and other accessories)							
Transportation play (playing with cars and lorries, riding bikes, skating, etc.) *continued*							

	Mon	Tues	Wed	Thurs	Fri	Sat	Sun
Music (playing rhythm instruments, dance, singing games, musical games such as musical chairs, etc.)							
Fantasy play (dolls, miniature figures, dressing up, puppets)							
Nurturing play (playing school, imitating family roles, playing restaurant, etc.)							
Large muscle activities (soccer, bean bag toss, rounders)							
Play with animals (playing fetch, chasing each other, careful rough-and-tumble)							
Hobbies (collecting, science, crafts, computers)							
Board games							
Solitary play (imaginative play, pencil and paper activities such as art)							
Play with one other child							
Play with a group of children							

The stages of play

Like other aspects of the secret language of children, your child's play will change from one age to the next. At each stage his play will have a significant influence on his cognitive, language and social development, and parents can facilitate this development when they participate in their child's play activities.

While most parents play a lot with their children when they are babies and toddlers, they tend to play less with their children when they enter school, and their participation in play activities diminishes with each passing year. By the time that children become teenagers, few parents play on a regular basis with their youngsters. For the remainder of this chapter, I will discuss how you can be an active participant in your child's play at every stage, using play to help shape your child's emotional, social, language and cognitive development.

Baby play

Within a week of coming home from hospital, Alison received a cupboard full of toys for her baby, Kimberly. Most of her friends were new mothers and they had read all the latest books on infant development and all of the purchases they made were educationally and developmentally correct. There were black and white soft blocks and a black and white mobile (babies pay more attention to high contrast colours in the first months of life). There was a tactile cube with six different textures (a baby explores the world more through his sense of touch than through his eyes or ears) and a tape of 'Mozart for Babies' (classical music, particularly Mozart, is supposed to stimulate mathematical ability and spatial reasoning). There was also an assortment of rattles, stuffed animals, nesting cups and so on. This was a lot of stuff for baby Kimberly to play with, but none of it was really necessary.

Like other infants, baby Kimberly came into the world with the three best toys ever invented: her mummy, her daddy and her own body. While there is now a burgeoning industry of playthings designed to stimulate infant development, researchers tell us that none of these mean much compared to the gifts that Mother Nature has provided. Most of the games that you play with your baby are passed on from generation to generation because we intuitively know they are appropriate in giving your infant exactly the kind of stimulation she needs. Consider these common games played with babies:

- *This Little Piggy Goes to Market* provides babies with tactile stimulation, a singsong rhythm and an element of surprise.

- *Peek-a-Boo* is a favourite game, because there is nothing more interesting to your baby than your face. Seeing your face come and go is much more exciting for your baby than any toy.

- *Who's that Baby?* is played holding your infant in front of a mirror. He loves seeing your face and because he is a very social animal he enjoys seeing the baby in the mirror (not realizing just yet that he is looking at himself).

- *Pat-a-Cake:* Babies love repetitive songs and repetitive motions. By twelve months, your baby will try to imitate your hand motions, as he enters a stage of imitative play.

For the first twelve months of your baby's life, his main interest in toys is to manipulate them. Within a year, your infant will start to use toys and other objects to serve their intended function. Blocks get stacked, buckets get filled, baby dolls and stuffed animals get fed, put to bed and, of course, cuddled.

Between nine and twelve months most infants have a favourite soft toy that must accompany them everywhere, particularly when they sleep. These special toys – usually a stuffed bear or other animal, but often a blanket or soft piece of cloth – are called 'transitional objects', and are particularly important to your child's emotional development. These favourite toys act as a bridge between an infant's need for a parent to provide comfort, and the infant's ability to comfort himself. Children often develop such a strong bond with these toys that parents can not pry them away, even to be washed. Many children carry around these playthings until they are four or five, only giving them up when they are finally convinced that they are too babyish.

TRY IT

All of us like to play with babies and that is just what they want and need. Every playtime encourages your infant's development: social, emotional, cognitive, motoric and language. Here is a list of some of my favourite ways to play with babies. Keep a similar list hung in your baby's room for other adults to see so that she will get everybody in on the play. Your baby will let you know which one she likes the best.

- *Target practice:* Hold a pie tin in front of baby while she lies on her back and let her kick it. She will like the noise and your reaction.
- *Ball roll:* Roll a ball in front of baby and let her watch it go by. As she learns to crawl, she will try to chase it.
- *Aeroplane game:* Lie on your back and hold baby above you, making her fly like an aeroplane.
- *Rhythm band:* Put on some lively music. Give your baby a rattle and you take one, too. Shake the rattle in time to the music, encouraging your baby to imitate you.

Toddlers and pre-school children

At around eleven or twelve months children begin playing pretend games where they imitate the activities of those around them. By eighteen to twenty-four months toddlers have progressed to a point where they will pretend to perform multiple acts in a meaningful sequence, such as pretend cooking, playing shops or caring for a baby doll. Parallel play begins at fifteen to eighteen months. This is the stage where one child will engage in similar activities to a child next to him. While the toddlers may talk or smile at one another and offer each other toys, they do not really interact in their play.

As your child reaches its second birthday cooperative play begins. At this stage children organize their play around a distinct theme and take on special roles based on it. They typically prefer to play with members of the same sex and are clear about the types of toys and the types of play that they think are appropriate for boys and girls. Children vary considerably in their ability to play with others at this age. Some children are very aggressive. Many have a hard time sharing their toys or waiting for their turn. Adults make the difference in helping children develop more socialized play. Studies show us that virtually all children play more cooperatively and longer when adults are present to iron out conflicts and guide children in their play.

Between the age of two and three, children enter the world of make-believe. Make-believe allows young people to explore topics that frighten them, to deal with aggressive feelings, and experience the entire range of human emotions.

There was a time when it was thought that the children who had imaginary playmates were shy and socially awkward, but researchers tell us that far from being a sign of emotional immaturity, imaginary friends are a healthy and appropriate part of a child's development. Girls are more likely to have imaginary girl friends. Boys are more likely to have animal friends. Imaginary playmates are a way for children to practise language as well as social skills and may actually be a predictor of early social success.

By three, children are ready to learn simple games. They like following rules, but they also like to win. Helping children learn to be a good sport is an important goal of this age.

TRY IT

I hate to hear children say, 'I have nothing to do.' I hate it even more if I hear a parent respond, 'Why don't you go and watch television or put on a video.' There are so many ways for young children to play, they should never feel bored. Over the years I have found that children never run out of ways to play when their parents take the time to make them an 'Idea Box'. Take a shoebox and write down twenty-five or more play ideas on small slips of paper. I have written down twenty-five things that my pre-school age daughter likes to do, but you should vary this list according to your child's interests. Now when your child needs something to do, just have him close his eyes, reach into the box, and pick three play ideas. Then he should choose the one he likes best. When you show your enthusiasm about the Idea Box, and substitute new activities every few weeks, I doubt that you will ever hear any more complaints of 'I have nothing to do.'

Idea Box		
Build a block house.	Pretend cooking a meal.	Pretend writing letters and delivering the mail.
Play rhythm instruments to music.	Put together a puzzle.	Dress up toys or dolls.
Colour a shoebox and put your 'valuables' in it.	Make snakes out of clay.	Pretend that you are going on a trip and pack up what you will need in a box.
Play hide-and-seek.	Play dressing up with old coats, shoes and hats.	Play catch.
Blow bubbles.	Roll cars or lorries down a hallway into a pretend garage.	Create a zoo out of stuffed animals.
Make a house out of pillows and boxes.	Decorate pretend clay biscuits.	Trace your hands or feet on paper and colour them in.
Play a simple board game or card game.	Finger paint.	Set up a gymnastic course (tumbling, running, jumping, etc.)

School-age children

When children enter school they still enjoy imaginative play. Girls may prefer dolls and a doll's house and boys may prefer playing with action figures or construction toys, but both enjoy acting out dramas in their miniature worlds. With each passing year, children bring more diversity to their play. By seven or eight they should begin participating in organized sports. As their intellectual abilities increase they enjoy strategy-oriented board games, card games and, of course, video games. This is also a time that they will take pleasure in hobbies and crafts. Anna Freud noted that hobbies are exactly halfway between play and work; they are pleasurable to do, and yet they also teach important cognitive skills as well as self-discipline. Consider Sean, who at ten took up the hobby of performing magic. Sean collected magic tricks, saving his pocket money for regular trips to a magic store in a nearby town. He read books on the history of magic. He practised his tricks in the mirror over and over again. He put on shows for his parents and his brother and sometimes for his friends. He searched the Internet for ideas on magic tricks he could make. He joined a young magicians' club.

Between the ages of seven and twelve, children often become passionate about a play activity, such as a sport, a craft or a hobby. These should certainly be encouraged as long as they stimulate the mind, require social interaction and, like Sean's hobby of magic, involve a variety of different kinds of interesting tasks. Video games, an increasingly popular activity for millions of children, do not meet these criteria. Although non-violent video games, like television, can be an entertaining activity, this type of play should be limited to no more than one half hour a day. If you find that your school-age child is spending more time than this playing video games, then I recommend visiting a library and looking for books about the hundreds of activities in which your child could become involved that would stimulate his development. Here are just a few:

- Collecting
- Sewing
- Community service projects
- Taking care of animals
- Sports
- Build a science kit
- Start a garden
- Be a clown (or comedian)
- Puppetry

Playing with teenagers

Josh was a trying teenager. He was bright, but since he rarely did his homework his grades were only average. He rarely respected the limits and curfews that his parents set for him. If he was supposed to be home by 11 p.m., you could be sure that he would show up after midnight. If he was told not to go to a party, then his parents were confident that he would be there. They finally sought counselling when they found marijuana and a bottle of whisky hidden in his room. Josh's parents hoped that the family therapist could help them find a way to make Josh follow their rules. Josh hoped that the therapist would tell his parents to be less strict and 'cool out'. Josh explained that his other friends did not have early curfews, and some of their parents knew that they 'partied hard' and thought that it was all a part of growing up. But the therapist had another goal in mind. She explained, 'I want you to play more as a family. That's my prescription for working things out.'

This family therapist knew that in spite of their protests, the vast majority of teenagers like to spend time with their families. The therapist also knew that teenagers who spend more time in pleasurable activities with their families are less likely to participate in high risk behaviours and typically do better in school. The trick is to find activities that will build a sense of belonging and togetherness.

Although many teenagers enjoy playing board games or sports with their parents, the competitive nature of these activities can sometimes do more harm than good. Competitive games, by definition, pit one player or team of players against another, and this conflict can often lead to hurt feelings or resentment with teenagers, particularly when there are already grounds for friction like in Josh's family. Cooperative games are almost always a better alternative when teenagers are involved, because they teach families to work together towards a common goal. Terry Orlick, in his book *The Second Cooperative Sports and Games Book*, explains that common competitive games can readily be changed into cooperative games by simple rules changes such as having one collective score, instead of individual scores, or by requiring that all players must have a turn before a point is scored. In this case, the therapist assigned Josh's family a game of 'Cooperative Basketball', knowing that basketball was a sport that Josh and his father had enjoyed in the past, and that they had a basketball net in their driveway. The rules were:

1. All shots for each game must be made from one spot (such as the foul line). Each person gets a shot, taking turns, with the oldest player starting first.
2. The ball must be passed to each member of the family before a shot is made.
3. The game is over when ten baskets are scored by the family.

The therapist gave Josh's family the assignment of playing this game three times a week. She further explained that if they got tired of playing this cooperative game, then they should make up another one. The only rule had to be that everyone wins by playing together.

Of course, she also asked them to sit down and discuss the family rules and the consequences for breaking them, and she suggested to them: 'When you learn to play and enjoy each other at play, then every problem will seem easier to solve.'

Chapter 6

Understanding the Language of Your Child's Play

The world of play

Play is as essential tool used by psychologists who are trying to help children understand their emotional and behavioural problems, but it is certainly not the sole province of the professional counsellor. For over forty years parents and other non-professionals have been taught how to use therapeutic play techniques to help children with an array of common emotional and behavioural problems, from shyness to dealing with a trauma, to coping with a divorce.

Many magical things happen when a caring adult plays with a child. Tens of thousands of children have had the directions of their lives changed by adults using the same techniques that I will describe in this chapter.

Helping children through the secret language of their play promotes their self-confidence, their ability to communicate their emotions and their desire to understand the emotions of others. Playing with your child, using the same techniques as professional counsellors, will help him face and overcome both the common and the uncommon problems of childhood. Studies have also shown that this type of play not only helps children with their present problems, but it can actually prevent problems from occurring in the future.

There are many forms of play therapy, but the one I most commonly prescribe for parents is called 'Special Play'. Special Play uses five different play therapy techniques which adults use to create a miniaturized world of unconditional positive regard for their children. It is a world where children receive support and acceptance from adults no matter what they do. It is a world where there are no wrong feelings or bad thoughts, so anything is possible. When parents enter this secret world through regularly scheduled Special Play times, they learn to listen to their children's needs and concerns in an entirely new way. When children experience their parents entering the secret world of their play, they are often able to approach their problems and try out new solutions which were never before possible.

Play therapy in the home

I have recommended Special Play for many types of childhood problems, but I have always felt it is particularly beneficial for children with behavioural problems. Sometimes these children are labelled as having an Attention Deficit Hyperactivity Disorder (ADHD), sometimes they are diagnosed as having an Oppositional Defiant Disorder (ODD). Many times they are diagnosed with both. But no matter what the label, parents and professionals are all too familiar with the troubling reasons that cause these children to be referred for help: stubbornness, a quick temper, uncooperativeness, problems in anger control and a negative attitude.

Most clinicians agree that the more difficult and challenging a child's behaviour, the more he will benefit from play therapy in the home. This type of play helps parents enjoy their children in a way that many had thought impossible. It can repair a relationship with a child that has been worn thin by constant disagreement and conflict. It gives children the message that even though they may have problems, they are truly valued and loved for themselves. In addition, when parents are taught the techniques of Special Play, they begin to feel that they can once again make an important difference in their child's life.

For example, I remember treating Alex, a 7-year-old diagnosed with ADHD, who was brought in by his harried and distraught mother at the request of his headteacher. Alex's single mother,

Robin, was a corporate lawyer, and truly a self-made woman. Abandoned by her own mother and raised by a foster family, Robin had put herself through college and law school. When she found herself pregnant at age twenty-eight, by a man whom she really did not want to see any more, she decided that she would embrace the challenge of raising a child as she had met every other difficult problem before, with unwavering commitment and enthusiasm.

But Alex had presented Robin with a different type of challenge than she had ever encountered. He was a fairly easy baby who was well cared for at a high quality nursery near Robin's work. But as Robin liked to say, 'When Alex took his first step, he decided he'd rather run, and he hasn't stopped since. Alex was asked to leave three nursery schools before he was enrolled in a special school for children with behavioural problems. Like so many ADHD children it was not just that he was very active and would almost never sit still, Alex was also uncooperative. At school he did not want to do what the other youngsters did. As one teacher diplomatically put it, 'He marches to the beat of a different drummer,' but what she really meant was, 'Why doesn't he act like all of the other children?' At home, Alex was on his own time schedule. There was an argument over every bedtime, bath time or homework time that his mother could remember.

I showed Robin some basic behavioural techniques to use with her son, but I knew that this would not be enough. 'I want you to start helping your son by just playing with him,' I explained and described the following technique of Special Play.

Special Play consists of five techniques that are used by professional therapists to create a relationship where troubled children feel valued, no matter what their problems. These techniques also encourage children to explore their feelings and actions, and to change their behaviour in order to secure the approval of the therapist. The five techniques I will discuss are easy to remember using the acronym PRIME (praise, reflect, ignore, model, esteem). The word 'prime', of course, means 'exceptional' or 'first' and you should think of Special Play as an *exceptional* way to communicate with your child, the *first* step in building a more positive way for him to interact with the world.

Most clinicians agree that Special Play, which helps shape a child's behaviour through positive attention, is the first step in any therapeutic programme. Russel Barkley, a leading expert on helping children with Attention Deficit Hyperactivity Disorder, has designated this special form of play as the first step of his eight step programme to teach children better behaviour. In his book *Taking Charge of ADHD* he notes:

> The first step of the program involves learning how to pay attention to your child's desirable behavior during playtime . . . don't take control of the play or direct it [but] . . . after watching your child's play, begin to describe out loud what your child is doing to show your interest . . . Ask no questions and give no commands . . . Remember that this is your child's special time to relax and enjoy your company not a time to teach or take over the child's play.

Although different therapists emphasize slightly different techniques that parents should use during Special Play, the most important element in helping children with behavioural problems is to re-establish a positive, mutually rewarding, relationship with them. In the remainder of this chapter, I will discuss how you can use Special Play to help children three to twelve years old, but as you will see, many of the principles can be applied to helping your teenager as well. The techniques are:

- *P*raise your child for positive thoughts and actions and feelings: As the child plays the parent praises him for socially appropriate comments and decisions.
- *R*eflect your child's feelings: As the child plays, the parent reflects and describes the feelings that he believes are part of the child's play.
- *I*gnore inappropriate statements, feelings or behaviours: As the child plays, parents ignore the things that might contribute to a behavioural or emotional problem.

- *Model* appropriate statements, feelings and behaviours: The parent describes what the child is doing, showing that he is paying close attention and heightening the awareness for the child.
- Show *E*steem for your child: During the play sessions, you show your esteem for your child by giving him unconditional attention and affection, both verbally and non-verbally.

You should begin by setting aside fifteen or twenty minutes during the day when you and your child are alert and relaxed. Select some of your child's toys and put them out on the carpet. Choose toys which are likely to stimulate imaginative play, which could include: action figures, dolls, dressing-up clothes and costumes, puppets, art materials, play animals, cars and lorries, building blocks or other construction toys and so on. You can ask older children to choose their own toys or playthings. As long as you encourage active play, as opposed to video games or watching TV, the same principles will work. Tell your child that you are going to have a Special Play time together for twenty minutes and that he can play any way that he wants. Then use the following Special Play techniques.

Praise your child for positive thoughts and actions and feelings

Praise is a powerful tool for you to use to teach your child your values and reinforce the behaviours that you think are important. You undoubtedly praise your child already to express your affection for him, but the type of praise I am referring to is more focused. Think of praise as an important reinforcement for behaviours which reflect your child's emotional and social development. As you participate in your Special Play sessions be specific in showing your approval for the play activities that will build your relationship with your child. Remember that with every comment you make about your child's play, you are also making a general comment about his day-to-day behaviour as well. For example, when you say, 'I like the way you have your dolls talking to each other,' you are giving your child the message, 'Talking is really important to me.' When you tell your child, 'It's great that you keep trying to sort out your puzzle, even though it is hard,' you are reinforcing his persistence and patience with a difficult task.

Scientists believe that the reason that praise and other forms of positive attention are so reinforcing to children is that they stimulate the production of the neurotransmitter dopamine in the brain. Dopamine is the biochemical equivalent of what we experience as pleasure. The brain produces dopamine when you have a good meal, or when you meet someone that you are attracted to or when you take a walk on a beautiful spring day. When you praise your child, your approval triggers dopamine production in his brain and he experiences your praise as pleasure just as you do when you receive a sincere compliment.

You should be aware, however, that with praise, just like with many other things, children can get too much of a good thing. When parents praise their children for everything that they do, this powerful technique seems to lose its value. During Special Play you should praise the specific statements, behaviours and feelings that you feel will encourage your child's emotional development and his ability to cope and overcome everyday problems.

Take, for example, Caitlin, age five, whose mother was taught Special Play to help her daughter deal with a difficult divorce. Caitlin was very upset by the announcement of the divorce, and when her father moved out of the house, she started to show signs of depression. Wisely, Caitlin's mother sought immediate advice before things got worse. The counsellor felt that Caitlin's reaction was appropriate to the circumstances, but prescribed Special Play as a way to help ensure that Caitlin (and her mother) learned the best way to handle this difficult situation.

Caitlin's mother was asked to make a list of the three most important thoughts that she wanted Caitlin to have on a regular basis. The counsellor explained that when children change their thoughts, they change their feelings and behaviours as well. Caitlin's mother wrote down three statements:

The divorce is not your fault.

Your dad and mum still love you.

You will be fine even though there will be changes ahead.

Then Caitlin's mother was asked to write down the three behaviours that she thought were most important to help Caitlin overcome her sadness regarding the divorce. She wrote down:

To do things that are fun, even though the situation is difficult.

To talk about your feelings.

To tell Mum or Dad when you need help.

Finally, she was asked to write down the three emotions that she felt were now missing from Caitlin's day-to-day life. She was asked to be specific in describing how she would recognize the behaviours that might indicate Caitlin had these emotions. She wrote:

Joy – her face lights up and she laughs out loud.

Assertiveness – she stands up for herself and has a very confident tone in her voice.

Calm – she looks relaxed and seems to be enjoying herself . . . not anxious and sitting on the edge of her seat all of the time.

Caitlin's mother had an old doll's house and thought that this would be a fun thing for Caitlin to play with. She gathered a shoebox full of Caitlin's dolls and figurines and put them in front of the doll's house. These are some of the ways that she praised Caitlin during her Special Play time.

Caitlin was excited to see the doll's house.

Her mother said, 'I love to see you so happy!' She was reinforcing Caitlin's expression of positive feelings.

Caitlin had two dolls talking to each other and planning a party.

Her mother said, 'It's nice that your dolls are able to talk to each other about their feelings.' She was reinforcing Caitlin for talking about her feelings.

Caitlin took a plastic monster and called the monster 'the ugly sister'. Caitlin said, 'This is the ugly sister that never goes to the parties.'

Her mother ignored this statement and said nothing.

In communicating with your child through Special Play, you should just ignore comments or behaviours that are negative or contrary to your goals. As we shall see below, ignoring inappropriate comments or behaviours can be just as important in Special Play as using praise.

TRY IT

Make a list of the thoughts, feelings and behaviours that you want to reinforce with praise during your child's Special Play. You may want to refer to this list before each play period.

List three positive thoughts that you want your child to have. You can state these yourself during the play when you have a natural opportunity, then reinforce them if your child repeats them. Do not state them as 'lessons' to learn, but rather as casual comments.

1. _____

2. _____

3. _____

List three behaviours that you want your child to show in his play (e.g. kindness, nurturing, concern for others, patience, etc.). Praise these behaviours during your child's play and, of course, at other times, as well.

1. _____

2. _____

3. _____

List three feelings that you want your child to show more often. Try to provide situations during the play where these feelings will come naturally, and then reinforce them with attention and praise.

1. _____

2. _____

3. _____

Reflect your child's feelings while he plays

Part of a play therapist's job is to reflect or mirror the feelings, conflicts and desires that we believe the child is trying to show us through his play. When we describe the behaviours that we see or paraphrase the child's own words, we help him to talk more about his feelings and to develop a better understanding of them as well.

Psychologists believe that when children (or adults) learn to express their feelings in a supportive relationship, it helps strengthen the neural pathways in the brain that connect the thinking part of the brain (the neocortex) to the feeling part of the brain (the limbic system). This will eventually make it easier for children to control their feelings through conscious thought, a key ingredient in mental health.

As your child plays, you can reflect his feelings by simply commenting on what you see, much like a play-by-play commentator on a sports broadcast (but without the hyperbole and forced enthusiasm). Just be natural in your comments and observations and most of the time you will probably be right on target. You will know you are successful because your child will respond by talking more about his feelings or commenting on them himself. Sometimes you will be mistaken and you may even say the wrong thing. Do not worry, this happens to even the most seasoned play therapist. If you reflect back a feeling that your child believes is inaccurate, he will correct you. Then you should just repeat back his correction.

For example, Connie was using Special Play to help her son Oliver learn to control his temper. Oliver would talk back to his parents and erupt with angry outbursts while playing with his friends. He would have an 'explosion', according to his parents, almost every day. The school counsellor suggested that Oliver's mother use Special Play to help understand why he was so angry, and to give him practice in more acceptable ways of expressing his feelings. Here's a sample of Oliver's play and his mother's reflections.

Brad: [talking for a female puppet in a raspy witch-like voice] 'I'm Oliver's teacher, mean Mrs Potter. I hate Oliver. He's stupid.'

Oliver's mother: [reflecting the feeling] 'You feel angry at your teacher.'

Oliver: [using the teacher puppet] Oliver's a bad little boy. He gives me a headache.'

Oliver's mother: 'You think the teacher doesn't like you.'

Oliver: [taking out a puppet of a dog] 'I'm Oliver. Nobody likes me. My teacher is mean to me.'

Oliver's mother: 'Oliver says that nobody likes him.'

Oliver: [turning to his mother and saying angrily] 'No! I said my *teacher* doesn't like me!'

Oliver's mother: [remaining calm with a neutral voice] 'Your teacher doesn't like you.'

Oliver: [talking to himself] 'Yeah, my teacher doesn't like me.' [Now talking to the teacher puppet] 'Why don't you like me Mrs Potter. I'll try to be better.'

Oliver's mother: 'You want to try to be better.'

Oliver: 'Yeah. I will try.'

When you make reflective statements to your child during Special Play, you express your uncritical acceptance of his feelings, and this helps build his self-confidence. Hearing you express his concerns also helps make his feelings seem more legitimate and provides a platform for both accepting them and exploring them further. There is also an emotional release that seems to happen for children in this kind of play. Children, like adults, simply feel better when they talk about their feelings, and by reflecting and describing your child's feelings you will be encouraging more intense play. Finally, this type of play helps children deal with their feelings on a symbolic level. In the above example, Oliver explored his anger and disappointment related to his teacher by using puppets, rather than acting out these behaviours in real life where he certainly would not get unconditional support.

Another way of reflecting your child's feelings is by imitating or 'mirroring' his behaviour. If you are not sure of what to say, or maybe there is not anything appropriate for you to say, just mimic the kind of play that your child is doing. Imitating your child as he plays makes him feel that you are not only paying attention, but that you are connected to him on an emotional level. When you imitate a child's play you are saying, 'I like what you are doing. I like it so much that I'm going to do it too!'

As you reflect, describe and imitate your child's feelings and behaviours, remember to be objective. Unfortunately, this is not always as easy as it sounds. We are used to constantly judging the behaviour of others, and it is human nature to divide what we see into that which we approve of and that which we do not. But objectivity is absolutely essential in communicating your positive regard for your child in the secret language of play. Being totally objective in your words as well as your voice tone and body language may be a little difficult at first, but you will soon get the hang of it. It just takes practice.

TRY IT

Most parents that learn the techniques of Special Play need some practice in being objective with their children. See if you can change the following judgemental statements into ones which are more objective. I have given you examples of how to do this for the first three statements.

Judgemental statement: 'If you build that block much higher, it's going to fall.'
Objective statement: 'That's a high tower that you're building with your blocks.'

Judgemental statement: 'That dress doesn't go on Barbie, it belongs to your other doll.'
Objective statement: 'Your Barbie is putting on her dress.'

Judgemental statement: 'You're going to break that doll if you bang him on the floor like that.'
Objective statement: 'You look as though you are really mad with that doll the way that you are banging him on the floor.

Now you try it:

Judgemental statement: Be careful with your scissors, or you're going to cut out an important part of that picture.
Objective statement: _____

Judgemental statement: That music is too loud.
Objective statement: _____

Judgemental statement: Don't you think you should use more crayons than just one colour?
Objective statement: _____

Judgemental statement: Why do you always sound so angry when you play?

Objective statement: _____

Judgemental statement: Do you not like it when I play with you?

Objective statement: _____

Ignore inappropriate statements, feelings or behaviours

In communicating with your child through Special Play, you should just ignore comments or behaviours that are negative or contrary to your goals. Psychologists know that ignoring inappropriate behaviour is every bit as important as giving praise and attention to positive behaviour. In real life situations this may be difficult. If your child sticks his tongue out at you, or makes a smart remark, or has horrible table manners, I think that you do need to enforce your household rules and apply reasonable consequences to this kind of misbehaviour. But Special Play is truly special, and we treat problems in the world of play differently. Remember that this is the child's world you are entering, not yours, and the rules and logic of the world of play are different. Your goals are to reconnect with your child and communicate in his most natural language, not to manage his behaviour. When your child does or says things that you don't agree with or even like, just remain objective and ignore them.

If you think that your child's comments or behaviour are inappropriate you can turn away and play by yourself in a different way (we'll talk about the modelling technique in the next section). The only exception to the principle of ignoring what a youngster does is if a child presents a danger to himself or others, or wilfully destroys property. In this case, of course, you must immediately intervene and say something like: 'The only rule I have in our Special Play is that you can't hurt anyone or anything. If you break this rule, I will stop you right away and we will have to stop our playtime together.' (See the next chapter for a discussion of what to do when children persistently play aggressively.)

Model appropriate statements, feelings and behaviours

If your child consistently does not play in ways that you feel that you can praise, then you should model the type of play that you want to reinforce. As it turns out, imitation is a two-way street. When you imitate your children while they play, they begin to imitate you, too. Looking at the list that you made (pp. 94–5) of the goals of your Special Play, try to introduce these thoughts, behaviours and feelings into your play by doing them yourself.

For example, John Williams used Special Play with his daughter, Vanessa, to help her with an extreme form of shyness referred to as selective mutism. Like most other children with this disorder, Vanessa simply refused to talk when she was not in her own home. No matter what her teachers did, no matter how much encouragement she got from her classmates, Vanessa would not say a word. At home, Vanessa talked as much as any child her age, except when the subject of school was brought up. Because Vanessa spoke only with her parents, it seemed logical to her school counsellor that her parents would be the best people to help her. Her father was selected for the Special Play sessions because he seemed to understand her best. 'I was very shy when I was young,' he told Vanessa's counsellor. 'I guess I still am kind of shy,' he confessed. 'But I've learned how to cope with my natural shyness and I wish Vanessa would too.'

The counsellor suggested that John buy a miniature schoolhouse from a local toy shop and 'play school' with his daughter using Special Play techniques. This is an example of how he used modelling to show his daughter new ways to cope with her excessive shyness.

Dad: 'Let's play a game of school, Vanessa. Here's a teacher and a group of kids. We can play with this classroom and see what happens.'
Vanessa: 'I don't like school. I don't want to play with the schoolhouse. Let's play Secret Squares.'
Dad: 'I know that you don't like real school and that you don't like to talk there. But this is just pretend. You don't have to

worry about talking in pretend school. Let's see, I'll be a student and you be a teacher.'

Vanessa: 'OK. [Somewhat reluctantly she takes the teacher figure.] Sit down kids, it's time to do your reading groups. You kids go over there and you kids over here. Now I'm going to walk around and check on you.'

Dad: 'I'll be this boy. [He takes a figure.] He's not a good reader. He says to his friend, "I hope the teacher doesn't ask me to read."'

Vanessa: [to her father] 'Should I ask him?'

Dad: 'Sure, let's see what happens.'

Vanessa: 'OK. [She now seems more interested in the play and what will happen next.] James, it's your turn to read. Will you read in front of the class.'

Dad: [in the role of James] 'I don't really want to, teacher. Can you ask someone else?'

Vanessa: 'I know you don't want to read. But you have to.'

Dad: 'Can I read just once sentence? I know that I can read just one sentence. OK?'

Vanessa: 'OK. You can read just one sentence.'

Dad: 'And the next time you call on me I'll read two sentences. OK?'

Vanessa: 'OK. Fine. That's good that you're trying.'

Vanessa's father is modelling what the counsellor told him to do with Vanessa – encourage her to take one small step at a time. In pretend play, children can practise doing things that may be difficult for them in the real world, but doing so will always be easier when you show them how.

TRY IT

Think about a scenario in the real world and create a pretend drama with your child during his Special Play time. Choose small figures or puppets so that the drama can be acted out. Now take a role that might be similar to your child and demonstrate the thoughts, behaviour and feelings you want your child to imitate. Invite your child to play out this drama using the modelling technique along with the other four techniques that make up Special Play.

Show your child that you hold him in high esteem

When children are infants and toddlers we constantly hug them and kiss them and play with them. Nature has made our little ones so adorable that we cannot get enough of them! This nearly constant expression of our caring builds the foundation for their sense of self-worth, and also sets the pattern for how they will express caring and affection towards others when they are older.

But as children grow, we become less physically and verbally affectionate towards them, even though this is still an important way that they build their self-esteem. As a psychologist, I often tell parents to shape their child's behaviour through praise and affection and to 'catch them being good'. But sometimes parents retort, 'I'd like to "catch them being good", but they never are good!' Special Play is my answer for parents who seem to have lost the knack for showing their children how much they care for them. Special Play helps re-establish the all important bond between parent and child; the bond that will be the prototype for every relationship in the child's future.

The most important way that you can show your esteem for your child using Special Play is simply by doing it consistently. Too many times parents start off with the best of intentions, but one thing or another interrupts their scheduled play sessions until all of a sudden parents realize that they have not shared this experience with their children in weeks. You must keep your commitment to your child by using Special Play on a regular basis, at least several times a week, if not every day. Find a time (remember it is only fifteen to twenty minutes) that you can commit to, just as you would commit to an important business appointment. Do not let day-to-day pressures keep you from this important way of helping your child's emotional development.

When you play, make sure that there are no distractions. Find a place where you will not be interrupted. Turn off the phone or answering machine. Let other people in your home know that this is an important time.

Finally, you should know that your non-verbal behaviour speaks louder than your words. Here are some ways that you can show your child your esteem and positive regard non-verbally, as well as through the other Special Play techniques.

- *Eye contact:* When you play with your child, make sure that you are on the same eye level. If she is playing on the floor, then that is where you should be, too. If you are at a table, make sure that you are facing her.
- *Facial expression:* Your child is always watching you, even when she is doing something else. Remember, when you feel interested, you look interested, and if you feel bored, then you will look like you are bored.
- *Posture:* Lean towards your child. This shows your interest in what she is doing.
- *Gesture:* You can use gestures as a way to show your praise for your child, like the 'thumbs-up' sign, patting him on the shoulder, clapping your hands and so on.
- *Clothes:* The clothes you are wearing communicate to your child about your desire to play. Take a few moments to change into your 'play clothes', just as you would have your child do.
- *Physical distance:* A child's personal space is about an arm's length away, but when you play, you are usually closer than this. Be aware of her non-verbal signals that indicate when your child wants you to be closer or when she wants more physical distance.
- *Voice tone:* Your enthusiasm for the play should be reflected in your voice. If you are distracted or even bored, your child will pick this up in your voice tone.

If you have scheduled a Special Play session but you are distracted and stressed, then suggest another time for you and your child to play when you can give your full attention and energy. Tell your child that you have had a hard day and that you want to have your Special Play time later the same day (but not later than the next day). If you are sincere, your child will understand. But make sure that you carry through with your commitment to play at the soonest opportunity. Remember that your child knows the secret language of play better than you, and nothing speaks louder than a broken promise to play. If you can make Special Play a regular habit, I can guarantee that you will create experiences for you and your child which neither of you will ever forget.

Chapter 7

Troublesome Play

We normally think of play as the most natural part of child-hood. What could be a more innocent picture than a five-year-old girl dressed in her mummy's shoes, playing with her dolls and tea set, or a 9-year-old boy lounging on the staircase and throwing a tennis ball against the wall, again and again? But as with other aspects of the secret language of children, there may be a hidden meaning to a child's seemingly innocent play, a meaning which responsible adults must both interpret and respond to.

Most parents recognize when their child plays differently than other children, but they are not always sure about whether this difference is a sign of a problem or not. Consider the common parental concerns below. Which ones do you think could be signs of trouble?

- Sam, age four, wanted to 'play baby' after his sister Alison was born. Sam liked to drink from a bottle, talk in gibberish, and he tried to make himself a nappy out of construction paper and Scotch tape.
- Maggie at age six had a typical fascination with dressing-up dolls. But her favourite activity was to take the clothes off of all her dolls and have them do 'naked dances'.
- When Malik was nine, he moved into a new neighbourhood where there were no other children who had a Pakistani back-ground. Although he was a good cricket player, the popular sport in his new school was football, and he was not particularly good at it. He spent most of the time at break by himself while the other children played.

• Katy went through a difficult time when her grandfather died. Normally a happy and outgoing child, she now preferred to spend time playing by herself, having pretend funerals for her dolls and burying them in a sandbox.

So which of these children revealed signs of emotional distress? All of them. Sam's regressive play shows his anxiety about being replaced in the affections of his parents. Maggie's doll play shows that she has had at least some exposure to adult sexuality. Malik's social isolation will interfere with his social development. Katy's sudden change of mood and the repetitive nature of her play reveal her deep grief at the loss of her grandfather. Yet while each of these children showed signs of emotional conflict, none of them went on to have serious problems. Children's play will often reveal emotional distress, but that does not mean that they will necessarily develop a psychological problem. On the contrary, observing your child's play can be an early warning system for preventing psychological problems, calling you to action long before actual symptoms appear. In each of the examples mentioned above, an adult paid attention to the child's play and gave each youngster the appropriate guidance.

In some cases, your child's play may indicate a need for professional help. Every serious childhood problem – from over-aggressiveness to depression – first reveals itself in play. If we consider that an estimated 5 to 10 per cent of children exhibit some form of a serious emotional problem in childhood, then it is likely that many of the readers of this book will have children who have emotional and behavioural problems that need professional attention. If you find that some aspects of your child's play are troublesome to you, do not hesitate to seek professional guidance. Remember that your intuition is your best guide in understanding the secret language of your child. In this chapter we will look at the most common forms of troublesome play that may indicate an emotional or a behavioural problem, including: aggressive play, sexualized play, ritualistic play, children who can not play alone and children who can not play with others.

Aggressive play

It is normal for young children, particularly boys, to show some aggression in their play. Many of the toys that boys like to play with are designed to bring out their aggressive impulses, so it is only natural when their play includes fighting, shooting and games of war. I have known many parents who have tried to discourage their children from any form of aggressive play, in the hope that they will raise more peace-loving and compassionate boys. But forbidding any form of aggressive play rarely gets the intended results. If children want to play aggressively, they will find a way. Many years ago, a friend of mine told me about an incident when her 2½-year-old son wanted a toy gun that he saw in the store. 'I won't get you a gun,' his mother told him, 'but I will buy you a doll to play with.' When they got home, the boy took the doll out of its box, pointed it at his baby sister, and said, 'Bang, Bang!' He continued to use the doll like a gun for the rest of the day.

This mother assumed that if her son played with guns and war toys, then this would predispose him towards aggression as the boy grew into a man. But this is not the nature of play. In fact, this boy, now twenty-five, grew up to be a gentle, kind-hearted young man even though he played with guns and action figures throughout his childhood. Similarly, many children, both boys and girls, are able to play very aggressively in sports, or in competitive intellectual games like chess, but that aggression does not spill over into their day-to-day behaviour in a negative way. In fact, researchers tell us that children who are slightly more aggressive in their play are also more popular with their peers. The trick, of course, is in being able to handle different, even opposing feelings at the same time; to be assertive, but to also be kind, helpful and respectful of others.

Anger and aggression in play is not the same thing as anger and aggression in the real world. I remember vividly a time when a young mother brought in her 5-year-old daughter for an evaluation because when the child played with her doll's house, she regularly stuck the 'mummy' doll's head in the play toilet, saying,

'There, that's what you deserve!' When I interviewed this mother, she did not reveal any clues that this girl had any problems with anger or aggression. I reminded this mother that play is a world of imagination and fantasy, where any feeling can be explored. When children have serious anger control problems, they can be observed not only in their play, but it invariably affects behaviour relationships in the real world.

Eight-year-old Jason is an example of a child with true anger control problems. He was sent to a counsellor for his uncontrollable outbursts of temper. Jason had difficulty in any type of play. If he was playing with his electric trains, and a piece of track did not fit properly, he would completely destroy the train setup, throwing the tracks and cars across the room. If he lost while playing a board game with his parents, he would storm out of the room, slamming the door behind him and vowing he would never speak to them again. Anger is a problem in a child's play when the child is not able to see and respect the limits of the play. Anger is a problem when children, like Jason, destroy toys. Parents should be concerned when play with other children leads to arguing or physical confrontations. They should also be concerned when a child does not respect rules, or limits, or the needs and desires of others.

If your child has problems in anger control then there are many things that you can do. First, you should look at your child's environment and lifestyle and determine if there are things happening which may be contributing to excessive anger and his inability to express it appropriately. We know that some children are temperamentally more prone to being impatient or having angry arguments, but this tendency is exacerbated by factors which are within a parent's control. Here are some things you can do to help your child learn to control his anger in the secret language of play.

Eliminate violent video games and violent television shows

There is no question that the violent content of television shows and video games encourages aggression.

Play cooperative games

Most children with anger control problems have difficulty in playing competitive games. There are many games, however, that build trust and cooperation. For some ideas, I recommend Dale Lefevre's book *Best New Games* for dozens of great ideas.

Have more family playtime

Children with problems in anger control frequently have at least one parent who is quick-tempered. Sometimes both parents behave this way. More family play is my prescription whenever there is excessive arguing or conflict in the home. Find activities that everyone enjoys. Keep playtimes short – just ten minutes is enough – and make sure that everyone has a good time. If anyone gets angry during the play, immediately stop, and try a new activity the next day.

Use play as a way to set rules and boundaries

By definition children with problems in anger control have a hard time with limits and rules. In many families, this is in part due to the difficulty that their parents have in setting clear rules and giving appropriate consequences if those rules are broken. Play gives parents many opportunities to set rules and enforce them. Consider the following rules and consequences from the Harris home who had two spirited boys, ages seven and nine. You may want to come up with a similar list for your child's playtime:

Rules for playtime	What happens if the rules are broken
You must not argue during playtime.	Both boys must sit quietly for fifteen minutes.
You must put away your toys or other things when you are finished with them.	Toys not put away are taken away and put in the cupboard for one week. *continued*

You must be careful not to hurt anyone during any sport or playtime.	When one brother hurts another, he must do that brother's chores for one week.
You must stop playing immediately if a parent says it is time to do something else.	You must go to bed fifteen minutes earlier for each time you have to be reminded to stop playing.

Finally, if you have a child with problems in anger control, you can use games to teach him specific anger control skills. In the next chapter, I will talk more about emotional learning games that can help children with anger control by teaching them better ways to express their feelings, understand the feelings of others and control their impulses. But if you cannot wait, try this game for helping children learn to ignore the teasing or taunts of others.

TRY IT

The Ignoring Game

What you are teaching: Children with problems in anger control are typically more sensitive and responsive to the negative things that they see around them. They are more likely than other children to interpret actions or words as provocative, even when nothing was intended. When you ask a child who has just had an angry outburst or confrontation with a peer, 'Why did you do that?' you may hear a response like: 'Because he gave me a dirty look,' or 'Because he called me a name,' or simply, 'She started it.'

I designed the 'Ignoring Game' to help children practise ignoring the taunts and teasing of others, rather than reacting with anger. You will also find it appropriate to play with any child who is learning to deal with teasing.

What you need: A deck of cards; a stopwatch, kitchen timer or wristwatch.

How to play: The youngest player goes first. She attempts to build a card house for three minutes. The second player verbally or non-verbally teases the player trying to build the card house. No touching is allowed. If any player building the card house is touched, she automatically wins the game. The player building the house gets one point for each card standing after three minutes. But she gets one point deducted every time she looks at the player who is doing the teasing. After three minutes the roles are reversed. The first player to get twenty points is declared the winner. (*Hint*: It is easier to build a card house on a carpet than on a slippery table. If younger players have difficulty building a card house, use a combination of blocks and cards.)

The sexual side of play

One Saturday afternoon I received a frantic call from the mother of a 6-year-old girl, who had been a patient of mine about a year before. The child had run into the house complaining that her friends were 'playing sex', and that they would not let her play.

'What exactly did she mean by that?' I asked the mother, trying to quickly shift into my professional mindset, even though I had been pulling weeds from the garden. 'She said that they were playing with their dolls and taking their clothes off and "playing sex" with them,' the mother said, not trying to disguise the growing panic in her voice. 'But Emmy said that one of the girls had her clothes off, too, so I'm not really sure what went on.'

This mother's concern was certainly understandable. Statistics tell us that tens of thousands of children are sexually abused each year, most of them girls. Surveys also tell us that abuse is not limited to adults abusing children. All too frequently sexual abuse comes from older children, either in the home or in the neighbourhood, and it often starts out as some form of sex play.

In this case, as in any situation where sexual abuse or exploitation is suspected, the first rule is to keep calm and gather the facts. I advised Emmy's mother to sit down with her daughter and ask her to describe exactly what the girls were doing while they played. I suggested that she ask the parents of the other girls to have similar conversations with their children. In this case, the play had not gone very far, and all the parents involved were advised to monitor their children more closely and have discussions about appropriate kinds of play. In other situations I have encountered, when sexual abuse was discovered in an initial conversation, I urged parents to immediately seek professional advice for the family and the child and to report the incident to the appropriate authorities.

While parents can discover sexual abuse through play they can also turn to play as a way to prevent it. For example, I advise parents of children five years and under to use dolls to explain to their children the 'bathing-suit' rule of safe touching. The 'bathing-suit' rule states that: 'The areas covered by your bathing suit are private and not to be touched by anyone unless you're being washed or examined by a medical doctor.' Young children are very concrete thinkers, and they are also very curious about their bodies and the bodies of the opposite sex. Dolls can be a good way to answer their questions, as frankly and honestly as you can.

One of the keys to good parenting is being able to articulate your values to your child, and to do that you need to be clear about them and comfortable in expressing them. This is certainly true when it comes to your child's sex education. Most psychologists feel that there is no longer such a thing as a 'Big Talk', where children are told the facts of life, but rather children learn about sex and sexuality a little bit at a time, and each stage of development brings a new layer of understanding.

Play gives you a unique opportunity to talk to school-age children about the many aspects of sex and sexuality. During Special Play, as described in the previous chapter, you can not only share your values, but you can also teach your children how to handle difficult situations. For example, a former client, Harry Wentworth, read in his newspaper about three 9-year-old boys who had cornered a 6-year-old girl in the stairwell of their elementary school, and they had made crude remarks to her while trying to lift up her skirt. Harry's daughter Patrice was also six, and he wanted her to know what to do if she was ever confronted by a similar situation. During his Special Play time with his daughter he suggested: 'Let's act out a play about someone teasing you because you are a girl. Sometimes girls get teased by boys and it is important to know what to do. You take the boy doll and I'll take the girl doll and you tease me about being a girl and let's see what happens.'

Assuming the role of the girl in this little drama and letting his daughter take the role of the boy accomplished two things. First, it gave Harry an opportunity to find out what Patrice had already experienced around teasing. Letting her take the lead and listening to the language that she used told him clearly about her experience regarding gender-based teasing. Secondly, by taking the role of the girl doll, Harry had a chance to model appropriate responses for his daughter. Through pretend play, he responded in ways which demonstrated how a 6-year-old might handle teasing such as: Don't be alone at anytime. Tell an adult immediately if someone says or does something that upsets you. Walk away from a situation that makes you uncomfortable.

For older children communication board games are particularly useful in creating an atmosphere for parents and children to talk openly about sexuality or other awkward topics. One commercially available game, the 'Ungame' (Talicor, Inc.), was invented by a speech and language therapist for exactly this purpose. The Ungame has been used by tens of thousands of families to create an atmosphere where thoughts and feelings are shared without fear of criticism. In the next chapter I will teach you how to make your own communication board game for use with your family, using the Make-a-Game technique, where you and your children can write your own question cards to cover any topic imaginable.

Ritualistic, repetitive or odd play

Occasionally parents will observe their children during play and report that they seem 'strange', or in 'another world'. One parent called me because he was worried that his 6-year-old built exactly the same Lego house every day. The boy would spend hours using exactly 58 pieces, 32 blue and 26 red, and would arrange them precisely the same way each time. Then the boy would observe his toy house, staring at it for fifteen minutes or so, then carefully take it apart, mix up the pieces, and start all over again. His father reported that he had been doing this for at least a month, and that he had been showing some other odd behaviours as well, like staring at his digital watch for a half an hour at a time.

Ritualistic or odd play is always a concern. On the one hand, it is common in certain stages of childhood. On the other hand, when it lasts over an extended period of time, or it interferes with other aspects of a child's development, it may be a warning sign of serious psychological problems like Obsessive Compulsive Disorder (OCD) or Asperger's Syndrome, a type of autism that is characterized by eccentric play and very poor social skills in children who typically have a high level of intelligence and language skills. Ritualistic play can also be a characteristic of children who have been physically abused, or who have suffered some other trauma.

This, of course, is not to say that all young children who partic- ipate in odd and ritualistic types of play have emotional problems. One 3-year-old I know liked to line up every one of her twenty- three dolls on the bed, in the exactly the same pose, before she would go to sleep. This night-time ritual began to spill into a day- time habit, and Rachel used to play 'line-up' every day. But this seemingly rigid form of behaviour only lasted for a few weeks. When an older friend saw Rachel's game of 'line-up' she said, 'That's a stupid game, let's play kitchens,' and Rachel acquiesced. After that she rarely played 'line-up'.

I have known many other children who like to play with their toys in a very formalized and repetitive way, and this usually does not indicate a serious problem. Sometimes doing the same thing over and over again brings children comfort. Other times this type of play allows children to try to master complex feelings. For example, Gregory lived in a small New Jersey town, a suburb of New York City, where many parents commuted to the city every day. Gregory turned five years old on 13 September 2001, two days after the terrorist attack on the World Trade Center in Manhattan. Gregory did not know anyone who died that terrible day, but his parents seemed to know many people who had lost loved ones, and, of course, Gregory saw the grim images of the planes crashing into the Twin Towers and the buildings collapsing on repeated news- casts. For months Gregory played 'protection' with his toys. He would surround a particular toy, or figure, or even a framed photograph of his family, with all of his best 'fighting men'. Then he would build a tall 'anti-gravity fort' to repel attacking aircraft. He played like this once or twice each day. It was his magical way of keeping his family safe. But as the months passed, Gregory played this game less and less. By the new year, he hardly played the game at all and preferred to play with a new toy he received for Christmas.

Repetitive and ritualistic play serves a magical purpose for children just like repetition and rituals do for adults. Perhaps you go to the same coffee shop in the morning, or use the same special cup every morning at home. Perhaps you wear a particular sweater or tie to an important meeting or carry around a lucky coin and rub it for confidence. Ritualistic and repetitive behaviour is a common occurrence in nearly every stage of development, but it is only a problem if you cannot stop doing it, or if you do not have more realistic ways to deal with anxiety. If you are at all concerned about a child's odd or ritualistic behaviour, then certainly consult a professional.

When children have difficulty playing with their peers

Not too long ago, I was giving a lecture to a group of parents about the importance of playing with your child, and a parent of a 7-year-old came up to me and said: 'Dr Shapiro, you said that it is important for us to play with our children, but all I do is play with my child! I play with him at least three or four hours a day! Whenever I'm around he wants to play. Whether I'm cooking dinner or trying to make the bed, it doesn't matter. I can't get anything done and frankly it's driving me crazy. You say that parents should spend time playing with their children every day, but is it possible that I'm playing too much?'

The problem that this mother faced was not really about too much play, it was about too few limits. She needed to learn to say, 'No, I'm too busy to play with you now, you'll have to find something else to do.' The problem was also that this child (who was five years old) did not know how to play independently.

It is natural for children to want their parents' attention as much as they can get it and, of course, want you to participate in activities that they enjoy. But children go through many stages of play as they grow and they should be seeking the company of other children in their play as early as two-and-a-half or three. By age five they should enjoy playing in different ways with different people. They should play with their parents, with their peers and by themselves in about equal amounts. By seven, children usually prefer playing with their peers to any other form of play.

But unfortunately many children have difficulty making the shift from playing with family members to playing with peers. Of all of the different problems that children tell you about in the secret language of their play, the most common is: 'Nobody wants to play with me, I'm lonely.' There are many reasons why children feel isolated and alone, including behavioural problems, shyness, physical or cultural differences, even family problems that keep children focused on their relationships in the home rather than on their peer group.

Most of the time there is some combination of situational and temperamental factors that keeps a child from being successful at meeting age-appropriate social challenges. Take, for example, Noah, an overweight 11-year-old, who rarely played with other children. Noah was naturally shy, but his embarrassment over his weight problem made things worse. When the other children in his school played together at break, Noah sat and read a book. When others in his class got together for play dates or sports at the weekends, Noah stayed home and watched television.

Every age of development has important milestones which we expect children to achieve. In the area of social development, we expect children to have at least one 'best friend' between the ages of seven and nine and to have a group of friends (usually of the same sex) by age eleven. But Noah did not even have a single friend. Aside from the fact that he was lonely, his inability to find friends portended serious long-range consequences. Children who are socially isolated are at risk of a wide range of psychological problems as they enter adolescence, from depression and eating disorders to drug and alcohol abuse. We sometimes think of intellectually precocious 'eggheads' as being loners in school, but in actuality most socially isolated children are underachievers and have a much greater risk of academic problems and school drop out.

If your child is between six and twelve years old and does not play with other children on a regular basis then you should certainly be concerned. From a developmental perspective this age range is the 'window of opportunity' where children learn relationship skills which they will use to meet the social challenges of adolescence and adulthood. You should make every effort you can to see that they learn the secret language of playing with others. Here are some things you can do.

Play with your child more yourself

Adult 'playmates' are not the same as having friends of the same age, but play is a language that can be spoken at any age. When your child plays with you or other adults in the home she can still learn important social skills, such as creative thinking, taking turns, being a good winner or a good loser and so on. As she practises these skills with you, encourage her to use them with other children as well.

Encourage your child to find a hobby and seek social opportunities related to that hobby

Children find it easiest to make friends with other children who have similar interests. It does not matter what the hobby is – collecting comic books, playing chess, skateboarding or spelunking – every hobby has some elements of play and playfulness.

Teach your child the skills he needs to help him make and keep friends

There are reasons why some children are more popular than others. Popular children have better social-play skills than other children, and unpopular or isolated children typically lack these skills. Aaron, for example, was a typical child with Attention Deficit Hyperactivity

Disorder. He had only an occasional friend and was never invited to parties because he was considered 'bossy' and boastful. In fact, Aaron was not particularly bossy or boastful for an 8-year-old boy, but he came across that way because of his poor judgement in social situations. If Aaron saw a group of boys playing football, he might yell, 'I'm a great player. I have two footballs at home! Can I play?' Then the boys would just ignore him. Aaron might ask them if he could play again, but eventually he would just walk away. Aaron's parents were naturally concerned about his lack of friends and they asked his teacher for advice. The teacher recommended a social skills training group that they had in his school where children were taught specific skills to help them make friends and play well with others. For example, instead of just shouting out to a group of children Aaron wanted to play with, he was taught to find one person who looked friendly and to go up to that person, make eye contact and ask politely if he could join in. Social skills groups of this type are very helpful to children with ADHD and other behavioural problems, just as they are helpful to children who are shy or socially awkward. Many counsellors feel that this type of training would benefit all children (and some argue that it would help most adults, too). If your child has difficulty in speaking the secret language of play with his peers, then you should inquire at your school as to whether social skills groups are available. If not, here are some suggestions that you can do yourself.

TRY IT

Begin by observing your child at play with other children. Try not to intervene, even if things are not going well. Then review the list below and see if there is one thing that would help your child be more successful at playing with others. Practise this skill by role-playing with your child. If you can, videotape the role-playing so your child can observe himself practising a newly acquired social skill. Keep encouraging your child to spend time playing with other children, no matter what the circumstances. Most children with problems in social skills play better with slightly younger children, since they themselves are socially immature. Remember that play is the best way that your child will develop the relationship skills that will last him a lifetime, so make sure that he spends time every day learning these skills.

Ten Critical Social Skills that Children Learn at Play

1. How to invite another child to play.
2. How to take turns.
3. How to follow game rules.
4. How to be a gracious winner.
5. How to be a gracious loser.
6. How to share toys or other playthings.
7. How to behave to get positive reinforcement from peers.
8. How to be flexible about one's needs.
9. How to evaluate one's social successes and failures.
10. How to read non-verbal cues of others.

Chapter 8

Fifteen Minutes of Play a Day: A Prescription for Happier, More Confident Children

I have been prescribing emotional learning games to children for over twenty years. I have invented board games, card games, word games, pencil and paper games, outdoor games and games you play in the car. Because I teach these games to other psychologists and therapists, I know that they have been used with tens of thousands of children in the United States and around the world.

Each game I invent is designed to teach children a specific emotional or social skill, such as: communicating feelings, respecting the rights of others, resolving arguments peacefully and so on. Of all the techniques I have used to reach children in their secret language, games have been the most effective because of their ease of use and universal appeal. Emotional learning games are now considered a standard treatment for helping children by most in professional settings, but there is no better place I can think of using them than in your home.

Emotional learning games are for the most part modifications of games that are already familiar to children. This is what makes them so easy for children and their parents to learn. Take, for example, the game of 'Mummy Says' (a derivation of the familiar game of Simon Says) that I used to help 6-year-old Ray become more cooperative with his parents.

Ray's mother, Rosemary, brought her son to me for counselling with the complaint, 'He never listens to me. He never does a thing

I ask him to. He's the most stubborn child I have ever seen.' As his mother talked, Ray just sat there with his arms crossed over his chest. He seemed completely detached from his mother's accusations, as if she were talking about a different child entirely. Rosemary began to tell me about Ray's background – her divorce when he was two, his problems in school – but I interrupted her. 'Just what do you want Ray to do that he is not doing?' I asked. 'Do you want him to pick up his toys? To get ready for bed without a fuss? Tell me just one thing that is important to you, and I'll show you how you can get him to cooperate immediately without a struggle.'

Rosemary seemed surprised at the directness of my offer. She did not think that Ray would become more cooperative so easily. 'Well, I'd like him to clean up his room,' she said tentatively, not sure what I was going to do or say. 'It's a mess and I'm tired of yelling at him.'

'OK then, I'll show you how to get him to clean up his room,' I replied matter-of-factly. 'I'll have him clean up my office for me, which as you can see could use a good straightening up.'

I turned to the boy and said, 'Ray, do you know how to play "Simon Says".' I got up from my chair indicating I was ready to play.

'Sure,' Ray said warily, but ready to see what was going to come next.

'Well, this is a game called "Dr Shapiro Says". It's played exactly the same way, but when you play, you'll be helping me do something important. OK?'

'OK,' Ray agreed and we began.

'Now Dr Shapiro says: "Stand Up."' Ray did.

'Dr Shapiro says: "Take the three books on my desk and put them on the book shelf."' Ray did.

'Now Dr Shapiro says, "Pick up the pieces of the game over there, and put them back in the box."' Ray did. I glance at Ray's mother and saw her staring at him with a mixture of pride and amazement. It was as if she had never seen her son be cooperative before.

'Now raise your right hand.' Ray did not because I did not say 'Dr Shapiro says.' 'Very good,' I said, 'you're a good listener.'

'Twirl around.' Ray did not.

'Now, Dr Shapiro says: "Straighten out that crooked picture over on that wall."' Ray did this.

'Good! You straightened the picture on my wall, put away a game and put my books back on the bookshelf. Thanks! Dr Shapiro says "Sit down."'

Ray sat with a look of self-satisfaction. He had done exactly what I asked him to do and he seemed happy to show that he could be cooperative when he wanted to. I explained to his mother, 'Now it is your turn to play a game of "Mummy Says". I'm sure that Ray will do whatever you ask, because that is how he'll win the game!'

We played 'Mummy Says' a few times in my office and Ray was equally cooperative. Then I took a pad and wrote a 'prescription' to play this game at home three times in the next week.

I have taught 'Mummy Says' and other behavioural games to hundreds of parents over the last twenty years. Using similar games, I have helped children deal with every problem you can think of, from coping with bullies to overcoming shyness. Like Ray, in the context of a game children will behave in ways which parents and teachers never thought possible. Why do they do this? Because humans have an inborn desire to follow the rules of a game. With very few exceptions, children between the ages of three and twelve get immediately caught up in any game that you present to them. The fact that a game is designed to help them with an emotional, social or behavioural problem does not seem to make a difference.

Many child therapists use emotional learning games in their sessions to help children learn new ways to overcome their problems, and youngsters like playing these games so much that they begin to look forward to seeing a counsellor. But games are also ideally suited for use in the home. They require little or no equipment. They are simple to do and they are fun for both parents and children. Parents like them because they have immediate results.

But emotional learning games are not just for children with problems. As I wrote in a previous book, *An Ounce of Prevention: How Parents Can Stop Childhood Behavioral and Emotional Problems Before They Start*, emotional learning games are just as important in preventing problems. Emotional learning games are the best way I know to enrich your child's emotional intelligence in three critical areas: teaching children to understand and communicate their feelings; reinforcing important behaviours like helpfulness and kindness; and developing a positive attitude and values.

In this chapter, I will teach you my favourite games to help children in these three critical aspects of their emotional development. All of these games take just fifteen minutes or less to play and they are fun so that your children will want to play them over and over again. This is an important point, because repetition is really the key to their success. As you know, when you are acquiring any new skill, whether it is a better golf swing, learning a foreign language or playing a musical instrument, it takes a lot of practice. If you practise every day when you begin learning that skill you will soon reach at least a basic level of competency, and that will give you a sense of accomplishment to acquire an even greater level of proficiency. This same principle holds true when learning new emotional or behavioural skills. Practice – at least fifteen minutes a day – is needed to really make a difference in your child's development. Then after a few weeks, whatever new emotional or behavioural skills you are working on should get easier. Set aside just a quarter of an hour each day to increase your child's emotional intelligence, just as you set aside some time every day to help your youngster learn reading, history, maths or another important subject. I am certain that this will be time well spent.

Begin by teaching children new ways to understand their feelings and the feelings of others

Emotional skills are best taught to children the way that academic and athletic skills are taught, one step at a time. Take, for example, the emotional skill of learning to talk about feelings. You may not think of this as something that has to be taught and yet I am sure you know many adults who have not acquired this skill. Most young children need to be taught that talking about your feelings is a way that others will understand your needs and desires. They need to learn that talking about feelings is not only a more direct route to getting what you want, but that it also makes you feel better (many adults need to be reminded of this, too).

Children should begin learning a 'feelings' vocabulary when they are three or four years old. By five or six years, they should be able to understand more than ten basic feelings (sad, happy, afraid, brave, surprised, angry, calm, confused, shy, lonely, etc.) and to identify situations when these feelings are likely to occur. Between eight to ten, children should be able to recognize the signs of different feelings in others. By adolescence they should understand the subtle differences of dozens of different feelings and they should be able to see that their feelings can be changed by the different actions that they take.

Researchers consistently tell us that being able to talk about feelings is one of the most important measures of emotional intelligence at any age. The more children talk about their feelings and respect the feelings of others, the more popular they will be among their peers and with adults outside of the family. Children and teenagers who are able to reflect on their feelings and are sensitive to the feelings of others invariably have more social and academic success. This is a key aspect of good mental health.

Helping children learn to express their feelings is particularly important when children have behavioural problems. Consider Diana, who at age six was considered a 'wild child'. Since the age of two-and-a-half or three, Diana had been wilful and aggressive. She talked back to her parents, threw tantrums, sulked and was hostile towards other children. She had been asked to leave her nursery school because she was constantly in the time-out corner, although it seemed to have no effect in reducing her difficult behaviours. Within a week of entering infants school, Diana was referred to me for counselling because she was teasing other children and talking back to her teacher.

After an evaluation, I told her parents: 'Diana doesn't talk about her feelings, she just acts on them. I honestly don't know why she is such an angry little girl, but I know that she needs better ways to deal with her anger. She also needs to learn how to recognize and explore other more positive feelings that she has. Behavioural programmes do not seem to have worked in the past, so let's try something new. Let me teach you a game that will help Diana, and the rest of the family, talk more about feelings.' And with that I reached behind my desk and took out my Feelings Ball.

The Feelings Ball game is great at getting children to talk about any feelings that you think are important for them. I am sure that it will work for your family the first time that you use it and that you will be surprised at how easy it is to get your children to open up. I have used this game as a warm-up exercise in large lectures with more than 500 people attending and I always get three or four audience participants to stand up and talk about their feelings and experiences – and believe me they do not want to do this! I have prescribed this game to many families, and to teachers as well. It never fails in helping children at any age talk about their feelings. When you play it often, it gets children into the habit of talking about their feelings, instead of just acting them out.

Here is how to play:

TRY IT

The Feelings Ball Game

Object of the game: To get children in the habit of talking about their different feelings.

Ages: 5+

Number of players: 2–10

Preparation: You will need a beach ball and a permanent marker. Inflate the ball and write down different feelings around it, such as happy, sad, angry, afraid and so on. Choose feelings that are appropriate to your child's age level. You can write down the same feelings three or four times to fill the space on a large ball.

Rules:
1. An adult goes first, to model how the game is played. Throw the ball up in the air and then catch it with both hands. Look

and see which 'feelings' word is closest to your right thumb.

2. Now talk about the last time that you had that feeling.

3. Then throw the ball to the person on your right who must do the same thing.

4. Do not comment on what another person has said – just listen.

5. Continue until each player has had at least two turns.

The Feelings Ball game is a great way to get your family to talk about feelings, but there are many other variations that you can do with this game to teach other emotional intelligence skills. Get additional beach balls and try these games using the same rules as the Feelings Ball game.

The Funny Ball game – write down funny things to do on the beach ball, such as: 'tell a joke', 'make a funny face', 'tickle another player', make a strange sound' and so on.

The Calming Ball game – write down different ways to relax on the ball, such as: 'listen to quiet music', 'take ten deep breaths', 'massage the hand of another player', 'describe a peaceful place' and so on. With this game, rather than one player doing what it says on the ball, all players must simultaneously do what the Calming Ball says.

The Make-a-Friend Ball game – write down different things that help children practise simple social skills, such as: 'Shake the hand of the player to your right'; 'Give another player a compliment'; 'Ask another player about the events of his/her day.' This game can be played by the family, but it is even better if you can get a group of children together to practise friend-making skills.

The anger control game

Once Diana had begun to verbalize her feelings on a regular basis, the next thing she needed to learn was to control her anger. It is an unfortunate commentary on our times that almost every school I visit these days has anger management classes to help children like Diana who are prone to outbursts of temper, verbal assaults or physical aggression. There are complex reasons why so many children these days seem to have problems with anger control, but rather than dwell on the causes, I prefer to look at solutions. The best solution I can think of is to give every child some help in learning about anger, long before there is a problem. After all, everyone gets angry at sometime and everyone needs to know how to express anger appropriately. So why not teach all children how to understand and control their anger as part of their emotional education? And what better way to do it than the secret language of play! This game is used to teach children nine things to do to help them with their anger: talk about what is bothering you with a friend; listen to quiet music; play a game with someone; find something to make you laugh; draw a picture of your anger; take five deep breaths; think of two alternative solutions to your problem; walk around in circles until you cool down; sit down and relax your muscles.

I taught these anger control skills to Diana by using a simple coin toss game. As you can see in the illustration below, the angry faces have negative point values and the anger techniques have positive point values.

TRY IT

The Cool Down Game

Objective: To teach children nine anger control techniques.
Ages: 6 to 12
Players: 2

Preparation: Copy the illustration above on to an A4 sheet of paper. You will also need ten 2p and ten 1p coins. You will play this game on a table or other flat surface.

Rules:

1. The object of the game is to get the highest number of points by throwing coins into the Cool Down Circles.

2. Each player gets a pile of coins.

3. The youngest player goes first and tosses a coin, trying to get the coin on a Cool Down Circle. If he gets a coin at least halfway in the circle, he gets the number of points designated by that circle if he answers the question or demonstrates the technique in that circle.

4. If the player lands on an angry face, then the designated number of points is taken away.

5. Then the next player goes and play continues taking alternate turns.

6. When all the coins have been tossed, the player with the most points is the winner. The winner can get a small prize.

Emotional learning games can teach children new behaviours

At the beginning of this chapter I described a game of 'Mummy Says', a derivation of the classic childhood game of 'Simon Says', which teaches children to listen and follow directions while performing some task or chore that they would not ordinarily do. Over the many years that I have been prescribing emotional learning games, I have found that this is a much more effective approach to teaching children better behaviour than standard discipline techniques like the time-out corner or taking away a privilege. As I frequently tell parents: 'It is easier to teach children to be good, than to prevent them from being bad.' And the best way to teach a child something new is through a game.

As the games below will demonstrate, you can teach children good manners, you can teach them to be more helpful and you can teach them to be more attentive to adult rules, and much more. Most importantly, I think that you will find that these games are a welcome alternative to constant reminders, reprimands and punishment. It is always better to help children through the language of play, a language which they already understand.

Teaching children manners

Good manners are the most basic way that children get the approval and acceptance of others and yet so many children these days have poor manners. One survey found that 70 per cent of parents believed that children today have poor manners as compared to prior generations and yet, ironically, only 20 per cent of these same parents felt that *their* children had poor manners. This leads me to conclude that parents have high expectations for the behaviour of other people's children, but low expectations for their own youngsters.

Whatever your perceptions of your own child's manners, I can tell you that the more politely, considerately and thoughtfully that your child behaves, the better she will do in the world. Everyone likes well-behaved and well-mannered children and so it follows that they get more positive feedback and social approval, which in turn gives them a sense of self-confidence and self-worth. You can make sure that your child gets an emotional head-start in life by simply emphasizing good manners in your home. If your child resists, then perhaps this game for young children will help.

TRY IT

Games can take many forms. Young children in particular love games that involve music and singing. When they learn a new song, particularly if the song is based on a familiar melody, they will sing it over and over again – which is exactly what you want to help them learn a new behaviour. If you have young children in your home, you might want to play this game several times a week. It certainly beats constant lectures about good manners.

Manners are the way that we show we care

Objective: To remind young children about the importance of good manners and encourage them to find new ways to show that they are considerate of others.
Ages: 3 to 7
Number of players: 2–12
Preparation: None.

Rules:

1. Gather the players in a circle.

2. Explain that you are going to teach them a 'good manners' song to a tune that they probably already know. The song is sung to the tune 'This Is the Way We Wash our Clothes'.

3. Then say, 'This song is called, "This Is the Way We Show We Care." We will end each verse with something that shows we have good manners.'

4. Sing the first verse yourself:

> This is the way we hold the door,
> hold the door, hold the door.
> This is the way we hold the door,
> so early in the morning.

(Note that the time of day may change depending on the good manner in each verse.)

5. Continue singing the song using such phrases as: 'eat with a fork', 'use a napkin', 'catch our sneeze', 'say, "excuse me"', 'flush the toilet' and so on.

6. Use movements to demonstrate each phrase.

7. Give each player a point each time he or she adds a new verse.

8. When a player adds a new manner that has never been used in the song before, they should get two points.

9. At the end of the 'game' add up all the points and say, 'Thank you for playing!' It's good manners!

Remember that all new behaviours also need positive reinforcement in the form of praise and non-verbal cues in the real world. Make sure that you continually reward your child's good manners when they use them.

Teaching children to be more helpful

Some children seem to be naturally helpful, but others are not. Unfortunately we live at a time when being viewed as a helpful or kind person is not as important as possessing physical beauty, material wealth or athletic ability. Until the time that we hold Good Samaritans at the same level of esteem as movie or rock stars, parents will have to make an extra effort to teach the value of helpful behaviours.

Altruistic behaviours are taught to children in many ways. Most of all, children look at their parents and imitate what they do. Secondly, children are influenced by both the stated and the unstated rules of their home. One child I knew several years ago was required to save half of his allowance to give to a charity. This was an important value in his home and there was no choice about it. Another child was simply encouraged by her parents to look for ways to help other people. On a daily basis, she was shown helpful and courteous behaviour like holding a door for someone, or offering to help someone carry a heavy bag. Both these children grew up to be kind and helpful teenagers and young adults.

A third way to help children learn values is through their own secret language, particularly their art, their stories and their play. The following game is designed to encourage children to think about how to help others.

TRY IT

Follow the Helpful Leader

Objective: To make helping behaviour a daily routine.
Ages: 4 to 8
Number of players: 2–4
Materials needed: None.
Preparation: None.

Rules:

1. Set a timer for five minutes and explain to the child or children that you are going to play follow the leader.

2. Begin by doing some warm-up activities, like skipping, clapping your hands, twirling and so on.

3. Now go around the house or the garden and do simple helpful things. Pick up some rubbish. Straighten a chair. Put away a book or toy. Unpack the groceries. Be enthusiastic and have fun and get children into the habit of helping out.

4. Then ask your child to be a leader, by cleaning up his room. Do what he does, but do not do more. Concentrate on having fun, rather than on getting the room in perfect order. Keep the time period short. Remember that actions speak louder than words.

Play this special game of follow the leader often and you will see how much easier it is for children to be cooperative and helpful.

Teaching children social skills through games

Emotional learning games are particularly useful in teaching children new social skills, but they are naturally most helpful when they are played with other children of the same age, which may be difficult for you to arrange in your home. For this reason, I advocate that emotional intelligence training be a part of every child's school experience; every day in every class. Recently I had the opportunity to address a group of parents and teachers in a small school district outside of Philadelphia. The superintendent of the school district had made emotional intelligence the number one priority in every school for the year. He knew, as other school districts have found out around the country, that teaching emotional intelligence, which emphasizes teaching children social awareness and respect for others, reduces many common behavioural problems, from teasing and bullying to truancy. An added benefit of this type of programme is that it also improves the overall academic performance of students. This superintendent also realized that the best way to approach emotional intelligence training is through a partnership between parents and teachers, in the same way that parents and teachers form a partnership in teaching children academic subjects.

Social awareness games, like other emotional learning games, can teach children any one of dozens of social skills, including: how to make a smooth entry into group activities, how to play fair and how to resolve disagreements. The game below, a simple modification of the game of 'Hot Potato', is designed to teach children the importance of showing respect for others.

TRY IT

No Place for Disrespect

Objective: To teach children the importance of respecting others, as well as specific behaviours that show respect.

Ages: 5 to 10

Number of players: 3 or more.

Preparation: Make one copy of the Disrespect Card and 24 copies of the Respect Card shown in the illustration below.

You will also need a kitchen timer.

Rules:

1. Players sit in a circle.

2. This game is played like the game of 'Hot Potato', except that you pass around the 'Disrespect Card'.

3. The adult sets the kitchen timer for one to three minutes and players pass around the Disrespect Card.

4. If the timer goes off while a player is holding the Disrespect Card, then she must think of a way that you can show respect to someone.

For example:

    a. Be quiet when others are talking.

    b. Wait your turn.

    c. Say 'please' and 'thank you'.

    d. Hold the door for someone who is behind you.

5. If the player thinks of a way to show respect, then she gets a Respect Card and hands the Disrespect Card to another player.

6. Now the timer is reset and both the Respect Card and the Disrespect Card are passed around the circle.

7. This continues and each time a player gets a Disrespect Card and gives an example of how to show respect for others a new Respect Card is added to the circle and passed around.

8. When all the players have a Respect Card (e.g. there are five Respect Cards in the circle for five players), then the game is over because there is no room for Disrespect!

Emotional learning games teach children new ways to think

Every psychological problem can be defined in part by a distortion in normal ways of thinking. Children with Attention Deficit Hyperactivity Disorder, for example, do not typically plan ahead or think things through like other children of the same age. Shy children characteristically think that if something goes wrong it will be their fault, but if something goes right it is due to the efforts of someone else. Children who are outgoing typically have the opposite way of looking at the world.

Children who suffer from depression are negative or pessimistic thinkers. They believe that the difficult times that they encounter will continue to occur, while happier periods will be temporary. Youngsters who have an optimistic way of thinking, believe that the opposite is true; bad times are temporary and good times will continue to reoccur.

Most psychotherapists believe that if you want to effectively help children, you must change the distorted thinking patterns that underlie their emotional disorder. Emotional learning games are ideal ways to help children to learn and practise new ways of thinking for nearly every emotional problem of childhood. There is also evidence that teaching children different ways to think about themselves and their world can help 'inoculate' them against future emotional or behavioural problems.

Daryl, for example, did not meet the criteria for any specific psychological disorder, but he was considered at risk of developing problems. His parents had recently divorced and he was having difficulty in both maths and reading. His teachers observed that he seemed 'sad and unhappy' most of the time. Concerned that he may, in years to come, develop more serious depressive symptoms, they enrolled him in a special prevention programme. In group sessions, along with six other children, Daryl played emotional learning games at every meeting. His favourite was the Positive Thinking game. Here is how to play.

TRY IT

The Positive Thinking Game

It is important to note that optimistic thinking is not just about being your own 'cheerleader' as some self-help books recommend. It certainly does not hurt to say things to yourself like, 'Go for it' or 'You can do it', as a way of encouraging yourself to perform a difficult task, but Martin Seligman, author of *The Optimistic Child*, points out that a true optimistic style of thinking involves a realistic way to think about causes and effects. This game is designed to teach children that even when bad things happen, they can make them better.

Objective: To teach children how to change pessimistic thoughts into realistic, optimistic ones.
Ages: 7+ (adults can benefit from this game too)
Number of Players: 1 to 8

Preparation: You'll need two dice and the list of sentence starters below.

Rules:

1. Players sit in a circle.

2. Begin by explaining that the purpose of the game is to teach children how to turn negative thoughts into realistic positive ones. Give several examples of how to do this. The adult playing the game will be the judge of whether responses will win points or not.

3. The youngest player goes first and rolls the dice.

4. She reads the incomplete statement that corresponds to the sum of the dice, completing the sentence (e.g., if she rolls a three, then she reads statement no. 3 from the twelve statements below).

5. Then the player on her right must give a positive rebuttal to the statement, from the first player's point of view. For example, for statement no. 1, a player might say: 'Sometimes I feel sad when kids pick on me.' The next player might say: 'But I have a good friend that is fun to play with.'

6. If the second player gives an appropriate response, then both players get a point. If the adult feels that the response is not a positive one, then only the first player gets a point.

7. In addition, if a player rolls the dice and two even numbers that are the same come up (e.g. 2 twos, 2 fours, 2 sixes), the two players get 3 points each, instead of just 1 point.

8. If 2 ones are thrown, then that player loses a turn.

9. Play for fifteen to twenty minutes, and the player with the greatest number of points is declared the winner.

Statements for the Positive Thinking Game

1. Sometimes I feel sad when . . .
2. Sometimes I get angry when . . .
3. Sometimes I want to give up when . . .

4. Sometimes people get at me because . . .

5. Homework can be hard when . . .

6. Making friends can be hard when . . .

7. One thing I don't like about myself is . . .

8. One thing that bothers me at home is . . .

9. I really have a bad day, when . . .

10. The thing that bugs me most about the children in my class is . . .

11. I'm really not very good at . . .

12. One problem that I keep having is . . .

Let me re-emphasize that emotional learning games like the Positive Thinking game are not just for children with problems or even for youngsters who are at risk of problems. These games build emotional intelligence skills for all children and teenagers. According to research done by Martin Seligman and others, optimistic and realistic thinking leads to better performance in school and at work. It promotes better relationships with others because at every age people respond better to positive people. An optimistic attitude helps children cope with the common and uncommon obstacles that occur at every stage of life and even seems to help many people recover more rapidly from illness, potentially adding years to a person's life. And you can give your child all these advantages and more with a simple game.

Emotional learning board games

Of all the emotional learning games that you can play with children, the most successful are adaptations of simple board games. These games teach specific emotional skills like how to resolve conflicts or how to make friends. Because you write the cards for the game, they can really be used to address any problem at all.

Although emotional learning board games are widely used by mental health professionals, they are not commonly found in homes, where I believe they are most appropriate. Let me show you how easy it is to construct this type of game and to use it to teach your child important values like honesty, charity and responsibility. In a world where parents constantly worry about the influence of the media on their children's values, and where dangers of drug and alcohol abuse or other high risk behaviours seem unabated, here is a simple way you can guide the moral development of your child in the secret language of play. I call the game: the Good Character game.

TRY IT

The Good Character Game

I have always believed that the main reason why emotional learning board games are so popular with mental health professionals and children is that they are easy to play. Like many other board games that are popular with children, you roll the dice, move your counter forward, pick cards and do what the card says. That's all there is to it. But the cards in this type of game are different than children usually encounter. They ask children to think about their feelings, to consider new ways to relate to others and to practise new behaviours.

With you as a good role model, being open and honest with your answers to the game questions, children start to talk and think about things that will really surprise you. Remember, however, that this is a game and it is supposed to be fun. Do not use this as an opportunity to lecture or criticize your child. Just listen respectfully to the other players' answers and show your genuine appreciation when players share their thoughts and feelings.

Objective: To teach children the values that are important to their emotional and moral development.
Ages: 8 to 12
Players: 2–4
Preparation: You will need two dice, four counters or game markers, 100 poker chips or lp coins. You can use the dice and the counters from a game that you already have. You can also use little figures for the counters. Make a copy of the game board below.

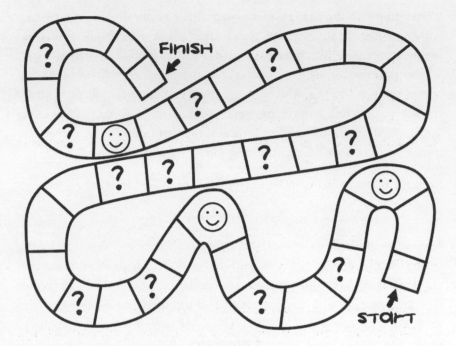

Copy the board on to a piece of cardboard to give it durability. You and your child may want to colour in the board with markers or crayons to make it more appealing. Make twenty question cards copying the list of questions below or making up your own questions. You can write the questions out on small 2 × 3 in. cards or if you want to use your computer, get perforated blank business cards from an office supply store and follow the directions for printing out cards.

Although you have written twenty questions for use in the game, you should feel free to add your own questions, creating them with your children. Making up questions can be just as instructive as playing the game.

Rules:

1. Each player puts his/her counter on the Start square.

2. The youngest player goes first and rolls the dice. If he lands on

a square with a question mark, he picks a card and answers the question. If he answers the question with an acceptable answer he gets one chip. If he lands on a square with a lightning bolt, he gets two chips.

3. Then the next oldest player takes a turn, rolling the dice, moving her counter and answering questions.

4. When the first person gets to the Finish square, the game is over.

5. The player who has the most chips is the winner.

Questions for the Good Character Game

(Copy these on to small 2 × 3 in. cards)

1. Why is it important to be honest?
2. Name a rule that is important in your home.
3. What would you do if you saw someone stealing sweets from a store?
4. Why is it important to have good manners?
5. Describe a time that you shared something of yours, even though you didn't feel like sharing.
6. What is a way that you can show your respect for someone older than you?
7. Name something that you would like to change about yourself.
8. If you were the Prime Minister, what would you do to make things better for people who are poor?
9. Name someone that you admire because he or she is generous.
10. If you wanted to do one really kind thing for another player, what would you do?
11. Name the thing you like most about your father or mother.
12. Talk about someone that you think of as a 'hero'.
13. What would you do if you saw someone cheating at a game?
14. Why is it important to obey traffic rules?

15. What is the nicest thing that anyone ever did for you?

16. What would you say to someone who wanted you to do something that you knew was wrong?

17. Why is it important to do chores on time?

18. What would you say to someone who teased other people to get them to stop?

19. Talk about something that you do that shows that you are responsible.

20. Talk about something that happened in your life that made you feel proud of your values.

When you play the Good Character game you will be amazed at how seriously children act when discussing their values and behaviour, even while they are enjoying the play. Emotional learning board games have a unique way of getting children to communicate at a level of self-awareness that rarely comes out in day-to-day conversation.

Of course, the most important part of all the games in this chapter is your participation. As you show your interest in your child's answers and as you express your values through your own answers, you have an opportunity to model your own feelings, behaviours and thoughts through the secret language of play.

Part summary

Any type of play is helpful to your child's emotional and social development. From the first weeks of life you can begin to teach your child through the secret language of play, stimulating his cognitive, language and emotional development. Play continues to be an important part of a child's emotional development throughout childhood, which is why it is such an important medium for professional counsellors to understand and help children.

But helping children through play is much more effective when it is done in a child's home. No one knows a child as well as his parents and no one has the same investment in his development. By spending just ten to twenty minutes a day you can learn to listen to your child's emotional concerns just the way a professional does. Just as importantly, through simple games and activities you can teach your child important emotional and behavioural skills and have fun doing it.

There is really no wrong way to speak the secret language of play with your children – just have fun.

Part III

The Secret Language
of Your Child's
Stories and Dreams

Chapter 9

Stories That Never End

Stories have a much greater influence on a child's behaviour and emotional development than most parents realize. Stories help shape the emotional life of children. They teach children values. They provide examples of how children can deal with common problems. Stories give children the words that they need to solve difficult problems. They open worlds of possibilities and foster a sense of purpose and hope.

There is no question that the stories we hear and read in childhood can influence us for years to come. For example, a successful lawyer told me how a childhood classic, *The Little Engine That Could*, still helps him prepare for speaking in front of a jury. 'I know it sounds sentimental,' Jonathon explained, 'but that story is one of the things that most influenced my life. My mother read *The Little Engine* to me every night for weeks, when I was five or six. It was the first book that I learned to read by myself. I still say the words to myself sometimes when I'm feeling down or when I lose confidence in myself. "I think I can. I think I can. I think I can. I know I can. I know I can." Sometimes I say this to myself to overcome butterflies in my stomach when I'm going to make a presentation to a jury. There is nothing else I know that can instantly give me confidence.'

Some psychologists believe that the classic tales of childhood actually enter our psyche and shape our values and the standards for our behaviour. They point out that fables and other stories are passed on from one generation to the next, barely changing because they are ingrained in the very essence of the culture. They reason that the longevity of these stories reflects their ability to tap into deep unconscious issues that affect all children. Stories like *Sleeping Beauty* or *Cinderella* introduce children to the primitive struggle between good and evil. Stories like *Hansel and Gretel* and *Pinocchio* tell children that they can learn to be brave even in the face of their worst fears. Fables like Aesop's *The Tortoise and the Hare* or *The Ugly Duckling* by Hans Christian Andersen teach children lessons about virtues such as patience and accepting differences.

In the introduction to his best-selling collection of stories, *The Book of Virtues*, William Bennet points out: 'If we want our children to possess the character traits we most admire, we need to teach them what those traits are and why they deserve both admiration and allegiance.' Bennet's book consists of classic stories, history lessons and poems, which he feels should form the foundation of every child's 'moral literacy'.

The stories that your children hear and read will influence their development whether you do anything or not, but in the next four chapters we will also examine ways that you can use stories and dreams to be a positive influence on your child's life. When you understand the secret language of your children's stories you will develop new insight into their emotional as well as their intellectual and moral development. The stories that your children tell you can make you aware of early signs of problems. The stories that you tell them or help them create, can teach them new ways of coping with their problems and help through difficult times. To begin, I will look at one of the simplest and most effective ways of using the secret language to communicate with your child by just reading books.

Read books to your children to help them understand their emotions and to develop ways to to cope with their problems

For over twenty-five years mental health professionals have been using books to help children with a wide variety of problems. They have even coined a term for the technique of using books to help children with their problems – they call it bibliotherapy. In my experience there are few ways to speak the secret language of emotions to children which are simpler and more effective. There are now hundreds of storybooks available to help children understand and cope with such diverse problems as divorce, living with chronic asthma, handling bullies and many more. The primary intention of this type of book is to provide a positive role model for children and to give them realistic examples of how to cope with life's difficulties. These books are typically about children with problems who find realistic and positive ways to overcome them. They provide children not just with good role models but they also offer children examples of how to behave and even think. These stories are most effective when they are read by loving parents or other caring adults, who give children added emotional support with their presence. The fact that children like to hear the same story over and over again makes this a particularly valuable way to impart emotional messages.

I have written over a dozen of these 'self-help' books myself in an effort to extend my voice from my office and speak the 'secret language' of emotional healing to children I have never met. One of my own favourite books deals with a common concern of counsellors, helping children find appropriate ways to express their anger. In *The Very Angry Day that Amy Didn't Have* I wrote about two girls, Amy and Margaret, who both had difficult days. Amy stubbed her toe getting out of bed. Margaret forgot her homework. Amy was teased by other children in her class. Margaret left her lunch at home. But through all her difficulties, Amy kept her temper. When she made a mistake she corrected it. If someone picked on her friend she stood up for him and then walked away. Margaret, on the other hand, let her anger get the best of her. She threw tantrums, took her anger out on other children and even stuck her tongue out at her teacher. As you might expect, the day gets worse and worse for Margaret, while Amy learned the importance of keeping her cool and having a positive outlook.

Bibliotherapy books are also used to help clarify common misconceptions that children have which can lead to emotional problems. For example, many children whose parents are divorcing feel that they are the only ones going through this heart-wrenching experience. But in *Dinosaur's Divorce: A Guide for Changing Families*, by Laurene and Marc Brown, children can enter the imaginary world of a dinosaur family getting a divorce. The parent dinosaurs fight, the children dinosaurs worry, cry and get angry. But finally the dinosaur family resolves most of their conflicts and the children adjust to living in two homes. As in other bibliotherapy books, the dinosaur family learns emotionally healthy ways to handle difficult times. They learn how to handle holidays and special occasions, what to expect when parents begin to date, how they might react to step-parents or step-siblings. The best bibliotherapy books legit-imize feelings for children and help them see new and realistic solutions to their problems or concerns.

TRY IT

Begin building a bibliotherapy collection for your child today. Start with books that you already have around the house. If your child has some special concerns such as a health problem like asthma, or a family problem like having a sibling with a disability, ask a public or school librarian to recommend some books on these topics. There are storybooks about almost any childhood problem that you can imagine, but these are not likely to be found in a bookshop, since many are from small publishers. I advise parents to set aside a spe-cial bookshelf for books that teach the secret language of dealing with emotions as opposed to books that may just be for entertainment.

Positive stories teach children, negative stories scare them

Bibliotherapy books differ from most classic fairy tales because they offer only positive solutions and positive role models. Many classic fairy tales and certainly many Bible stories and parables use the 'fear factor' to steer children into better behaviour. Many parents have experienced hearing stories designed to scare them into better behaviour when they were young and they in turn try to use this technique with their own children. I have never seen how scaring children with stories helps them.

One parent I was working with, we will call her Lois, told me that she regularly told her son stories to try to get him to behave. I saw her for a session after she was having one of those days when everything that could go wrong did. Her 5-year-old son, David, was not making things any easier. David was having one of his 'wilful days', as Lois called them. She saw these days as a struggle of his will against hers and all too often, she confessed to her friends, David won these battles.

On this particular day, David had made a trip to the supermarket seem like one of the twelve tasks of Hercules. David had pulled biscuits off the shelves and begun to eat them, even though Lois had specifically forbidden him from doing so. He said that he had to go to the potty three times in ten minutes but as soon as he got to the toilet he changed his mind. In the checkout queue David had a full-blown screaming tantrum because he wanted some gum which his mother would not buy him.

On the way home in the car Lois fumed, her heart racing and her head aching, while David sulked in the back. 'Let me tell you a story,' she started, 'it's about a little boy that never listened to his parents. Wherever the family went this boy was uncooperative. He complained all the time. They went to the beach and he said it was too hot and too sandy. They went to the movies and he made too much noise and the family had to leave. His mother took him to the supermarket and even though she was tired and in a hurry, this little boy didn't care and he behaved very, very badly. His parents gave this little boy everything he wanted and do you know what he said?'

David made no response and this just egged Lois on.

'He said, "I don't care." That's all he said, "I don't care." So his parents got together and agreed that if their son didn't care about them, then they shouldn't care so much about him. They stopped buying him toys and giving him nice clothes. They fed him plain yucky cereal everyday for every meal. They stopped taking him on nice holidays and doing nice things. So what do you think of that story?' Lois queried with some degree of self-satisfaction that she had made her point.

David made no reply, but he looked even more sullen.

Lois was very aware that there was a secret message behind her story. The moral of her story was: 'If you do not treat your parents better then we will not treat you so well.' She told the story more as a punishment to her son than as a means of instructing him. In truth, she had no intention in the world of loving her son less, or giving him less, but she was angry at David for making a hard day even harder.

Certainly Lois was not the first parent to tell a story to her children with a negative or punitive secret message. I have known parents who tell stories to their children about witches and monsters who carry 'bad' children away and they relate tales about children who are locked in the cellar until they learn to behave. These stories are intended to frighten children into better behaviour but they do not work. Whether they realize it or not (and I presume that they normally do not) these stories are equivalent to standing a child in a corner with a dunce cap on his head and with a sign on his back saying 'I have been bad'.

Negative stories have no instructive value for children. At worst they are cruel and harmful and cause further mistrust to the parent–child relationship.

As David listened to his mother's story he became more sullen and upset. By the end of the story he was slouched down in his seat with his hands covering his ears.

What Lois really wanted David to hear was: 'I am really mad at you for being inconsiderate!' But this is not the message that her son heard. Of course, Lois could have just said this straight out. Then she could have given David an appropriate consequence for his misbehaviour, like taking away TV time for the evening. And she could have told him a positive modelling story, which would tell her son what she wanted him to do and say and even think.

This was the positive modelling story that I helped Lois write and then read to her son.

Once upon a time there was a boy named Peter who did not listen to his parents or follow their rules.

They told him to do his homework, but Peter said, 'I'd rather watch television.'

They told him to clean up his room, but Peter said, 'I like it messy, just the way it is.'

They told him to call his grandma and say 'Thank you' when she gave him a new pair of pyjamas for his birthday. But Peter said, 'I don't like the pyjamas, so why should I say "Thank you"?'

Peter's parents worried that they were raising a boy who did not care about others.

So they told him, 'We're going to help you learn to be more considerate.'

They helped Peter do his homework and checked it when he was done.

They showed Peter how to organize his room so that he could keep it clean, and they made sure that he had ten minutes before dinner to clean it up each night.

They talked to Peter about being polite, having good manners and being appreciative when someone is nice to you.

They spent a lot of time teaching Peter how important it is to think about others. He listened and learned.

Peter became the kind of boy that everyone liked and admired.

THE END

As you can see, telling your child a positive modelling story is not about creating great children's literature, it is about creating great children. A positive modelling story creates a recipe for success; it tells children (and their parents) how to behave to win praise and affection. In a positive modelling story, there are no threats, no warnings and no mention of misbehaviour at all. The simple steps to tell a positive modelling story are:

1. Choose a 'hero' for the story who has problems like your child.
2. Create a problem that the hero of the story has to solve.

3. Create a solution to that problem that details exactly how you want your child to think or behave.

4. Create a positive, realistic ending.

I will talk more about creating positive modelling stories in Chapter 10.

Tell your children positive stories about yourself

Family dinner time gives you a daily opportunity to tell your child a positive modeling story. But unfortunately many parents use dinner time to rehash the day's problems and concerns, serving as negative role models for their children. Even if it is not overtly stated, children often hear messages like: 'I am not happy with my job, my boss, my co-workers, commuting, my salary, bills, my life.' It is no wonder that many children want to get away from the dinner table as soon as possible.

This is not to say that children should be protected from our problems and concerns or the problems in the world. Children need to know that their parents have problems, just like everyone else, but that these problems can be coped with and overcome. A negative, pessimistic view of the world is contagious. So is a positive, optimistic one. If you are like many parents reading this book and wondering how you can help your children with their emotional development, then listen to yourself at the dinner table tonight and try to take at least a few moments to tell about the good things that happened during the day, the problems that were solved, the kind acts that were done or received, the humour that was enjoyed even in the moments of exasperation.

With just a little effort, you can use your family's dinner time to give you a daily opportunity to tell your child a positive chapter of the story of your life. Like other stories, this can be a powerful way to teach children values and a positive outlook on life.

Please do not feel you should never complain about your day at dinner time or any other time for that matter. After all we are only human! But do try to tell at least one positive story each day at dinner time, directed at your children. Let them see that you live the values that you teach to them. Children learn by watching and listening to their parents. It happens constantly whether we are aware of it or not. This is the essence of the secret language. Since we know that a positive attitude is so important in our ability to deal with life's stresses, make this a priority in your daily communication with your child.

TRY IT

For one week try to tell a positive instructive story to your family at dinnertime. You do not have to make it up. Just think about something good that happened during the day, even if it was a very small moment, and talk about it. Even on your worst days you will be able to think of something good. After doing this for a few days you may begin to notice your own attitude start to change. And I assure you this will make a significant difference in your life as well as the life of your children. An optimistic attitude towards life is a key to better mental and even physical health. It is also contagious. Pass it on.

Dreams are stories, too

After the terrorist attacks on the World Trade Center and the Pentagon on 11 September 2001, many children (and many adults) retold this terrible story to themselves in their dreams. Catherine, a 10-year-old from a Long Island suburb just thirty minutes from Manhattan, was deeply affected. She told her parents the following dream.

'I dreamed that I was on the moon, and I had a handheld television, and I heard that the World Trade Towers fell down and killed lots of people. I decided not to come home. But then I missed my mummy and daddy. So I built a machine to go to earth and bring them to me on the moon.'

Psychologists believe that dreams and stories have two levels of meaning: the manifest or obvious content, and the latent or hidden content. But when dreams follow an emotionally powerful event, there is usually a short distance between the surface story and the hidden meaning of the dream. When asked what the dream meant, Catherine said, 'I want to be as far away from New York as possible. I think my mummy and daddy should move us to Arizona.'

In the wake of a powerful emotional experience most people can remember their dreams, even though at other times they may say that they do not dream at all. In actuality everyone dreams all of the time. Since the amount that you dream is simply a function of how much you sleep, children dream much more than adults because they sleep more.

Dreams comprise memories of images and sounds and physical motion and snippets of conversations. As we awake, in the process of remembering the dream, we compose these bits of memory into a storyline. By the time children are three or four they can tell you what they were dreaming about but, unfortunately, their most memorable dreams are usually the unpleasant ones. A young child is much more likely to tell you that she was chased by a monster or hit by a friend, then that she had won a free trip to a sweet factory. This is particularly true of recurring dreams which can make a fear bounce back and forth from day to night until a child's life is filled with anxiety.

Parents are naturally most sensitive to the secret language of dreams when their children have nightmares. Like Catherine, the girl who dreamed she was stuck on the moon, many children have nightmares as a reaction to unsettling daytime events. Since children have different fears at different ages, it might be a clown who disturbs a 3-year-old's rest and an upcoming geography test that affects a 12-year-old. But children also have nightmares when there does not seem to be any immediate reason. According to Dr Richard Ferber, Director at the Center for Pediatric Sleep Disorders at Boston's Children's Hospital, dreams can also represent emotional conflicts typical of a child's age. A 4-year-old might be struggling with his aggressive impulses pitted against his desire to please you. A 14-year-old might be wrestling with the concept of death and might dream about her own funeral.

Most young children will interpret their dreams literally. Serena, aged nine, for example, said that she dreamed about being in a boat and the boat was suddenly attacked by sharks (she had watched the movie *Jaws* that night for the first time). When asked what her dream meant, she replied: 'Don't swim in shark-infested waters.' But it is the magical content of dreams that makes them so enigmatic. Dogs can talk and drive cars. Trees become monsters. Houses can fly like planes.

Often children dream that they have the same super powers that they observe in the movies or in the comics and they see themselves as able to fly, walk through walls or lift enormous weights. Frequently in a dream one odd idea is paired with another one. My own most vivid dream from childhood was walking through a 'haunted house' at an amusement park with some older children feeling very proud that I was not afraid. But when I reached the exit a skeleton walked up to me and began breaking eggs over my head!

Although some people believe that dreams are really a secret code that can be translated with a Dream Dictionary, most clinicians believe that the true secret language of dreams can only be unlocked by the dreamer himself. Each dream is a story that the dreamer has created and only the dreamer can tell you what it means.

For some children, dreams reveal a deeper anxiety and may contain a more serious message. One child I treated, whose parents were going through a particularly acrimonious divorce, had repeated dreams of falling into a river and being swept away. Another child I saw in counselling was considered to be an 'underachiever' by his parents and teachers. He kept dreaming that he could fly – but only three feet off the ground. As hard as he tried he could not fly higher and he told me that he would wake up exhausted from trying to fly around trees and people who were in his path. These children do not see that their dreams are metaphors for the troubles that they are having in their waking lives, but we do. If it is in our power (and more often than we realize it is), we should try to reduce the stress that children are experiencing. At the same time, we need also to help children see that they are the authors of their own stories, both sleeping and awake.

Stories and your child's development

Most of the techniques in this section are geared towards children aged between five and twelve. Younger children do not have the language capacity to participate fully in the secret language of stories. Teenagers, on the other hand, are acutely aware of the double meaning of stories and that their stories can be interpreted. They are typically reluctant to share their stories because they understand that their stories can have an unwanted effect on the reader.

But this does not mean that the secret language of stories is irrelevant for younger children. On the contrary, stories are an important way of communicating at every age because they are ultimately a reflection of the thoughts, feelings, wishes and needs for both parents and their children.

Baby stories

Researchers tell us that reading stories to infants as young as six months old will stimulate their language development and even help them become better readers by the time they are ready to enter school. Obviously infants are not able to comprehend the meaning of stories. Rather it is likely that when parents read to their babies, their additional exposure to language and perhaps the particular cadence and attitude that parents have when they read, may have a role in forming the neural networks in the brain that will later influence a child's reading readiness.

The attitude of parents is passed along to their infants by their body language and their voice tone, volume and inflection. As parents hold their infants in their arms, turning the pages and speaking in a 'sing-song' voice, babies get the message that books are important to parents and so they become important to them.

Babies also enjoy just being told a story by their parents. A parent's calm voice is like an oral security blanket and many infants find the particular tone and cadence of a parent's story is just the tonic to help them drift into a relaxing sleep.

Perhaps the most important aspect of telling stories to babies is the closeness that it promotes. At these moments the secret messages that parents speak to their children are most tender and poignant: 'I will take the time to teach you about life. I will explain things to you that you don't yet understand. I will be with you to help you as you learn.'

Telling stories to toddlers and pre-school children

Between the ages of two and five, children begin to develop basic reasoning skills and the stories that they hear start to make sense. They love to hear the same stories again and again, often until they can recite them by heart. This repetition is important to a child's growing understanding of language. More than conversational speech, stories adhere to a basic structure of language. This informally teaches toddlers about grammar, word usage and, of course, vocabulary. Reading and storytelling also help toddlers develop listening and cognitive skills in ways that television and movies cannot. The spoken word stimulates different centres in the brain which are associated with a child's developing cognitive abilities, including his imagination.

As all parents with a toddler in the house already know, young children are astute mimics. They copy the phrases and mannerisms of their parents, playmates, teachers and from television. So why not give them stories and mental scripts that build self-confidence and teach them respect and concern for others?

There is no wrong way or wrong time to read or tell stories to young children. Yet there are some things you should know that can make your storytelling even more effective.

Dr Craig Lecroy, a proponent of reading positive stories to children, suggests the following guidelines for reading stories that will make an impact on your child:

- Choose a time that you can make reading or telling stories fun.
- Select a time when there are minimal distractions.
- Pick a story that is short enough so that the child's attention will not wander. It is better to read or tell a shorter story and have the child ask for more, than to wait for a child to lose interest.
- Read and tell stories with enthusiasm and drama.
- Give your child frequent eye contact.
- If your child wants to talk during the story, welcome his doing so as a way of communicating.

- If your youngster's attention wanders, then stop reading and wait. When you resume, start back with renewed enthusiasm.

Stories and the school-age child

As children go to infant school they soon begin to read; first just a few words on a page, then simple sentences and then short books. Every month you will notice that your child will build his vocabulary, read more fluently and derive more meaning from what he reads. Simultaneously his handwriting will improve, he will learn the fundamentals of grammar and spelling and he will be able to express himself in more complex ideas.

But even though it is critical for your child to master the mechanics of reading and writing at this stage of development, you should also recognize that this is a important time for children to learn values and moral behaviour through the secret language of stories. The stories that your child reads, hears and writes will not only help shape his character. Recent studies of character education programmes in schools in the USA also suggest that they can aid in preventing many common psychological and behavioural problems, ranging from drug and alcohol abuse to suicide prevention. Many schools have begun to weave character education programmes (also called moral literacy or emotional literacy programmes) throughout the school curriculum. In curriculums like Character Counts, a nationwide programme in the USA that emphasizes the importance of teaching children six important virtues (trustworthiness, respect, responsibility, fairness, caring and citizenship), children are asked to read, dictate, write or even videotape stories about important values and virtues.

The character education movement is catching on in schools across the USA. It is important for you to bring this type of education into your home. The early school years are an important window of opportunity to shape your child's values and behaviour. Stories are both a positive and a simple way to do so.

The teenage years: when stories cause worry

Stories told by teenagers can be just one more reason for parents to be wary of this age. For example, I found this story on the Internet after doing a search on 'stories by teenagers'. It was posted on a website that described itself as a 'writers club for teens'. The author was Sandra, aged sixteen. The title of her story was 'Death of the Heart'. Here are the opening paragraphs:

> Do you know what pain is really about? Vince did. He knew what it felt like to have a broken heart and broken limbs. He knew what it felt like to be wrecked in a car accident and to have his back nearly broken in half. To come so close to Death, that he could kiss it. And he knew what it was like to hate. He hated so many people, he had lost count.

What do we know about Sandra from this story? Even in these few sentences you can see the disturbing theme of hurt, heartbreak and anguish. After reading the opening paragraph I was almost afraid to read what followed. The story went on to detail the feelings of a boy rejected by everyone he cared for. It ended with him running away to find a new place where someone might care about him. Would you say that this was the story of a depressed adolescent or just one with a vivid imagination? Was the author writing about her own loneliness and pain or just using her imagination? I have no idea and I will never know.

The stories that teenagers write in their diaries or for their English homework can sometimes be poignant and other times frightening. Of course, we recognize that it is normal for teenagers to seek extremes in their behaviour, in their music, in their dress, as well as in their language. During the teenage years your children will develop a hypersensitivity to their own feelings – although not typically to yours. The stories they write are likely to be dramatic, full of passion and more apt to be one extreme or another.

Many teenagers use stories or poetry or diaries as a way to struggle with issues of isolation, longing and anger. Unlike younger children, teenagers understand that their stories have multiple meanings and that they communicate a message to the reader which can take place on multiple levels. But what should adults do when they hear a message of pain or even violence in the story of an adolescent? There has been a renewed debate about how seriously to take these messages since the April 1999 slaying of twelve students and a teacher at Columbine High School outside of Denver by teenagers Eric Harris and Dylan Kliebold.

Dr Kelly Zinna, a former FBI psychologist and author of *After Columbine*, notes that months before the massacre Eric Harris had written an essay portraying himself as a bullet falling in love with a gun named Maggie. The essay was perceived as disturbing and so his teacher naturally talked to his parents about it. Everyone decided that it was related to Harris's plans to go into the military and that it was 'consistent with his future goals'.

It is hard to say whether an experienced psychologist might have seen the essay as a cry for help. Professionals have certainly made mistakes before in misinterpreting a child or teenager's hidden message. But today no educator or mental health professional will ignore a violent essay written by a teenager. In light of what we have learned from the Columbine shooting and other tragedies, we must assume that any story a teenager writes about harming himself or others should be considered as a serious warning sign.

Of course, violence is not the only adolescent theme that will prove upsetting to adults. Teenagers write about every high-risk behaviour imaginable and every heightened state of emotion.

Naturally there is a difference between a teenager's public or private writing. Private letters, e-mail and diaries will be more transparent than an essay or story written in an English class. The best advice I can give to parents if a teenager's words disturb them is to talk to him about it. Studies have told us that even when teenagers actively try to distance themselves from their parents through their limit-testing behaviour and sarcastic attitude, they still want their parents involved in their lives. They still see their parents as the first place to turn when they are in trouble.

If you continue to be concerned about your teenager's writing after trying to talk to him then you should certainly seek professional advice. Action is always better than inaction when it comes to preventing a teenager's life story from turning tragic.

Make time for stories in your life

As you begin to use stories as another part of understanding and speaking in the secret language of your child, take a moment to think of how stories have affected your own life and how they continue to do so. Are you the type of parent that likes to read to your child? Are you a storyteller? Do you keep a diary? Are you a voracious reader, or are you the type of person who cannot remember the last time that you read a book?

TRY IT

- Make a list of the books and stories that influenced you as you grew up. How old were you when you read them? How many have you read to your child?

- Consider how much time you spend reading books to and with your child. Do you have a special time of the day devoted to reading and discussing books?

- Do you make up stories to tell your child? What do you teach your child through your stories?

- Do you influence your child's television viewing or selection of movies? When is the last time that you chose a television show or movie to watch with your child because you wanted your child to hear its message?

Chapter 10

Understanding Your Child's Stories and Dreams

At school Mattie told her teacher a story about a man who crept into her room at night and stared at her. The four-year-old insisted that this story was true.

Eleven-year-old Ben wrote a story about his parents getting married again, even though they had been divorced for more than three years. His parents wondered if this was normal or if he was showing signs of maladjustment.

Cara, aged five, liked to make up story plays with her dolls about princesses and knights in shining armour. But by the end of each play everyone always died. Her mother thought that it was strange that every story had an unhappy ending.

In each of these cases adults were perplexed about the meaning of a child's stories. They wondered if the stories were just fantasies, or did they reveal some inner problem or hidden longing? The answer to these questions lies in an understanding of the secret language of stories and dreams. For decades psychologists have realized that stories, as well as dreams, should not be taken at face value. Any made-up story – whether it is a dream, an oral or written story or a drama – reveals a great deal about a child's psychological make-up.

Mental health professionals often use storytelling techniques with children for diagnostic purposes. A psychologist will show a series of ambiguous pictures to a child, who then tells a story about what he sees. The psychologist will look for patterns in the stories and then see if the patterns fit what he knows from the other information he has gathered about the child from cognitive testing, drawings, observations and interviews with parents and teachers. The clinician recognizes that interpreting childhood stories is only one piece of the puzzle and any conclusions gathered from listening to a child's stories must be tested against information from the child's real world. Nevertheless, the stories that children tell give us important information about their view of their world and their place in it.

The examples at the beginning of this chapter help us to understand each child's point of view, to determine if there are problems and then to decide whether or not to take action.

Mattie, who told her teacher a story about a man who crept into her room, later said that it was her step-father. She did not like her step-father and resented his presence in the house. On checking, it was discovered that the step-father did occasionally go into Mattie's room, but just to say goodnight. Family counselling helped Mattie and her step-father find better ways to communicate.

The psychologist working with Ben, who had written a story about his parents getting married again, concluded that this was a perfectly normal part of the grieving process after his parents' divorce. Most children of divorced parents have a fantasy at some time that their parents will remarry. Some of them express this fantasy and others keep it to themselves. The psychologist suggested that Ben's parents read him several books about children adjusting to divorce, including Richard Gardner's *The Boys and Girls Book About Divorce*.

After a psychological assessment it was determined that Cara's repeated 'plays' about everyone dying suggested early signs of depression. A lack of concern about her school work, a loss of weight and a general disinterest in her friends and normal activities confirmed the diagnosis. As is sometimes the case, there were no obvious signs as to why Cara might be depressed. Cara began seeing a counsellor and was also referred to a paediatrician to determine if her depression had some physical cause.

As you can see, children's stories offer us only a part of the picture about their psychological needs and conflicts, but it is an important part nonetheless. In this chapter you will learn to listen to your child's stories in a new way. But if you suspect a problem you should not jump to conclusions. Stories and dreams are an amalgam of fact and fiction, an important way that children communicate their feelings and perceptions in the secret language.

The story game: a new way to understand your child's emotional development

Few children are spontaneous storytellers. Unlike the secret language of art, or play, or non-verbal behaviour, you must actively create opportunities to speak the secret language of stories with your child.

The Story Game is a simple and fun game intended for children from five to twelve. It taps into children's natural imagination and rewards them for their creative efforts. But most of all it is fun because you are playing, too! Children love to play games with their parents (see Chapter 8) and enjoy nearly any opportunity to do this. The fact that the game might be good for them as well is an added bonus.

It will only take you a few minutes to make the Story Game. You will need: a stack of index cards; about 100 poker chips or 1p coins; three shoeboxes (or other small boxes); some small toys; stickers or sweets to use as prizes.

To begin take a stack of twenty index cards and write down these 'story starters' on the cards.

Tell a story about:

1. Someone who is sad because he has no friends.
2. Someone who loves to read.
3. An animal who is lost.
4. A trip to an amusement park.

5. Someone who is fired from their job.

6. Finding lost treasure.

7. A circus that is damaged by a tornado.

8. A super hero.

9. A family who needs money.

10. A child who wins a contest.

11. A child who is afraid.

12. A child who loves animals.

13. A child who sees his parents fighting.

14. A group of children who go camping.

15. A child who is teased at school for being different.

16. A child who is a great athlete.

17. A child whose family moves to a new town so has to go to a new school.

18. A child who starts a business and makes a lot of money.

19. Someone who loses something important.

20. A child who becomes a great musician.

Now take the three small boxes and fill the first one with poker chips (or 1p coins will do if you do not have chips). Fill the next box with the Story Starter Cards that you have made and shake them so that the cards are mixed up. Fill the third box with some small prizes, like sweets, stickers or small toys. Now you are ready to play.

Tell your child:

'Let me teach you a new game. It's called the Story Game. You and I are going to tell stories to each other. You can go first, because you are the youngest.

'I want you to reach into the Story Box and pull out a card. The card will tell you what kind of story to tell. It will help you start the story but you must finish it yourself.

'When you tell a story you get two chips. Then I want you to tell me what the story means. This is the story's moral or lesson. When you can figure out a moral or lesson for the story, then you get another chip!

'Then I'll take a turn. I'll pick a card, tell a story and then think of a lesson, too. When you get nine chips, you can close your eyes and pick from the Surprise Box!'

I recommend that you write the stories down or tape record them if you want to become an expert in the secret language of stories. But it is not necessary to do this.

Now you are ready to play. You and your child should take turns telling stories and determining their morals or lessons. This game will stimulate your child's creativity and language development and, if you are like most families, you will find it an enjoyable and challenging activity. More importantly it will also open a window into the inner workings of your child's mind. Read on to find out the 'secrets' that your child's stories will reveal.

Interpreting your child's stories

The most important part of any story is the person who is telling it. When a child tells a spontaneous story, he is drawing not only from his own experiences, but his own values, wishes, concerns and needs. Psychologists call this process 'projection' because the child is 'projecting out' his inner self to be viewed by the outside world.

There are three important questions that you will ask yourself when trying to understand what your child's story reveals about his emotional life. These are:

1. What is the attitude of the 'hero' of the story?
2. How are problems solved?
3. What values does the story represent?

Your child is the hero of his own story

Psychologists assume that when a child tells a spontaneous story the hero or main character of the story represents the child himself. This assumption is supported by the remarkable consistency that we see as a youngster relates a series of stories. For example, Joel, aged seven, picked a card that said, 'Tell a story about an animal at the zoo.' He told a story about a tiger that got loose from his cage and ate all the people at the zoo. Then he picked a card that said, 'Tell a story about a storm.' He told a story about a thunder-cloud that looked for people to rain on while they were picnicking. When he picked a card that said, 'Tell a story about a child who was lost', he told a story about a girl who did not have any friends because all of the children she knew were 'stupid and mean'. When asked what the girl did in the story when she was treated meanly, Joel replied, 'She called her friends' parents and told on them.'

Reviewing the themes of Joel's stories you do not need a Ph.D. to see that he is a very angry little boy who wants to get back at people for his perceived hurt. Each of his three stories have the same theme. In every story that Joel tells the 'hero' of the story is angry and vindictive. And yet as obvious as this may be to us, Joel does not see that this is so. When he was asked if the little girl in his last story reminded him of anyone special, Joel replied, 'No. I don't know any girls like that.' His concrete level of thinking does not allow him to step back from his stories and see that they are really about his own feelings. His feelings are a secret from himself.

Now when you listen to the secret meaning of your child's story, think about what the main character in the story is like.

- Is he purposeful?
- Does he possess positive personality traits (friendly, helpful, kind)?
- Does he have predominantly positive feelings?
- Does he handle negative feelings appropriately?
- Does he have realistic goals?

As you listen to your child's stories, think about the main character and what that character reflects about your child.

How does your child solve problems?

Now, I want you to consider how the hero in your child's stories solves problems. You probably noticed that half of the cards written for the Story Game describe positive and fun situations and half of the cards describe problems. Take notice of how your child makes up stories that are positively or negatively slanted. Children with a negative attitude will typically make bad things happen even when the story starters describe a positive subject. Children with a positive attitude towards themselves and their world will address negative situations as problems to be solved. Their negative story starters will have positive endings.

You should also listen to the way that your child solves problems in his stories. Young children constantly hear stories where problems are primarily solved through the use of magic and so, naturally, that is the type of story they tell. A fairy godmother waves her magic wand and a bully turns into a frog. A boy develops super powers and flies away from the forest with the scary monsters.

According to Dr Richard Gardner, a prominent child psychiatrist and expert on helping children through the secret language of stories, stories where children exclusively rely on magic to solve their problems do more harm than good. Gardner points out that children need to have a realistic attitude about solving their problems and that this should be reflected in the stories that they hear and tell. For example, in his book *Stories About the Real World*, vol. 2, Dr Gardner wrote a story about a little boy and a monkey who visited a scientist's laboratory and found a machine where you put in a coin and get a banana. Both the boy and the monkey loved bananas and since there was a big pile of coins next to the machine they kept getting more and more bananas. But one day the scientist tried an experiment and he did not fill the machine with bananas. The monkey came and put coin after coin in the machine, but no bananas came out. Eventually he gave up and walked away, even though there were still many coins left. Then the little boy came in and tried to get more bananas. But there were no bananas in the machine, so nothing ever came out! Yet the boy did not give up hope. After putting in dozens of coins he began screaming and kicking the machine and calling it bad names. He kept on putting coins in the machine and screaming and kicking until the scientist had to drag him out of the laboratory. Dr Gardner's lesson: 'If at first you don't succeed, try, try again. If after that you still don't succeed, forget it! Don't make a big fool of yourself.'

As your child relates a story, listen to how he solves problems. Ask yourself these questions:

- What kind of an attitude does the main character have when approaching a problem?
- What is the main character's point of view?
- Is the problem solved by the main character or by someone else?
- Is the problem resolved in a way appropriate to the child's age?
- Does the main character of the story have different ways to solve different problems, or just one way?

The moral or lesson that a child tells will give you important clues about how he solves problems.

Here is an example of a story told by Susan, aged eight, when she picked a card that said: 'Tell a story about someone that loses something important.'

Once upon a time there was a man. He was a woodcutter and he made his living chopping down trees. He had an axe that he always took with him into the woods and he loved that axe very much. But one day, when he was alone in the woods, he lost his axe. He was very sad that he lost his axe. But the next day his mother saw that he was sad, so she bought him a new axe!

THE END

The moral that Susan told was: 'If you lose something your parents will get you a new one.'

On the surface, we can look at Susan's story and it seems pretty innocuous, a simple tale of loss and replacement. But when we just look below the surface at how the problem in the story is solved we can see that Susan's story indicates an unwillingness to deal with the conflict. The problem with the story is that the conflict is resolved by the woodcutter's mother, not by the woodcutter himself. Susan suggests in her story that loss (or perhaps all problems) will magically be resolved by an adult, suggesting a dependency on adults that is uncharacteristic of this age.

Asking a child to explain the moral or lesson will help you understand, see their point of view.

Here is an example of a story told by Tanya, also aged eight, where she shows both responsibility and initiative in solving a problem.

Once upon a time there was a boy who wasn't allowed to cross the street by himself. His mother and father said that if he crossed the street by himself then he might get run over by a car or a lorry. The boy always listened to his mother and his father so he was very careful and never crossed the street by himself.

But one day he saw a blind man on the other side of the street. The blind man looked unhappy and confused. The boy was afraid that the blind man was going to walk into the street and get killed. So the boy decided to cross the street and help the man. He waited for the light to turn green and then looked both ways. He knew that he was breaking his parents' rule, but he thought it was for a good reason. He got to the other side of the street and helped the blind man back across. The blind man said, 'Thank you very much. You were a great help.'

THE END

The moral: Sometimes you have to break a rule to do something that is right or to help someone out.

How does your child's stories reflect his values?

The third element of your child's stories that you should listen to is how the story expresses his values. Here are some important values that we would all want for our children:

- Honesty
- Trustworthiness
- Patience
- Kindness
- Charity
- Acceptance of others
- Respect for differences
- Courage
- Responsibility
- Unselfishness
- Leadership
- Persistence in the face of frustration

When your child tells you a story, listen to the values and the character traits of its hero, which, as I have noted, reflect his own view of himself and the world.

Consider this story told by Angie, aged 10, after picking the card, 'Tell a story about someone who needs money.'

Once upon a time there was a boy, Jack, who needed some money to buy a new bike. He asked his mother and father for some money, but they were too poor and didn't have enough to give him for a bike. So Jack decided to get at job at McDonald's where he could earn enough money. He worked there for two months and earned £150. (He also got free hamburgers and French fries, too!) After he earned the money he decided to buy the bike but continue to work at McDonald's. That way he could also get money to buy some CDs and some clothes.

THE END

The moral: If you need things and your parents can't afford them, get a job.

Angie tells an interesting and a positive story. Her 'hero', Jack, shows responsibility and initiative. But compare it to a story told by Teresa, aged ten, who picked the same card, 'Tell a story about someone who needs money.'

Once upon a time there was a poor family, whose last name was Jamison. The Jamisons never had enough to eat or to buy the things that they wanted. Then one day Mr Jamison was looking through his garage for things he could sell and he found a very old painting that had belonged to his great-great-grandmother. He saw a show on tv where people got money for old antiques and so he took it to an antiques shop in town. The man who owned the shop said that the painting was worth a lot of money and so he wrote Mr Jamison a cheque for £30,000! Now he could buy his family everything they needed.

Mr Jamison went home and kissed his wife and kissed his children and they all had a big party. But they decided that they needed to share their good fortune. Mr Jamison gave some of his money to the church to help other poor people. He gave some of the money to his brother who needed money to go to college. He even gave some money to his neighbours so they could go on a trip to Disney World with their sick child. The Jamison family put the rest of the money in the bank and invested it, so they would not have to worry about money again.

THE END

The moral: Money can solve a lot of problems for you and the people that you love.

Teresa's values – her sense of family, her desire to share, her concern for others and her desire to plan for the future – are reflected in her story *after* the immediate problem is solved. Her story shows that she is the type of child whose concern for others is almost as great as her concern for herself.

What are the values that you want to teach your children? Have they learned them? If so, they are likely to be reflected in stories like Teresa's, even if you do not see such altruistic behaviour on a day-to-day basis. As I have said, stories are internal representations of children's inner lives. Their sense of self is reflected by the 'hero' of their stories and their sense of initiative and purpose is reflected in the way that they solve problems in their stories. Children's values are reflected in how their heroes and other characters in the story act when the immediate problem is solved.

Now it's your turn! Telling positive modelling stories back to your child

When you learn to listen to the messages underneath the stories that your children tell, you will learn a great deal about them. But that is just the beginning of the Story Game. When it is your turn to tell a story, you can tell positive modelling stories that will influence your child's self-image, his ability to solve social problems and even his moral development.

As I explained in Chapter 9, positive modelling stories are just what they sound like: stories that present your child an idealized way for him to think, act and feel. The easiest way to create these stories is to think about the same elements that I explained in understanding your child's stories.

- *Create a positive hero:* Tell stories in which the hero portrays a positive attitude towards life and accepts his feelings as well as the feelings of others.
- *Emphasize problem solving:* Introduce a realistic conflict in the story and a realistic solution. Avoid fairy tale endings where problems are magically solved. The hero should take appropriate steps to solve the problem.

- *Teach values:* Emphasize the values that are important to you. State the values in the lesson or moral of your story.

Here is an example of a story told by Nancy, the mother of 8-year-old Denise. Denise was a shy girl who did not like new situations or meeting new people. Notice how the heroine in Nancy's story acknowledges Denise's problem with shyness and presents appropriate ways to deal with it. Nancy told this story when she picked the card: 'Tell a story about a trip to an amusement park.'

Once upon a time there were two sisters. One sister loved excitement and she loved to run and jump and ride her bike very fast. The other sister was brave in her own way, but she didn't like to do things where she thought she might get hurt.

Then one day the whole family went to an amusement park. The first sister wanted to go on all the scary rides. She particularly wanted to go on the Viper roller coaster, which was said to be the biggest, scariest roller coaster in the whole world. But the second sister said that she was too scared. She was afraid that she might fall out. She preferred to go on the merry-go-round.

Their parents said that both the girls had to go on the rides together, so they definitely had a problem. The second sister said, 'I don't want to go on the Viper, because I'm not ready for that. But I will go on the Ferris wheel with you.' (She said this, although she had never gone on the Ferris wheel before.) 'OK,' said the first sister. 'That's a compromise. And we can scream and scream if we want. That makes it more fun.'

So the two sisters went on the Ferris wheel – ten times! Maybe next time they would try the roller coaster, too.

THE END

The moral: Sometimes if you are afraid of one thing, you can find something not quite so scary to try.

When you make up stories for your child, whether they are spontaneous bedtime stories or whether you are playing the Story Game, keep in mind that you are giving your child a message with your story. Be positive, but also be realistic. Do not worry about happy endings, even if your child insists on one. Remember that the secret language of stories can help you explore many different emotions with your child.

Chapter 11

The Problems That Stories and Dreams Can Tell Us

Are you concerned about your child's stories? Do you find them strange or unsettling? What about dreams? Does your child have frequent nightmares or anxiety provoking dreams?

Most parents have good instincts about their children's stories or dreams. They know when their child is acting a little differently, even though they cannot always define exactly what the problem may be. For example, a parent recently told me that her son was having more frequent nightmares after they had moved to a new house. She explained, 'He has always been prone to having nightmares when he is upset. But now it is pretty much every night.' If you sense something is wrong you should follow your instincts and try to do something about it. With this child dinner-time discussions about how to make the transition to his new home and school easier reduced his nightmares within a week. Children tell you in many different ways when they are emotionally troubled. You need to listen and react.

In this chapter I will talk about some of the things that psychologists look for when listening to a child's story. You can listen for the same things and hopefully take the appropriate steps to help your child. If you find yourself worried and not sure what you should do, do not hesitate to ask for a professional's opinion. You have the advantage of being an expert on your child, but trained professionals have the advantage of seeing many children at different ages and they will probably be able to tell you whether your child really has a serious problem and what steps you should take, if any, to address it.

Just as with other parts of the secret language of children, you should not really be concerned about a single story. Rather you should look for trends or patterns in a child's stories that might indicate signs of trouble. Stories should also be viewed in the context of other aspects of the child's behaviour. For example, Melissa, aged 11, wrote a short story about a girl who had no friends.

Once upon a time there was a girl named Katie. Katie was sad all of the time and she didn't like to talk to anyone but her dolls. Katie had five dolls, but she liked an ugly one named Berta the best.

Katie only wanted to talk to Berta. She stopped talking to her mum and her dad and her friends. Only Berta understood how Katie felt.

Then one day Katie couldn't find where she had put Berta. She looked all over the house and the neighbourhood. Katie thought to herself, 'Had Berta run away? Had she been kidnapped?' She couldn't even ask for help in finding Berta because she had stopped talking to everyone!

Katie decided that she would tattoo a picture of Berta on her hand. Then when she needed to talk to someone she would talk to her hand. And that is what she did.

THE END

Melissa's English teacher read the story and became quite concerned. She thought Melissa was a happy, friendly and well-adjusted student. But now she began to wonder whether Melissa had some deep dark secret that she was unconsciously revealing through her story. She referred Melissa to the school counsellor who called her parents in for a conference. They were also surprised that Melissa would write this kind of a story. Next the counsellor had a meeting with Melissa, 'just to talk about things'. Melissa gave no indication that she had any problems. Finally, the counsellor showed her the story and told her that her English teacher wondered what the story meant. 'It's just a story,' Melissa replied. 'I just started to write it and that is how it came out.'

In this example everyone did the right thing. Teachers should be aware of signs of trouble. Counsellors should consult parents before they jump to conclusions. Information should be sought to determine whether a child's out-of-character behaviour is a call for help.

While it is important to keep in mind that you should be cautious about over-interpreting a child's stories, when children tell certain stories over and over again, this is typically a signal that a problem exists. These include: stories that lack imagination; tales that reveal an excess of anxiety; violent stories of any nature; and stories that lack organization and detail.

When stories lack imagination

Every time I talk to parents who have problems with their child I ask them about their child's television, video game and computer habits, what many psychologists now refer to as 'screen time'. There are many mental health problems than can be exacerbated when a child spends too much time in front of a television set or a computer, but one that is not often considered is the influence that these activities have on a child's imagination. Many experienced teachers I know have noticed that the play and stories of children seem to be less creative than they once were. They believe that this is largely due to the amount of time that children spend watching TV instead of participating in creative activities which foster their imagination.

For example, when 7-year-old Jennifer was asked to make up a story as part of her diagnostic assessment, she told a story about a mermaid who longed to have legs and run and play on the land. The plot and even some of the dialogue was straight out of the Disney cartoon *The Little Mermaid*. At a follow-up interview, Jennifer's mother told the psychologist doing the testing that Jennifer had watched the videotape of the cartoon 'hundreds of times' since she was two years old and that she could even play out scenes, taking the voices of multiple characters. When asked to make up an original story, one that no one had told before, Jennifer drew a blank. 'I don't know one,' Jennifer admitted, without embarrassment.

These days too many children tell and write stories that are undisguised re-enactments of popular movies and videos which they have seen over and over again. When parents allow a child to have too much screen time they fail to provide opportunities to stimulate their child's imagination. This passive activity can hinder children from developing their creative thinking, which in turn can prevent children from learning problem-solving skills that are necessary for both their academic and social development.

WHAT TO DO

Parents rarely argue with me when I point out that their children are watching too much TV or playing too many video games. The average British child spends three hours a day in front of the TV, more time than any other single activity except attending school. Aside from the negative influence that television can have, think of all the things that children are missing: reading books; sports; creative play; pursuing hobbies; helping others and so on. But when I ask parents if they can reduce their child's screen time, I often get a discouraged or even an angry look, as if they want to say 'Why don't you try it!'

My response is that too much screen time is a bad habit, like too much junk food. Then I ask them to put their child on a 'TV diet', which includes video games and videotapes as well regular television. If you feel that your child spends more time watching TV or playing video games than in active and creative endeavours, consider putting him on a TV diet. Cut back an hour a week for a month or two. If you do this I am sure that you will see a change in your child's attitude and approach to himself and to others.

Stories that reveal anxieties about real life problems

Most of the problems expressed in a child's story are fairly transparent. For example, Paul's father was a corporate executive in a multinational company. This meant that the family had to move every few years to a new city. Paul's father had announced that they would be moving to a new country and Paul was obviously unhappy. 'But this is important to my career,' his father explained. 'When I get a new job I make more money and then we can have more nice things.' But this argument did not address Paul's anxiety about going to a foreign country where he did not even know the language. When Paul played the Story Game (see the previous chapter), he picked a card that said: 'Tell a story about someone who wins a contest.' He related the following story:

> Once upon a time there was a man who played the lottery. He played the lottery every Wednesday, every week of the year. Then one Wednesday night he watched the lottery draw on TV with his wife and his sixteen children and he won! His ticket matched every one of the numbers in the lottery and he won £10 million!
>
> The man quit his job the next day and he took his family on a cruise around the world. They went to many places and did everything the man and his wife had dreamed about doing. But the sixteen children weren't happy. There was no TV on the boat and they didn't have all their stuff with them. They even missed going to school! At the end of the trip the man asked his family what they wanted to do next with the money. They all decided they wanted things to be just the way they were.
>
> So the man decided to give all of his money away to charity (except for maybe £500,000) and have things just the way they were.

THE END

The moral: Sometimes being rich is not as good as it sounds.

When children have things that they worry about it frequently comes out in recurring themes in their stories as well as in their dreams. One unmistakable sign for concern is that even when the story starts out on a positive premise, like winning the lottery, there is still a bad outcome. Another common indicator that a problem exists occurs when children in the made-up stories repeatedly end up unhappy. This is a sure signal that your child is trying to tell you something.

WHAT TO DO

It is important to note that it is perfectly normal for your child's stories to sometimes reveal anxiety about a difficult situation like a divorce or a family move. Children like things to be the same. Even if things are not great, children prefer the predictability of the status quo to the possibility that things could get much worse. It is also worth noting that a little anxiety is not a bad thing. Anxiety makes all of us, even children, more aware of problems.

Under the best circumstances anxiety can stimulate a child's coping mechanisms. Throughout this book you will find dozens of techniques to help your youngster cope with stressful times. And each time your child learns to cope with a problem, his self-confidence and resiliency should improve.

But if signs of anxiety continue for more than three months then this is usually a cause for concern. These signs may be revealed in your child's story, his art, his play or in other ways. Use the list below to look for signs that a child's anxiety has overwhelmed his ability to cope.

Anxiety checklist

Anxiety reactions are much more common in children than most people realize. Look for a combination of signs in the secret language as well as changes in the real world. If you feel that your child is overanxious, by all means check with a counsellor or other mental health professional. Anxiety disorders are much more easily treated when they are caught in the early stages.

Story characteristics:

• Stories are negative and pessimistic.
• The stories themselves may be short and unrevealing.

- The hero of the story is powerless or meets repeated failure.
- The environment of the stories is bleak and depressing.
- Problems are rarely resolved.
- The moral of the story suggests victimization.

Symptoms:

- Frequent physical complaints (headaches, stomachaches, fatigue).
- Avoidance of school, friends or other normal activities.
- Changes in sleep or eating habits.
- An increase in nervous habits like hair pulling or skin picking.
- Increased reliance on 'escapist' activities like watching TV.

If you have spotted more than two 'signs' of anxiety and you have already tried to reduce the stress for your child, then you should consider seeking professional guidance for you or your child.

Stories that have a persistent theme of violence

Few people would disagree that children are exposed to too much violence. Video games, movies, television, rap music . . . even the simple pleasures of youth soccer have been tainted by parents who get into shouting matches with coaches or other parents. It is no wonder that problems in anger control are one of the most frequent reasons that children are referred for counselling.

Still, most children show an amazing capacity to compartmentalize their experiences and their feelings. The vast majority of children learn to differentiate between pretend violence and real aggression and they are successful at developing appropriate values and behaviours in spite of negative cultural influences. But when children fail to compartmentalize cultural or personal exposure to violence, you need to be immediately concerned. If children repeatedly tell violent stories or if they tell stories which are extremely gory in nature, you should interpret this as a call for help from children at any age.

Take, for example, a story told by Christopher, an 8-year-old I once worked with from a rural area of Colorado.

Pudgie the Cat

There once was a boy who loved cats. Cats were his very best friends. He had cats all over his house, even in his bed. Everywhere he went, he took his cats.

But there was one cat that he didn't like, Pudgie the Cat. Pudgie was a bad cat. He smelled and was always in the way. He scratched the boy and raised his fur at him. The boy started to hate Pudgie, even though he loved cats. The boy – his name was Michael – decided to teach Pudgie a lesson. He threw rocks at Pudgie and sticks, too. He threw lighted matches at Pudgie and squirted him with a squirt gun. Pudgie ran away from Michael, and one day he ran away from home altogether.

THE END

Christopher was referred to me because he was the school bully. Nearly every day he was in trouble for picking on younger children. He certainly had problems at home – his parents were divorced and his father rarely visited him – but there was no clear reason why he would have so much anger and aggression. About three months after telling this story, Christopher's neighbour called the police complaining that they had seen him torturing cats. After investigating, the police found that he had hung two cats in his basement and had maliciously killed other small animals as well.

WHAT TO DO

Why do children act like Christopher? Frankly, we do not know. A small number of children, mostly boys, are diagnosed each year with a serious psychological condition known as Conduct Disorder. These children and some teenagers have very serious behavioural problems that range from cruelty to animals to arson and stealing. Some of these children come from violent backgrounds and have witnessed constant fighting or abuse in their home. Some have experienced abuse themselves. But other children with Conduct Disorder come from perfectly normal homes with loving parents and siblings who show none of these problems. Obviously children like Christopher need immediate professional help; and they need it as early as possible. Violent stories and play typically precede violent behaviour. Listening to the secret language of these children, as disturbing as their ideas can be, is the best way to help them avoid a tragic fate of anti-social behaviour and continual rejection.

Stories that lack organization are developmentally immature

From very early on, children learn that stories have a clear organization – a beginning, a middle and a resolution. They also learn that adding detail to stories makes them more interesting to others.

Analysing the organization of their stories can reveal a great deal about children's thought processes and whether or not their thinking, creativity and problem-solving abilities are age-appropriate. Sometimes stories can reveal a learning problem or other cognitive problem.

Young children, of course, tell very simple stories. At age three, Darren told the following story:

> Once upon a time there was a boy who lived in Chicago. He liked dinosaurs.
>
> THE END

As children grow older their stories should reveal more complex thinking, detail and organization. At age eight, Darren told another story about dinosaurs, which his parents wrote down:

> Once upon a time there were two dinosaurs, a Raptor and a Tyrannosaurus Rex. The Raptor was called Ganga and the T-Rex was called Ram. Ganga and Ram were best friends. The liked to roam through the forest and chase the other animals. Everyone was afraid of them and would run away. But they

just wanted to play! They decided to have a big dinosaur party and invite all the dinosaurs in the forest and in the lake. They sent out invitations and a thousand dinosaurs came to the party. They played tag and hit a piñata and everyone went home with a goodie bag. Now Ganga and Ram had lots of friends. When they walked through the forest, all of the other animals said 'hello' and 'how are you doing.' That made them walk tall.

THE END

As you can see, 8-year-old Darren's story follows a logical sequence of scenes. He introduces his characters, tells you something about them and then follows a simple storyline setting up both a conflict and its resolution. Even though the story is only 136 words, you get enough information and detail to picture the different scenes in your mind. You can envision these two dinosaurs walking together and talking. You can think of what a thousand dinosaurs might look like waiting in line for their party bags.

With every passing year you would expect Darren to tell more complex stories which parallel his increased cognitive development. By the time that Darren is a teenager, he will be telling and writing stories with subtle meaning, vivid description, irony and paradox. Probably they will be about other things besides dinosaurs.

But what about when children continue to tell or write stories that lack age-appropriate detail, organization or complexity? Sometimes this can be a sign of a learning disability and other times it can be a sign of an emotional problem. As early as seven, children should be able to tell and write stories for different audiences. By eight they should be able to look at a story they have written and revise and edit it. By nine children should be able to develop a plan for writing, using a variety of strategies to generate and organize ideas. They should be able to write several paragraphs on the same topic and produce a well-organized composition. They should show consistent progress in understanding the rules of punctuation and grammar.

If your child gets poor marks in written expression, make an appointment to talk to his teacher. Learning problems are defined as the inability of a child to perform up to his potential and if your child's teacher feels there are problems in his written expression and other areas of language arts, then you should ask for a psychological screening to determine if in fact there is a problem.

WHAT TO DO

If your child needs help in written or oral expression, there are many things you can do. First of all look at his reading habits. By nine children are typically reading at least one book a week. If your child does not have an interest in reading his school assignments, then find other kinds of reading that can interest him.

Secondly, have your children write more stories. There are several computer programs which teach children how to write stories that stimulate both creativity and writing skills (see www.superkids.com for suggestions and reviews of commercially available programs).

You can stimulate the imagination of a reluctant writer by having him dictate his stories to you. Ask him questions about the people, the places and the events of the story. Help him see that there are many choices to be made in creating a story and each one will take the story in a different direction. Then on another occasion teach him about the rules of writing. It is usually better to let children learn the skill of developing their imagination before working on punctuation, word usage, grammar and so on.

Troubling stories of the night – helping children with nightmares

When children have occasional nightmares your immediate presence is the best prescription. Hold your child or even lie down next to her if she wants you to. This is not the time to worry about setting firm limits or regular bedtime habits.

On the other hand, if your youngster is having recurring nightmares, then some form of daytime help will be required. The first thing you should do is to address the causes of the problem, which many times are fairly obvious. One mother consulted me about her

8-year-old who was having nightmares almost every night. When I asked about his bedtime habits, she said that he went to bed with a pile of comic books and read himself to sleep. When she showed me one of his comics at our next meeting, she seemed embarrassed. 'I had no idea how graphic these images were,' she admitted as she flipped through the pages to reveal a cave of skulls, a hulking two-headed monster with a mixture of blood and saliva dripping from his lips and even worse images. That day the boy's comic books were consigned to a sealed box in his parents' wardrobe, where they were to stay until he was older.

Even if your child is not having bad dreams, I would suggest that you review the images that he is seeing in his day-to-day life. Sit down and watch the television shows that he is viewing. Watch the video games that he is playing and look at the books or comics that he is reading. Consider if these are really the images and stories that you want to shape your child's day- and night-time.

The second step to take in reducing your child's nightmares is to examine the stresses and problems that your child might be encountering. Is she worried about her schoolwork or making friends at school? Is there something happening in the family that might be causing the child concern? Does she have a hurried lifestyle, running from one activity to another? Children experience stress just the way that adults do and sometimes it can spill over into their dreams.

If looking at the daytime influences on your child does not help, then you may want to help your child deal with nightmares within the secret language of his emotions.

Helping children change their dreams

Jonni Kincher, author of *Dreams Can Help*, offers several techniques that children can learn to take a more active part in the stories of their dreams. Kincher tells children that when they have bad dreams they can call on 'dream friends' for help. Dream friends can be animals or real people that they know, or even super heroes! She suggests that children make up stories while they are awake where their dream friends help them with the 'bad' people in their dreams. She tells children that they can 're-dream' their dreams while they are awake, writing a new ending that turns out the way that they want. Then they can try and have this same dream while they are asleep.

This technique is referred to as 'lucid dreaming'; teaching children to change their dreams while they are dreaming them. We all have lucid dreams at sometime. When you are dreaming and suddenly, while you are dreaming, you realize that you are dreaming, that is a lucid dream. Researchers believe that both children and adults can train themselves to do more lucid dreaming and literally solve problems while they sleep. By mentally rehearsing a new positive dream just before sleep, children can be helped to actually change their nightmares.

Dr Stephen LeBerge, who studied lucid dreaming with volunteers at the Stanford University Sleep Research Center, says that he had his first lucid dream when he was just five. In his dream he found himself starting to drown, but when he realized that he was dreaming he knew that he could not drown. He swam beneath the waves and enjoyed his swim.

Using a dream diary to help children control their dreams

Encouraging children to keep a dream diary can also be a useful way to give them the message that they can control their nightmares. For example, 12-year-old Margaret began having nightmares after her father had a heart attack. Nearly every night she woke up from a dream crying. She began begging to sleep in her parents' bed. When they said she was too old to sleep with them, Margaret would bring her pillow and blanket and sleep outside their bedroom door. In the morning Margaret rarely remembered her upsetting dreams.

The school counsellor suggested that Margaret start writing down her dreams as soon as she woke up. Margaret kept a diary of her dreams and found that she remembered many good dreams along with the bad ones. During the day she would talk to her parents about her dreams and what they meant. This gave Margaret an important opportunity to feel closer to her parents in an appropriate daytime activity, rather than in their bed at night. Within a few weeks her nightmares stopped.

Not only do dream diaries help children develop a sense of mastery of their emotions, they can also stimulate their problem-solving ability and their creative thinking. Physicist Niels Bohr reported that he had a dream in which he saw himself on a sun of burning gas with planets rushing by. Suddenly the gas cooled and solidified and the sun and planets crumbled away. When he awoke he realized that he had seen the model of an atom. Robert Louis Stevenson dreamed about a criminal who drank a potion to change his appearance, inspiring him to write the classic, *The Strange Case of Dr Jekyll and Mr Hyde*.

What to do if your child has night terrors

If your child is having frequent night awakenings, it is important that you determine if they are nightmares or night terrors, because they should be handled differently. Nightmares are dreams which occur in REM (rapid eye movement) sleep, which repeats itself in cycles throughout the night. Night terrors – which can range from moaning and thrashing, to calm sleepwalking, to full-blown terror episodes – do not occur during REM sleep and so they are not a by-product of dreams. We do not know exactly what causes night terrors in some children; however, we do know how to handle them.

While you should try to comfort a child who awakes from a nightmare, this response would not be appropriate for a child having a night terror. The best strategy is simply to be present and to make sure that your child does not hurt himself. If he is walking around, try and guide him back to bed, but do not try to wake him. When he wakes up he will not have a memory of what happened and will usually be able to go right back to sleep. Often he will barely be aware of your presence and the comfort that you would give after a bad dream is not needed. Since night terrors are not dreams and there is nothing for your child to remember, there is also no need to talk about what happened or to question your child.

Generally speaking night terrors in children under six are not thought to have any psychological significance. They will often disappear when children get more sleep, so consider getting your child to bed a little earlier, or reinstating a daytime nap. If partial awakenings occur repeatedly in older children or teenagers, it is thought that they might indicate some emotional stress, although these problems still may not be serious. Researchers think that some people simply have a predisposition to express their anxiety in these night-time episodes, just the way other children might be biologically predisposed to develop an ulcer or a stutter. Counselling may be indicated if the night terror episodes keep occurring, particularly because it may be upsetting to the child or teenager to know that they are 'out of control' while they sleep. Medication may sometimes be prescribed if the child's sleepwalking becomes a danger to him.

Chapter 12

Speaking to Children Through the Secret Language of Stories

Telling stories that change the way your child thinks

For many years psychologists have known that one of the most effective ways to help children with emotional and behavioural problems is to teach them new ways to think about themselves and their problems. Does this sound difficult? It is not. Whether you realize it or not you influence your child's thinking all of the time, because children model their thinking patterns as well as their behaviour on the people that they see everyday. If you are a person that becomes overwhelmed by problems or a person that acts without seeing different alternatives then your child is likely to have these same characteristics. But if you are a thoughtful and realistic problem solver then your child will be likely to develop this thinking style as he listens and watches you each and every day. It is not surprising that studies find that children who are good problem solvers have more friends, have fewer emotional problems and also perform better in school.

While most parents realize that children watch and imitate their behaviour and their language, they do not realize that they can influence their children's thought patterns and storytelling is one of the best ways I know to literally change the way that your youngsters think. In this chapter we will look at different ways to help your children learn stories that can change their lives: a fun game called the Problem-Solving Story game; creating Life Story books; creating self-help books for children; and a technique where children with problems learn to rewrite the story of their lives, called narrative therapy.

Teaching children problem-solving skills

According to Myrna Shure, author of *Raising a Thinking Child,* children can be taught to solve their own problems at a much earlier age than most parents realize. Consider 1-year-old Sabrina, who was offered a biscuit by her grandmother. She naturally took the biscuit in her dominant hand. Then Sabrina was given a second biscuit and she took it with her other hand. Now what do you think happened when she was given a third biscuit and both her hands were full? She placed one of her biscuits in her mouth and got the third one. She solved the problem of getting biscuits when your hands are full in a matter of seconds.

In the past, many psychologists underestimated children's ability to solve problems, because they conducted their experiments using problems which were not relevant to the children's experience. But when we give children relevant problems to solve (and what could be more relevant to a 1-year-old than getting more biscuits), we find that they have a remarkable ability to discover the solution to problems at a very early age.

With her colleague David Spivak, Dr Shure has conducted research for over four decades which demonstrates that children as young as 4 years old can be taught social problem-solving skills. They can learn to resolve their own arguments, avoid confrontations, even help other children learn to be better problem solvers.

I designed the Problem-Solving Story game to give children practice in seeing that there are alternative solutions to their common problems. When your children learn and practise this game you may see a dramatic difference in the way that you and your children relate to each other, particularly if you play it often.

You have probably played a game like the Problem-Solving Story game before, perhaps when you were a child. One person starts a story, the next person adds to it, then the next person adds another part and so on until the last person brings the story to an end. The story evolves through the collaborative imaginations of the players. But I have varied this classic game just a little to give children (as well as adults) practice in finding solutions to common problems.

The Problem-Solving Story game can be played by a family with three or four members or by a group of three or four children.

Here's how to play.

Each player contributes a different part of the story:

1. The first player starts by deciding on the main character of the story.
2. The second player adds to the story by creating a problem for this character.
3. The third player thinks of a positive and realistic solution to the problem.
4. If there is a fourth player, he can elaborate on the solution.

The youngest player starts the first story, the second youngest player goes next and so on. For the second story, the second youngest player starts and the youngest player takes the final turn, ending the story. Play continues until each player gets to start at least one story (in other words the group has told as many stories as there are players). You can continue to tell stories as long as you like. The important thing to remember is to model good solutions for your children. Be positive, but also realistic. Do not correct your children if they come up with solutions that are negative or unrealistic. Just be a good role model and your kids will catch on.

This is a very simple game that your kids will enjoy anywhere at anytime. It is a great game to play on short or long car trips. But the most important part of this game is the secret message that it teaches: 'There are few problems that cannot be solved by creative thinking and a positive attitude.'

Here are some examples of stories told by different families.

Eight-year-old Peter: Once upon a time there was a snail named Fred.

Mum: Fred was so slow that he lost every race.

Dad: So he bought himself some roller blades so that he could go faster than any other snail that he knew.

Seven-year-old Debra: Once upon a time there was a boy who lived in Alaska.

Mum: He lived in an igloo and they had a heatwave in his town and his igloo started to melt.

Dad: So his family put their igloo on a huge sledge and pulled it up north where the weather was colder.

Five-year-old Jasmine: Once upon a time there was a boy who was only five inches tall.

Eight-year-old Evan: [Jasmine's brother] He wanted to go to school like all the other children, but he was afraid that someone would step on him.

Mum: So he found a really tall friend to go with him to school and he rode on his shoulder. That way he was at the same height as everyone else.

Mum: Once upon a time there was a boy who didn't clean his room.

Ten-year-old John: He had really bad eyes and he couldn't even see that his room was a mess!

Seven-year-old Bethany: Wherever he went he would bump into things.

Dad: But he learned to feel when things were out of place. This was important so he didn't trip. Then he kept everything in its proper place.

Creating self-help storybooks

As I mentioned earlier, there are hundreds of books that have been written to help children better understand their emotions and their behaviour. Reading these books to children or having older children read them to themselves has proven to be so effective that it is one of the most popular counselling techniques in use today. There are many good self-help books that have been written for children and new ones are being published every year, but I am often asked to recommend the 'best' book for specific problems.

One father wanted to know of a book to help his 7-year-old who had suddenly developed a fear of death. A mother asked me to recommend a book that would help her older children understand that their 3-year-old brother had been diagnosed with autism. Another mother wanted a recommendation for a book for her ADHD son who did not like to take his medication.

Sometimes I can think of a particular book and sometimes I can not. But I often tell parents: 'There is one book that will help your child more than any other. This is the book that you write!'

Writing a simple storybook for your child is a very rewarding activity. I have recommended this technique to parents hundreds of times, always with positive results. Many parents tell me that they are not good writers. But I remind them that storybooks for children consist of just a few hundred words. I explain, 'If you can write a letter or even a long e-mail, then you can write a child's storybook. It is just a matter of organizing your thoughts and writing them down.' Then I give them a simple 'template' to show them how.

For example, Mary Jenkins came to see me on the recommendation of her daughter's school counsellor. She told me that her daughter, Georgia, had a mild stutter and that she was just diagnosed with a learning disability. Mary had noticed that Georgia's stutter became much worse when she was stressed. This was a particular concern because her husband was about to lose his job and the family would undoubtedly feel a financial strain. She asked me if I thought that her daughter needed counselling, and I replied that it sounded like she did need help, but I thought that Mary might be able to help her daughter much better than I ever could. I recommended that she write her daughter a self-help storybook.

To begin I asked Mary to think about what she wanted the book to teach her daughter. She replied, 'I just don't want her to worry so much about her problems. I want her to know that everything can be solved. I used to stutter myself when I was a child and I got help and got over it. I had trouble in school and I got help with that, too. Even if my husband loses his job, that has happened before and I know he'll get another one. I want Georgia to understand that no problem is too difficult to solve when you have people that love and support you.'

I explained to Mary that she should begin by telling Georgia just what she had told me – that she had had problems when she was a little girl and that worrying about them never helped. She should tell her daughter she would always love her and would show that love by helping her overcome any problem that came along.

I also noted that reassuring Mary was just the first step. The more important step would be to teach her daughter how to help herself. I thought that a self-help storybook would be a great beginning and I gave her the story template below (in italics) and asked her to fill it in.

In writing a self-help storybook for children you should keep just one specific problem in mind. Even though children may have more than one problem, as in Georgia's case, problems can become more manageable when children focus on one thing at a time. Confidence in solving one problem will then spread to other problems. Mary decided that the most important issue facing Georgia was her stuttering.

Here is my story template and what she wrote:

Start 'Once upon a time . . .' and introduce the main character with a different name to that of your child.
Once upon a time there was a girl named Ann.
Introduce the problem from the child's point of view.
Ann stuttered some of the time, particularly when she was nervous. She thought that if she stuttered, then other people would think that she was strange. She thought that the children at school might not like her.
Introduce a helping character, such as a parent, a teacher, a grandparent or a fictional character.
But Ann's mother wanted to help her understand her stuttering, because she didn't like to see Ann feel bad.

Give an example that puts the problem into a larger perspective.
Stuttering is a problem that many children have. Many famous people used to stutter when they were young or even when they were older. The great leader Winston Churchill, used to stutter when he was a boy. He grew up to be a great writer and a great speaker. Ann's mother used to stutter, too, but she learned how to handle it.

Write a positive and realistic way to solve the problem.
But Ann went to a speech therapist for help. Her name was Gwen. Gwen taught Ann to take a very deep breath and blow it out slowly when she felt nervous.

Write a second way to help solve the problem.
Gwen made up games to play with Ann to help her feel that she could control her stuttering. In a game with puppets, every puppet had a name that started with a 'W'. There was Wilbur, Wilhelm, Wendy, Warren and Wallace. Every time a puppet spoke, he or she had to say the name of another puppet and that was very funny.

Write a new way for the child to think about the problem.
Ann began to see that stuttering was just another problem that some children have, which they can overcome. Ann had a friend named Ella, who had poor eyesight. Ella wore glasses to help her see better.

Create a realistic conflict that the child might be concerned about.
One day Ann had to read her book report in front of her class. She was worried about stuttering in front of the class.

Have the child solve or cope with the conflict, showing a positive attitude.
She practised reading the book report over and over again. She practised in front of the mirror and she practised in front of her mother and father, and even in front of her dog. Her mother said, 'Ann, I want you to pretend that you are in front of your class and then *make* yourself stutter. Then stop, take a breath, say "Excuse me", and keep going. That is the worst thing that could happen, and when you practise the worst thing, then you will understand that even the worst thing isn't so bad.'

Resolve the conflict.

The next day Ann read her book report in front of the class. Her teacher said that she read it a little fast, but she did not stutter. Some of the other children did not read as well as Ann. One boy, Terence, did not do the book report and he was embarrassed.

State what the child has learned.

Ann went home and told her mother what happened. She said: 'Everyone has problems some of the time. I'm glad I had you to help me with mine.'

THE END

After Mary wrote the story she bought a small binder and copied her story on to the left-hand pages. On each right-hand page she asked Georgia to draw a picture.

Asking your child to join in creating the book with you will make it even more meaningful.

Don't be concerned about writing the 'perfect' story. Just be positive and give your child a vision of a new way to address a problem.

TRY IT

You can write a self-help book for your child, just like Mary did for Georgia. Here are the eleven steps she followed. Remember to make the book positive but also realistic. You may be tempted to write a story where problems are solved with magic and conclude with 'happy ever after' endings. But this is not the way the world works. Teaching your child new ways to cope with and overcome problems is the best way to help her find her own happiness and success.

1. Start 'Once upon a time . . .' and introduce the main character with a different name to that of your child.

2. Introduce the problem from the child's point of view.

3. Introduce a 'helping' character such as a parent, a teacher, a grandparent or a fictional character.

4. Give an example that puts the problem into a larger perspective.

5. Write a positive and realistic way to solve the problem.

6. Write a second way to help solve the problem.

7. Write a new way for the child to think about the problem.

8. Create a realistic conflict that the child might be concerned about.

9. Have the child solve or cope with the conflict, showing a positive attitude.

10. Resolve the conflict.

11. State what the child has learned.

Writing the story of your family

A few years ago a friend of mine decided to record her family's history as it was created. She started when her children were aged four and seven. Like most children, her two girls liked to hear stories about when they were babies and she knew they would not tire of hearing stories about their early years, even when they had small children of their own. My friend kept a weekly diary and scrapbook in a loose-leaf binder. She reserved every Thursday evening as a time to record the family's ever developing story. She invited her children and her husband to add their comments as well as their photographs and mementos. Her only rule was that it had to be able to be pasted on a page. Recently this mother told me it was one of the best things she ever did for her family.

She explained, 'A lot has happened in the past two years, mostly good, but some bad. I had a serious operation which I thought would be hard for my girls to handle. But everything went in our book (now six volumes and counting). When we wrote in the book, or when the girls read it, they talked with us and with each other. This is a very important activity that keeps our family glued together.'

Most families keep photo albums in some irregular fashion. Perhaps you should consider adding written comments to yours as well and recording the story of your family as my friend did. This type of activity is much more than just creating a 'keepsake'. It is an activity which will foster a sense of identity and belonging in children.

Writing your family's story is particularly helpful in families which do not fit the so-called 'norm' of two parents with one or more biological child. (In fact, there are almost as many families that do not fit this definition of the norm as there are families that do.) If you have a family with a foster child, an adopted child, children from another marriage, same sex parents, multi-generational families living together and so on, then writing your family's life story will help your children understand and accept these differences. My wife and I were taught about the importance of this technique when we were prepared to adopt our daughter Tess from China.

Telling a child that she has been adopted is never an easy thing to do. Just a generation ago many parents felt that they should not tell their children anything about their adoption unless it was absolutely necessary. Today psychologists feel that keeping secrets from children does much more harm than good. It is not only dishonest, but certainly in the case of adoption it robs the children of an understanding of their heritage and history. There is nothing more to this technique than recording the events, thoughts and feelings that shaped your family's life. But to your child it is the most important story they will ever read or hear. It is the story of their life.

TRY IT

There is no wrong time to start your family's life story. So why not start today! Get a journal, paste in a picture of your child or your family and write down anything that comes to mind. If you want, you can write about past events at some later time, but it is always easier to write about events as they occur. Take just fifteen minutes one day a week to write in your life story book and you will be amazed at the story you create.

Helping children rewrite the 'story' of their problems

Patrick was a 9-year-old boy who was at war with Madmoo, the Anger Monster. With his counsellor's help he wrote Madmoo the following letter:

> Dear Madmoo, the Anger Monster,
>
> I hope that you are learning your lesson by now. You have got me into trouble for the last time! You think that it is funny when you get me into trouble, don't you? Well it isn't funny. When I get mad and yell at kids and call them names, then people get mad at me and I get punished. You may like that, but I don't. I'd rather be liked by the other kids and not spend time in my room. I'm learning how to squeeze you out of my brain. When you crawl in and tell me to get mad, I take a long deep breath and when I let it out I can feel you coming out of my ears.
>
> All I have to say is, 'Get out and stay out!'
>
> Good riddance,
>
> *Not* your friend, Patrick.

Patrick was told by his therapist that he should 'go to war' with the anger that kept getting him into trouble. He was told to give his anger a name and then to drive him away for ever. Patrick decided to name his anger 'Madmoo'. 'You can write him letters,' the therapist explained. 'You can draw pictures of him and cut them into little pieces. You can make up a puppet show where you conquer him for good! Make sure that he never comes back.'

Patrick's counsellor was using a technique called narrative therapy, developed by psychologists Michael White and David Epson who practise in Australia and New Zealand respectively. Narrative therapy helps children rewrite the most important story of all, the story of their lives. The technique was developed from the observation that when children have problems, those problems become a dominant feature in the way that people treat them and the way that children think of themselves. When a child is suffering from a problem like depression, or shyness, or problems in anger control like Patrick, that problem becomes the primary lens through which the child is seen. It may seem as if the problem is shaping the child's entire life.

But narrative therapy posits that the 'child is not the problem, the problem is the problem'. With that important assumption in mind this technique then teaches children to separate themselves from their problem and then 'write the problem right out of their lives'.

In narrative therapy children like Patrick are taught to give their problem a name and even an identity. Patrick had been referred to counselling because, as the diagnostic report put it, 'Patrick is an angry child with poor impulse control.' But his counsellor convinced Patrick that he did not have a problem, that he was a good kid. It was something inside him that caused him to throw tantrums at home and storm out of his class at school at the slightest provocation. His counsellor explained, 'You've got to work to get this guy Madmoo out of your brain now and for ever. Let him go and get some other kid into trouble if he wants to.'

As Patrick learned to think of the problem as outside himself he was freed from self-blame and defensiveness. He was able to create a psychological space between his problem of anger control and his identity, a space that encouraged him to make new choices about his behaviour. He was no longer an 'angry child'. He was a child who was working on a problem.

This technique also encourages children to be more creative and light-hearted even about the most troublesome problems.

For example, Judith used narrative therapy to help her understand and cope with her obsessive compulsive disorder. At eight, Judith had many strange rituals that baffled both her parents and her teachers. She had to look over her shoulder three times every time she went through a door. If she wanted to raise her hand in class, she had to raise both hands together. She could not just raise one hand at a time. These type of rituals make no sense at all to anyone except the child with OCD. But to them they are the most important things in the world. OCD can be one of the most crippling of all childhood disorders and is one of the least understood. But even such a serious problem can be helped with a humorous attitude.

Like Patrick, Judith was told that she had to 'go to war' with her OCD to get rid of her habits and rituals.* With her mother she made a list of the rituals that bothered her. They counted fourteen. Like the other children using this technique, Judith was encouraged to come up with her own strategy for going to war with her OCD. Judith told her mother, 'I'm going to take a wad of toilet paper and every time I get rid of one of these poopy OCD things, I'm going to flush it down the toilet.' It took her six months and a lot of hard work, but her symptoms diminished significantly and Judith felt that she was well on her way to living a life without such disturbing behaviour.

TRY IT

If your child has an ongoing problem, try motivating him to work on that problem by having him write the problem out of his life. Here are some activities that will help:

1. Give the problem a 'persona'. It could be an unlikable person, an evil animal or a monster from outer space. The 'problem' should have characteristics that are particularly unappealing, such as a bad smell, ugly looks, as well as bad intentions. Children will typically be very imaginative in creating a persona for the problem.

2. Draw a picture of the problem. Children create visual images more readily than adults and they will automatically develop a picture of the problem in their mind. Help them draw the image or construct it from looking through magazines or comic books.

---

*Child psychiatrist John March has pioneered the use of narrative technique with OCD children at his clinic at Duke University. He calls his programme 'Driving OCD Out of Your Land' and urges children to 'go to war' with their OCD which is ruining their lives. To learn more refer to the book *OCD in Children* by Dr March, published by Guilford Press.

3. Make up stories about getting rid of the problem. You and your child can make up oral stories or create books about driving the 'problem' away. The more you tell the stories or read the books, the more you will motivate your child to change his behaviours in ways which will eliminate the problem.

Part summary

Stories have a much greater influence on children's development than most parents realize. Your child is constantly hearing stories which influence his attitude, values, behaviour and emotional life.

For more than seventy years psychologists have known that the stories that children tell reveal the secrets of their needs, conflicts and desires, but you do not need a PhD to use stories to understand your child's emotional development as well as to influence it. You can help your child by giving him books that will be models for him to understand his emotions and behaviours and if you cannot find the right book for your child, write it yourself. Self-help books are easy to write, no more difficult than writing a letter, but they can have a profound influence on your child's development.

There are also many ways to help your child create his own stories, which will give you a window into his emotional life. The Story game will not only help you understand how your child thinks but it will also help him build a positive image of himself and his world. The Problem-Solving Story game can be played just about anywhere in just a few minutes. Yet research tells us that making this type of activity a part of your child's daily life can improve his behaviour, his attitude and even his performance in school.

You can make a dream diary, write the story of your family and even use stories to help your child 'rewrite' the story of his emotional problems as an aid to reducing serious symptoms. Stories are a powerful tool in helping your child within the secret language of emotions. You are also likely to find that they help you in understanding your own values, emotions and behaviours. Just start: 'Once upon a time . . .'

Part IV

The Secret Language of Your Child's Art

Chapter 13

Why Children Express Themselves Through Art

There had been a terrible hurricane off the North Carolina coast. Carla's home had been totally destroyed. Nearly all of her toys and clothes and memories were swept away. Carla's mum and dad and baby brother drove three hours in stop-and-go traffic fleeing their coastal community along with thousands of their neighbours. The torrential rain pounded their car while the family listened to the police broadcasts on the radio.

Shortly after they arrived in the hastily converted church shelter, Carla and a group of other children were invited to sit around a table and draw pictures. A Red Cross volunteer passed around sheets of paper and a plastic bucket filled with crayons. Carla drew a picture of her family walking along the beach, hand in hand. In the right-hand corner she drew a dark ominous cloud waiting to ruin their fun.

Art is one of the first balms used with children to help ease the pain of an emotional trauma. Art has an almost magical quality of being able to contain the powerful emotions that are triggered by a trauma without burying them. It is part of the therapy for traumatized children in many hospitals, foster homes and shelters. It is also used in much less dramatic situations. It is part of a counsellor's 'tool box' in thousands of primary schools and local clinics. It helps children talk about their feelings of shyness, of anxiety over a test or the stress of being teased by other children. It is also a way that parents can communicate with their children about their innermost feelings.

It is hard to pinpoint exactly why art techniques are so useful in helping children express feelings that might otherwise be buried, or why it is so helpful at healing emotional pain. Like other aspects of the secret language it seems to form a bridge between the emotional part of the brain, the limbic system, and the thinking part of the brain, the neocortex. Certainly art techniques bring a sense of familiarity and comfort to children (and adults as well) in periods of stress. These activities help them recall times and experiences when they felt more safe and secure.

Although we think of art as a visual medium, when it comes to children it is really multi-sensory. The feel of a crayon on paper, the smell of play dough or clay, the soft squishing sounds and giggles of finger painting are all important emotional triggers which can connect the child to the wonderful world of his imagination.

Psychologists point out that art is a way of gaining symbolic control over what would normally be an overwhelming, even terrifying experience. For example, Laura, a girl of seven, was waiting in her hospital bed before her exploratory surgery. Laura's nurse placed a sheet of paper on the fold-out table by her bed and said, in a calm and reassuring tone, 'Let's draw a picture of what this room is going to look like just a few hours from now. You start out and draw yourself lying in this bed. Great! Now let me draw a cabinet over here and a table here and a chair in the corner. Now I want you to draw all the family and friends who are going to come and visit you this afternoon. Then draw some balloons and cards and teddy bears around the room. All of the children get lots of pretty things to decorate their room after an operation. When you come back after your operation we'll see exactly how your picture matches your room.'

In the following days Laura drew many pictures with the guidance and encouragement of her nurse. She drew a picture of herself lying on the operating table with her team of doctors holding hands and smiling in the background. She drew a picture of the inside of her stomach and intestines where her pain came from and then coloured it over with a pink marker, which Laura explained 'would make it feel better'. Laura also drew her room at home, a picture of her best friend and a picture of herself lying asleep and dreaming about going to Disney World.

With each picture Laura gained a little more control over her feelings. As she continued to draw she was able to visualize more positive concrete images. At the same time, she felt a little less anxiety and physical pain. Each picture helped her take another step towards better health. Psychologists point out that keeping hospitalized children involved in interesting activities takes their mind off their pain. Then subsequently they need less pain medication making them more alert and self-aware and better able to participate in their treatment.

Art techniques also provide a therapeutic benefit for children simply because they are part of a creative process. Studies have shown that the creative process provides an emotional discharge and purging that, in turn, brings about a sense of emotional relief.

Art can help your child cope with many types of problems or just add to an understanding of himself and others. It can also be of benefit to you. Before you begin thinking about how to use the secret language of art as a new way to communicate with your child, you may want to take a few moments to reflect on your own attitude and experience with art and how it might play a more important role in your emotional life.

TRY IT

The Scribble Technique was designed to be a quick and easy way for people to explore their imaginations. It is a good starting place for you to see what it feels like to use art for psychological benefit. The instructions are simple. Just take a pen or pencil and a sheet of paper. Now close your eyes and draw a scribble. Then open your eyes and make that scribble into a picture. Take as much time to draw as you like. Try it now.

Now before you take a look at your picture, think about your experience. Do you feel relaxed? Do you feel calmer and less worried about your day-to-day concerns? From a physiological point of view the creative process typically increases the levels of serotonin in your brain, and serotonin is a biochemical that acts as a mood regulator. Increased serotonin levels in the brain should give you at least a temporary lift in your confidence and sense of well-being. In other words, just doodling a simple scribble should make you feel better.

Now let us see what your drawing reveals about you. Interpreting drawings is an inexact science, but it certainly can be a first step to looking at your emotional life or the emotional life of your children.

First of all, let us take a look at how much time it took you to do the drawing. If you rushed with your drawing it might indicate that you are anxious or stressed. Perhaps you had a hard day or you are preoccupied with a problem. Perhaps drawing itself makes you uneasy. Or perhaps you do everything quickly.

Now consider how you filled up the paper. Are you an expansive personality that needs to fill every square inch? Or are you a minimalist with a sparse and exact style of interacting with the world?

Did you use thick or thin lines? Was your drawing detailed or did you just suggest elements of the drawing for the viewer to fill in? A great deal of shading or exceptionally thick lines may indicate anxiety or tension, even though art activities are intended to help you relax. A lot of detail might reveal that you are a concrete, precise thinker. An abstract drawing could suggest that you are a more conceptual thinker, more concerned with ideas than specific facts.

Did you draw a person or an object? Drawings usually reveal a person's interests and can give you a sign of where your mental energy is bound. Parents often draw people or children. Children most frequently draw pictures of other children, their family or animals. A fisherman would be more likely to draw a boat, a motor enthusiast a car, and so on. A person who repeatedly drew pictures that were violent or frightening or that were not even recognizable might cause us to be concerned.

As you can see, when we look at a person's art, whether it is done by a child or an adult, we do not have answers as much as we do questions. We form a hypothesis about what the art might reveal. Then we look at other evidence, either in the real world or the secret language, which might support or disprove

that hypothesis. Take, for example, the scribble above and the picture that was drawn from it.

It took less than a minute to draw. As you can see it shows a face, which suggests that the artist is oriented towards people. The face is smiling, yet the presence of teeth suggest that there is also some aggression in the smile. The scribble is 'realistic', suggesting that the artist has a concrete way of looking at the world. There is a moderate amount of detail. Certainly the artist is not a perfectionist, but is concerned that at least the basic elements are present: eyes; nose; ears; eyebrows; mouth; hair; even a chin. The face is oriented outward, possibly suggesting an outgoing personality and even an openness to the world.

Another psychologist might have seen something else in the picture, perhaps with a more negative interpretation. But since I was the artist, I naturally cast a positive light on my interpretation of my own drawings. With every drawing it is important to understand the situation in which it was made. For example, another psychologist might look at my drawing and say, 'Where is the body? Does this person have a poor body image?' But I drew the picture on a small scrap of paper, sitting in a coffee shop, at 7 o'clock in the morning, and I did not have room to fit a body in my picture! As I will remind you several times in this section, be careful about over-interpreting art, particularly if you are looking at a single picture.

Art as a way to express and understand feelings

The secret language of art has many purposes. One of the most important is to help children learn about their feelings. For example, once when I was working as a school psychologist, I was using the secret language of art to help Paul, aged eight, cope with the loss of his father who died of cancer. Of all the art materials that I kept in a box in my office Paul preferred clay. At one session, he took a red stick of clay and broke it into dozens of little pieces. I watched him as he intently made each piece into a red ball. When he was finished, I asked him what he had done. 'These are the cancer cells that killed my father.' Paul replied with undisguised malice in his voice. 'Now I'm going to kill them.' And he smashed every one of the 'cancer balls' with a small rubber mallet. With each stroke he made a comment like: 'There, that will show you!' or 'I got you stupid cancer.'

I have seen many children express their anger at the unfairness of life through the secret language of art. One boy I was treating for depression covered an entire sheet of paper with black crayon. 'What do you call this drawing?' I asked, trying not to reveal the concern in my voice. 'It's my life,' he replied matter-of-factly.

But helping children express their feelings is just the beginning. We can also use their art as a way to help them accept and then change their painful emotions.

For example, after Paul had smashed all his clay cancer cells I asked him if he wanted to take a different colour of clay and make healthy cells and then put the cells together to make a healthy person. 'OK,' he replied, 'but that's not going to help my father. My father is dead.'

'You're right,' I agreed. 'It won't help your father. But it will help you to build a happier life, and I know that is what your father would want you to do.' And that is what he did.

TRY IT

Art techniques can be used as a 'blank screen' for children to project their inner feelings or they can be used to direct children towards a specific emotion. The Family Museum is an example of what psychologists call a projective art activity, where children learn to 'project' their inner feelings into their drawings for others to see.

Begin by taking a piece of paper and drawing four squares to serve as pedestals in the Family Museum. Then ask your youngster to place objects in the museum that are important to the whole family. The objects that the child places in the picture will give you a sense of his beliefs about what he thinks is most important in the family. Now try this activity yourself and share your picture with your child. Place objects in your version of the museum that represent the values that you want to teach your child. Talk about what you are thinking as you draw.

Sometimes an activity like the Family Museum can show you how differently parents and children view their family. It can also be used to help find a shared point of view. For example, I used this activity with Rhonda, a single mother, and Melissa, her 9-year-old daughter. Rhonda had sought help because she was fed up with the constant fighting and bickering between her and her daughter. I asked Rhonda and Melissa to make separate drawings of their Family Museum, explaining that they should draw in the things that they thought were most important to their family. Rhonda put a vase of flowers on a pedestal, representing her garden, she drew a photograph of her own parents on another pedestal and she put a laptop computer on a third pedestal. Melissa drew a picture with a soccer ball on one pedestal, a television on another and a telephone on a third. When I looked at these two pictures, it immediately struck me how this mother and daughter were going their separate ways; neither one had drawn anything that represented a shared interest. As you might expect, their next artistic assignment was to draw a Family Museum together, drawing objects that represented things that they both enjoyed. They jointly decided to draw cooking utensils, a beach umbrella and a bicycle. This simple exercise made them start to think about things that brought them together rather than apart.

Art can be a way to fulfil a child's unobtainable wishes

Wendy, an 11-year-old patient of mine, insisted on drawing a picture of her family going on a trip at the beginning of each session. She drew her mother and father and herself on a train going to New York. She drew her family taking pictures of the Eiffel Tower in Paris and she drew her family on top of an elephant in India. Her pictures were colourful and detailed. She talked excitedly and happily as she created them.

The only problem was that her parents had been divorced for nearly two years and had not taken a trip together for at least two years before they separated. Now they hardly even talked.

One day while admiring one of her drawings of her family on a pretend vacation I commented to Wendy, 'I guess you'd like your parents to get together again and take you to one of these places?'

'No,' Wendy said. 'I don't want that.'

'You wouldn't want to go away with your parents on a holiday?' I asked again, hoping that she would tell me more.

'Nope. They'd just fight all of the time and it wouldn't be any fun,' Wendy said nonchalantly.

'But in the pictures they don't fight,' I observed. 'They are always happy.'

'Yup,' Wendy said, not looking up from her drawing. 'That's why it's more fun to draw pictures.'

In a child's pictures, just as in her play or her stories, anything is possible. Children can fly. Flowers can bloom in the winter. Parents who never have a civil word to say to each other can stroll together through a park, holding the hand of their 11-year-old daughter without a care in the world. Art is a way for children (and adults) to satisfy their basic emotional urges through fantasy. It is a way that they can fulfill needs that will never otherwise be met. For Wendy, art was a way for her to be with her parents without conflict. Through her pictures, Wendy could imagine situations which would give her the sense of calm and comfort that she could not experience in real life. Is this the same thing as having parents that truly enjoy each other's company? Of course not. But it is something. Humans have the unique ability to use their imaginations to help them find pleasures that would otherwise be denied. The ability to create positive thoughts and feelings even in a difficult situation is a hallmark of good mental health for children as well as adults.

Psychologists call the process of satisfying needs symbolically 'sublimation'. Sublimation is considered a normal way to cope with stress and a way to achieve a balance between ones desires and the limitations of the real world. It is one of the most satisfying aspects of art and other creative endeavours. Some people are probably drawn to art more than others because it helps them satisfy needs that are difficult or impossible to meet in the real world.

TRY IT

Ask your child to make a wish and then draw a picture of what she is wishing for. Does she want something for herself, like a new bike? Or does she want something for someone else? Perhaps she will wish for something abstract, like world peace. Notice your child's expression and body language as she draws and see if she is enjoying this activity. If she is like most of us, simply thinking about fulfilling a wish is satisfying. Do not feel that you have to bring this activity back into the real world with a comment like, 'Maybe you can save up and get your bike.' After all, wishes do not always come true. A comment like, 'I hope that your wishes always make you happy', will be enough.

Art as a way of helping children deal with loss

From the time that our ancestors lived in caves to the present, humans have used art as part of the grieving process. Psychiatrist Elisabeth Kübler-Ross, an expert on the grieving process, noted that throughout history people have frequently made spontaneous drawings or other artifacts immediately after a significant loss.

Therapists recognize that art is particularly useful for children who do not have the cognitive or language abilities to make sense of their loss and adequately express their feelings. If you have a child who has experienced the loss of a loved one, even a pet, art can help them through every phase of the grieving process.

Art gives children permission to express their feelings of grief in ways that they cannot put into words. For example, Amanda, aged eight, did not cry at her father's funeral. But later that evening she drew a portrait of herself drifting in a boat on an ocean of her own tears.

Art can also help children find a way to remember a loved one. Seven-year-old Jason never saw his grandmother again after he visited her in hospital. He was told that she had died and that he would only see her again in his memory. At school on the day of the funeral, Jason drew a picture of his grandmother in her hospital bed. But he told his teacher, 'I don't want to remember my grandma like this. I hate this picture.' Like other children of his age, Jason had a concrete way of thinking about death. Since his grandma was in hospital the last time he saw her, he felt that this was the way she had to be remembered. His teacher asked him, 'Why don't you draw a picture of your grandma that will make you happy to look at?' So Jason drew a picture of both of them walking in the zoo, a favourite activity.

Some sociologists have speculated that art is particularly important in the grieving process because of the knowledge that the finished art will occupy some part of physical space left empty by the loss. The art object also becomes a tangible representation of the emotions tied to the loss, not only for the person grieving but for those who view the art as a memorial.

No art project in history has shown us how significantly art can be an expression of shared grief as much as the AIDS Memorial Quilt. The idea for the quilt came from a group of San Francisco activists who were searching for a way to express the deep loss they felt for their friends and loved ones. The idea of many individuals contributing a quilt panel for each loved one and then sewing all the panels together started as a neighbourhood project. Within a year almost two thousand quilt panels were displayed on the Capital Mall in Washington DC. Even now, a decade and a half later, thousands of panels are added to the quilt every year and parts of the quilt tour the world as a continual reminder of the strength of the human spirit even in the saddest of times.

Talking to your children through art as they grow

Many parents use art to chronicle their children's growth. One parent I know has kept an art album for her daughter Kaitlin since she was two years old, adding one picture each month. Now that Kaitlin is almost thirteen, she likes to look through her gallery of 130 pictures and see how her interests and artistic skills have changed. Sometimes Kaitlin and her mother go through the album together, recalling memories and discussing the feelings that they engender.

Art can be an important part of your child's memories and there is no time like the present to start. Remember, however, that more than other parts of the secret language, art is bound up with other aspects of your child's cognitive and motor development. So gear your activities and expectations accordingly.

Art with toddlers

Children will be able grasp a crayon between the ages of fourteen and eighteen months. They will typically be able to draw a circle by their third birthday, a square when four and a triangle around the time that they are five. They are unlikely to be able to draw a diamond until after they have mastered writing the alphabet and can print their name and several other words at around seven.

It is important to remember that some children (particularly boys) are slower in their fine motor development than others. Although their pictures may look immature when compared to other children of the same age, this is not usually a problem. Most children catch up in their ability to draw and write by the time that they are eight or nine with a little extra practice. On the other hand, when a child has reached a certain stage of artistic ability and then begins to produce drawings like a younger child this can be a sign of trouble. An understanding of how children draw at each stage will help you evaluate whether or not your child's drawings are age-appropriate or a secret sign of trouble.

We call the age from eighteen months to 2½ years the Scribble Stage for obvious reasons. Children delight in simply moving a pen or crayon around a sheet of paper, taking interest in whatever appears. From a psychological perspective, this is a much more significant activity than you might think. To a toddler the simple act of drawing teaches them that they can have a visible effect on their world, which gets a predictable positive response from the adults who care for them.

Drawing is also a very 'grown up' thing for a toddler to do. A toddler does not really see the difference between drawing and writing, an activity in which adults are continually involved. For example, when 3-year-old Thomas was asked what he was drawing as he happily scribbled on a yellow legal pad, he replied, 'I'm drawing a list for Mummy to use when she goes shopping.'

There is no rhyme or reason to a toddler's scribbles. He experiments with lines and movement, much the way he babbled as an infant to experiment with sounds and noise. As he gains more fine motor control, the toddler's random designs begin to take form, but his view of what he has drawn may be a far cry from what an adult might see, as evidenced by 3-year-old Tanya's picture of her dog in his dog house:

Slowly the toddler's scribbles will become less random and consistent shapes will appear. Between the ages of three and five, children enter the Shape Stage, where they delight in being able to make pictures with circles, squares and lines. In this stage children will often draw the same picture over and over again, explaining that each picture is something different (even though adults may not see the difference). As toddlers begin to combine circles with lines and experiment with colour, they begin to see that they can make choices as they draw.

The power of a toddler's imagination allows them to see past their rudimentary skills in creating art. For example, 3½-year-old Caroline drew a picture of three circles with two small dots in each circle and presented it to her mother. 'What's this?' Caroline's mother asked, reading her daughter's sense of accomplishment on her face.

'It's you and me and Daddy going to Disneyland,' Caroline answered with pride. 'I'm giving it to you. Hang it up!' Every time Caroline walked past her picture, she would say with pride, 'That's a picture of our trip!'

(Note: If your child is not able to draw simple circles and lines by the age of four, this can be the sign of a developmental delay or visual impairment. Check with your doctor to make sure that there is no serious problem, or to see if some sort of stimulation is recommended.)

Art and the school age child

Between the ages of four and seven, children increasingly add detail to their art. When they draw pictures of people we expect to see arms and legs and basic facial features, even though they may be distorted.

Children can now draw pictures that tell a simple story. For example 6½-year-old Luke told his mother, 'I'm going to draw a picture of a dinosaur eating a hamburger.'

'Well that's an interesting idea,' his mother replied.

'Yes, I know,' said Luke, 'I'll draw in a milkshake for him to wash it down.'

We refer to this period in a child's development as the Sequence Stage, because now children will put a number of different elements in their pictures in a more thought out order. It is analogous to children learning to combine individual words into sentences and individual sentences into paragraphs to express an original idea.

Young children are most likely to draw what interests them. Their families are, of course, favourite subjects, as are dinosaurs, lorries, princesses and the cartoon characters that they see on television. As children reach the age of seven or eight, their cognitive and language abilities become more sophisticated and so do their drawings. Their art takes on a greater degree of realism and their images are usually immediately recognizable. More importantly, their drawings begin to reflect their feelings and thoughts as well as their concerns and conflicts. We call this the Fantasy Stage because children begin to use art the way that they construct stories and participate in dramatic play. This is the stage when children's art is most likely to symbolize their inner life.

TRY IT

Ask your school-age child to draw a picture of another planet. (You can do this, too, if you like.) Ask him to draw in creatures on the planet and to draw in the things that those creatures like to do. Then ask your child to make up a story about his drawing.

Here are some things to look for in the secret language of your child's drawing:

What mood does the picture have?

Art tells us a lot about the emotional attitude of children. Children convey their outlook on the world through the use of colour and, in particular, the representation of people in their drawing. School-age children with a positive outlook typically draw happy looking people doing interesting activities with other people. The figures are generally large and in proportion. (In other words children of the same age are approximately the same size, but smaller than adults.)

How complex is your child's drawing?

More detail shows greater creativity and perceptiveness and a longer attention span. Naturally these are also characteristics of children who perform well in academic subjects. Encourage your child to be creative in her drawings and this habit will be likely to carry over to other aspects of her life.

Does your child plan the picture out, or does he just start drawing? How much does he think about the drawing?

By the time that children are six or seven, they understand that drawing is a process that they have control over. They can decide what to put in the drawing and what to leave out. They can make multiple drawings, creating a series or improving the same drawing with each new effort. It is important to encourage a growing sense of mastery in your child's creative efforts. With every step he makes in controlling his self-expression in art, he makes a parallel step in learning to understand and control his emotional life.

Which part of the activity does your child enjoy more, the drawing or the story?

It is important to remember that some children show a strong preference for either visual motor or language based expression and learning. Most school-age children enjoy both visual and language oriented expression, but take note if this is not true of your child. If your child dislikes drawing, if she complains that she is 'not a good artist' like other children, or if her drawings seem particularly immature, then you may want to talk with her teacher to see if this is a symptom of a broader problem.

Art and the adolescent

By the time that children approach adolescence they become aware that their art can be 'read' by others and they may become acutely self-conscious of what they draw. This is a time that many children stop drawing altogether, even though they may have shown considerable talent when they were young. With encouragement, however, adolescents can use art to both communicate their feelings to others and to develop insight. As with children, art can be a particularly effective way for teenagers to express their emotions, to heal from physical or emotional pain or to grieve. With just a little positive encouragement and support, teenagers can also use art to explore and define their identity.

Over the years I have found that photography is a particularly helpful way to work with teenagers using the secret language of art. Photography has been called 'art for the non-artist'. Certainly it is a medium that appeals to those who want to create visual images but do not have training or a natural talent in drawing, painting or sculpture. The technique of using photography as a way to help people learn about and express their feelings is referred to as phototherapy.

Phototherapy has not had a wide following among mental health professionals, largely because of the expense and technical expertise needed for creative photography. But the growing popularity of digital cameras has begun to make photography a more popular hobby and many teenagers are beginning to find it is a unique medium for self-expression. For a £100 or less, teenagers can have access to a digital camera and software to create images which can help them view their world as never before. They can then share their images with their friends, families or classmates by printing their pictures, saving them in electronic form or publishing them on the Internet.

Although many older children and teenagers might benefit from simply being handed a digital camera and told to 'take pictures that mean something to you', I prefer giving more specific assignments which direct them to see the positive things in the world. We know unequivocally that having a positive attitude towards oneself and one's world has significant benefits for children, teenagers and adults. So we should promote this way of thinking at every opportunity. It stands to reason that parents, more than anyone else, should take every opportunity to communicate a positive attitude towards their children. Here are some phototherapy assignments that I have given to teenagers in an effort to orient them to a positive way of looking at their world. See if you think that any of these would appeal to your older child or teenager. Better still, make each assignment a family project in the secret language of art.

TRY IT

Look through the following photographic exercises and decide on the one that you think your older child or adolescent might respond to best. Of course, you can use a conventional camera, but a digital camera will give him more opportunities to express himself creatively. Collect the photos in an album or have an at-home photographic exhibit. Remember that the secret language of art is most helpful to teenagers when it stimulates conversation and insight.

The beauty of nature: Have your teenager take pictures of nature that show the beauty of the world
This activity encourages a positive attitude and an appreciation of beauty. There are so many aspects of our culture that focus young people on the 'darker' side of life, it is important to balance this with activities that help them see the beauty in their world as well.

Important details: Have your teenager take pictures of things that he sees everyday that bring meaning to his life
Have your child photograph anything that interests him. Encourage him to get as close to the 'subject' as possible, looking for what he might miss if he stood too far back or moved through his day too fast. This is also an exercise in flexible thinking. It teaches adolescents to be able to see things from a variety of points of view.

People connections: Have your teenager take pictures of family and friends
Ask your teenager to avoid posed pictures, but rather to take candid
photographs of the people that he cares about, doing something
that is important to them. Photography can encourage teenagers
to communicate in new ways, both in the process of taking the photographs and in displaying them for view. Remember that the secret
language of art is the language of emotions. As such it is an important part of your teenager's communication with others.

*Helping hands: Take pictures of people in your family or community who
help others (teachers, police, ministers, veterinarians, person holding a door
for another, etc.)*
This project produces some of the most emotionally evocative
images you will see: a child feeding his dog; a man helping a blind
woman across the street; an ambulance driver watching as his patient
is brought into the casualty. As every photographer knows, the
camera can capture 'the secret language of the heart', which in turn
produces an image that reminds each viewer of our common
humanity. But it is the heart of the photographer that is really on
view. When we direct teenagers to look for the good in people, they
will find it.

As we shall see, art can tell you many things about your child and
it can also create unique opportunities to help your child explore
himself and his world. Do not skip over this important way of communicating with your child just because you think of yourself as a
'non-artist'. Art is a natural way for your child to communicate with
you and you with him. So get out the crayons and markers and a
pad of paper and get started!

Chapter 14

Art as Communication Between You and Your Child

Participating with your child in art

Art therapists have pointed out that there is a significant benefit in just watching your child create art. Witnessing your child's delight in developmental achievements is one of the true joys of parenthood. When you witness your child's accomplishments with the natural pride of parenthood you send her the message: 'Yes, I see what you can do and I adore you for it.' What could be more important to a child's sense of self-worth?

Witnessing a child expressing feelings is in fact the essence of any therapeutic experience. Therapists undergo years of training to learn how to be a powerful presence for their diverse patients, but this is an easy task for parents. All you need to do is carve out some uninterrupted time to give to your child. It may seem simplistic but it is nonetheless true: just witnessing your child draw, or paint, or create something with clay, will have a significant emotional benefit.

On the other hand, when we view art as part of the secret language of emotional communication, we remember that all communication is a two-way street. I advise parents to participate with their child in creating art to make it more meaningful to them all.

First create an 'art friendly' home

When you go to a commercial district of a large city you pass shops with signs like 'French spoken here', 'German spoken here', and so on. These signs provide an important invitation to foreign visitors who might otherwise feel that they will not be understood. If you are serious about speaking to your child in the secret language of art, then you will need to create an environment at home that says, 'Art spoken here.'

The first step you will want to take is to get the art materials out of the cupboard and put them in a place that is more accessible to everyone in the home. An art box should include crayons, washable markers, scissors, plasticine and clay, water colours and finger paints. You will need several pads of paper. A variety of art materials allows your child to work in different art mediums which in turn encourages different emotional experiences.

Now pick a place in the home where you will feel comfortable doing art activities. Most parents prefer the kitchen table since it is easier to clean up. Certainly it should not be a place where you will be concerned about getting art materials on fabrics or rugs. Even though you should always use washable materials, worrying about making a mess will work against your efforts to use art as a way of opening up new channels of communication. Make sure your child has a large enough surface to work on. While working on the kitchen table the child should not have to worry about knocking over a vase or sugar bowl.

Choosing different art mediums

Different art mediums are associated with different ages, but that does not always mean that you should be restricted to only using art materials associated with that age. By selecting different art mediums you can actually make younger children express themselves in more sophisticated ways and older children and teenagers act as they did when they were younger.

Crayons and markers are the most common art materials used by young children. They have the advantage of being easy to use and always accessible. Suppose that you see your child looking upset or worried. Just say something like: 'You look like you are having a hard time today. Sometimes drawing pictures about your feelings or thoughts can make you feel better.' If your child seems reluctant to do this, do not force him. Some children have more difficulty expressing their feelings than others. Some children might even take this opportunity to tell you to mind your own business, but do not take it personally. Remember that any kind of communication is good for children and you can always take the first step and send the message that 'talking about your feelings can help'. If your child does not want to express his feelings through art (or through any other part of the secret language for that matter), then you can always take the lead.

For example, a friend of mine, who is also a psychologist, told me a story about trying to help her seven-year-old son, Ethan, after his baby brother had died of sudden infant death syndrome (SIDS). She handed her son some markers and crayons and suggested that he might want to make a picture about his feelings. But the boy told his mother: 'I don't want to think about that.' But his mother simply replied, 'OK, I understand. But I think I'll draw a picture of my feelings.' She drew a picture of herself crying. She said to her son, 'I'm very sad that Tommy is gone, that I won't ever see him again.' Then she took out another piece of paper. 'Now I'm going to draw a picture about all the things that make me happy', and she drew a picture of her older son, her husband, some friends, her bicycle and so on.

Ethan watched his mother with interest. Finally, he picked up a crayon and started scribbling. 'Are you drawing anything in particular?' his mother asked. 'No, I'm just drawing,' Ethan replied, but he looked relieved and seemed happy to just be sharing an activity with his mother. The point of this story is that children have their own ways of expressing and dealing with difficult times. Art is a very unique way for children to learn to handle their emotions, but it is important to remember that each child will find his own way of exploring and communicating his feelings. You can help by exploring and communicating your own feelings in the secret language of art and by creating opportunities for children to work their feelings through.

When children use crayons and markers to express their feelings as part of the grieving process, I suggest to parents that they keep their pictures in the pad or in a diary. The pictures then become a record of the process of one's feelings for everyone to look at.

To make art a part of your communication with your child, you will need to set aside time to do art projects. Remember that this is not an ordinary arts and crafts time where parents can just set up materials and then loosely supervise their children. This is an occasion for you to participate with your child in a new form of emotional communication. So it should be a time when you can devote ten or fifteen minutes entirely to your child. Turn off the TV. Turn on your phone's answering machine. Be ready to speak 'art'.

Art is a great activity for your child at any time, but to derive a true emotional benefit, to really speak the secret language of art, you will need to designate a fifteen or twenty minute period of time which is just for you and your child. Tell your child exactly when you will be doing art activities using language and time concepts that he can understand (e.g. after dinner and clearing up; first thing Saturday morning, etc.) and do everything in your power to make this happen. Prepare your art materials in advance and find a place where you will not be interrupted. This is worth saying again. Find a place where you will not be interrupted.

If you stop to answer the phone, if you need to leave your child to go to attend to a crying baby, if you need to go to help your husband find the car keys, then this will defeat the most important purpose of speaking to your child through the language of art, which is to make them feel that they are valued. If you cannot give your child fifteen minutes of uninterrupted time at home, then go out for a soft drink and take your art materials with you. Get up early with your child or stay up a little later. But find the time. It is worth it.

When your child has finished an art project, you should give some thought to how it will be preserved. A child's art has many levels of meaning and so we must respect each piece of art as a unique creation. I do not mean that every childhood drawing must be treated like a masterpiece and hung up for reverential display, but rather that art is a way that children express themselves emotionally and you should take care to ask them what they want to do with an art project once it is created. I suggest combining an art scrapbook and diary in one binder. On one page paste a picture that the child creates, and on the other page write down comments made by the child about the picture and its meaning. As we shall see, it is the combination of using art and words that can be so helpful to children in their emotional development.

TRY IT

Any aspects of the secret language will become more important to you and your child as you practise it. I know that finding another fifteen minutes a day in your schedule can seem burdensome at first. However, it will seem easy and natural once you make it into a habit. It is easier to start a new habit when you do it more intensely at first. Here are some activities that you can do with your child to explore the many ways you can communicate through art.

Draw a self-portrait

This is usually the first art activity that psychologists use when trying to understand the emotional life of a child. Many books have been written about how to interpret a child's drawing of himself, but for our purposes we will concentrate on how to see the self-portrait as a way of communicating.

The most important thing to remember is not to question your child about his picture, but rather just make objective evaluations. This is the best way to get your child to explore his own perceptions and feelings.

For example, Claudia was a 10-year-old girl who was referred to me for counselling because of her extreme shyness. Art activities are particularly useful in helping shy children, because there is no expectation for them to talk (even though every shy child I have ever worked with eventually does). I asked Claudia to draw a picture of herself. As she drew I commented on her work:

Therapist: 'That's you.'
Claudia: 'Mmm, hmmm.'
Therapist: 'You're drawing a very small picture of yourself. It only takes up a little corner of the page.'

Claudia: 'I like to be small.'

Therapist: 'I guess if you're small no one will notice you.'

Claudia: 'That's right. I don't want people to pay attention to me.'

Therapist: 'I see that you're smiling in your picture. I guess that you're happy even though you're small.'

Claudia: 'Yes. I'm happy when no one notices me.'

Therapist: 'I see you're drawing a dog in the picture next to you.'

Claudia: 'That's my dog. His name is Champion because his mummy was a champion show dog.'

Therapist: 'Champion looks happy, too.'

Claudia: 'Yes, he's happy when I'm around.'

Therapist: 'I wonder what else will make both of you happy?'

Claudia: 'We like to play in the garden. I'll draw my garden.'

By simply commenting on her self-portrait, Claudia was encouraged to think and talk more about herself and her world. In the weeks that followed, Claudia did many more self-portraits, gradually adding things that were important to her pictures and then adding other people, too. She became aware that the activity of drawing a picture of herself was a way of telling me about her sense of self-worth. One day she very deliberately drew a picture of herself with a huge head that filled the page. 'This is me having a good day,' she explained. 'I had a very good day today, I got the highest mark in my class on the maths test.'

'Good for you,' I commented. 'That is something to have a big head about.'

Draw four pictures that show four feelings:
happy, sad, afraid, brave

Most of the time when I counsel children I give them 'emotional' homework. You may not think that children should be getting home-work for their emotional problems, but these are always fun activ-ities for them to do, so they rarely mind. More importantly, it is their work in their home rather than in a counsellor's office that will make a difference in helping them with their problems. As I have said earlier, children learn new emotional and behavioural skills by practising them a little bit every day and there is no place better for that than in their home.

This activity is an example of how art can be used to explore specific feelings. The instructions are simple: draw four pictures, showing someone having each of the four emotions: happy, sad, afraid, brave (sometimes I will choose different emotions, depending on the situation and age of the child). In each picture, draw in the things that make you feel that way. Children respond much better to this type of art activity than they do to questions about their feel-ings. For example, Sonya was a child who was adopted from an Eastern Europe country when aged three. Her adoptive parents were told that it might take a while for her to make an adjustment to her new family, new language and new country, but she still seemed to have problems when she was eleven. Her mother described her as 'very moody' and 'exaggerated in her emotions'. Little things seemed to upset Sonya and she would react with a full-blown tantrum one day and inconsolable sobbing the next. If her father criticized her table manners she might burst into tears or she might throw her plate across the room. To her parents she seemed totally unpredictable.

Sonya's primary goal in counselling was to help her understand her feelings and to see that she could control them, rather than them controlling her.

Her parents were instructed to give Sonya a 'feelings chart' every day and she was to draw a picture of an important feeling that she had each day. They were asked to sit next to Sonya while she worked and to draw the picture themselves if they felt like it.

The change in Sonya was not immediate, behaviour change rarely is, but over the next few months her parents reported that her moodiness was diminishing and that they felt closer to their daughter than they had in years.

Draw a picture of a machine that helps people

Art can also be used as a way to help children learn new values. When I have asked children to 'draw a machine that helps people', I have seen some incredible contraptions, including a machine that made food from mud to feed the world's hungry and a machine that turned 'mean people into nice ones' by coating them in chocolate. Children are exposed to a constant barrage of negative images on television and in the media, but with only a little effort, you can get them to start thinking about positive values and the things that they can do to make a difference in their world.

The International Children's Art Foundation is an ambitious attempt to teach children values through art. Their 'peace through art' programme is designed to foster peace and multicultural understanding around the world through children's art. As they explain in their mission statement: 'ICAF employs the arts as a dynamic channel to nurture the creativity of children. As a language-independent medium, art links children around the globe. Children experience the power of collective creativity and the value of cross-cultural cooperation through our innovative programs.' The foundation sponsors an international art Olympiad, publishes a magazine to promote children's art and hosts exhibits of art from children around the world. They even have on-line activities in their efforts to reach millions of children around the world (go to www.icaf.org).

Here are some more ways to teach your child values through art.

Art as a gift

Have your child give her art as a gift. Everyone likes children's art and a framed picture makes a great addition to anyone's wall. There are also kits that can turn art into everything from ties, to plates, to placemats and computer programs that can create buttons, T-shirts and more.

Organize an art show

You can do this through your school or at home. You can have a 'one-child' show or get the whole family involved. To teach values, create a theme for the art show, like 'pictures of peace', or 'pictures of ways to be responsible'. Children enjoy having an 'art assignment' and when you give them a project which encourages them to think of important values, you make this a meaningful part of their thoughts and conversations.

If you want to stretch this valuable educational activity even further, you can set up a children's art gallery and sell the pictures, with the proceeds going to a local charity.

Have your child teach art to younger children

One of the best ways I know to help children with emotional problems is to provide them with opportunities to tutor children who are two or three years younger. Tutoring gives aggressive children the opportunity to be nurturing and thoughtful about the needs of others. Tutoring gives shy and anxious children the chance to be more outgoing and direct. Any type of tutoring is helpful to both the tutor and the tutee, but I have found that tutoring in art is particularly effective in fostering the emotional and social development of children. When children help other children with art there is no pressure to perform and no strict criteria to be evaluated on as with tutoring academic subjects. Both the tutor and the tutee can concentrate on developing a helping relationship without worrying about being judged. Always keep the art project simple (e.g., finger painting, sponge painting, using moulds to shape clay) and limit activities to fifteen or twenty minutes. Give the tutor instructions on how to teach younger children so he or she will be sure to have a successful experience.

There are many ways to communicate with your child through art when you take the time to explore your creativity. There is no question that this will be of benefit to you as well as to your children.

Chapter 15

How to Know When Your Child's Art Is Really a Call for Help

Steven, aged eleven, drew a picture of his sister with her head cut off. But this did not mean that he wanted to kill his sister. He was just angry with her. George, aged seven, drew a picture of himself drowning in a river. This did not mean that he was suicidal or even depressed. His parents had warned him so many times about going near the stream close to his home, he wanted to 'see' what it would be like to go into the water. So he simply drew himself there. Sarah's drawings, on the other hand, were a sign of her inner troubles. When she was five she had been sexually abused by a teenager in the neighbourhood. Now at seven, her drawings were sexually precocious. In fact, it was through her drawings that the sexual abuse was discovered. Sarah repeatedly drew pictures of herself in bed with the teenage boy, an image that would be unusual for a 7-year-old to draw.

Interpreting the secret language of a child's art can be difficult, even for a trained psychologist. You must always be very cautious about jumping to conclusions, particularly when looking at a single drawing.

There is an old joke I was told in graduate school about interpreting children's art. It still serves as a reminder to me to never jump to conclusions. This joke is about a child who would come home with a new drawing everyday that was always drawn with a black crayon. His mother, who had studied psychology in college, knew that a child's selection of colours reflected his emotional state and she began to be concerned. When her son drew a black butterfly she did not think much of it. When he brought home a picture of himself drawn in black she started to worry. Then he brought home a picture of a black dinosaur, a black house and a black garden. The boy's mother started to wonder if he was seriously depressed. Finally, when her son brought home a picture of a black rainbow, the boy's mother could not contain her anxiety. 'Why are you so unhappy?' she asked her son, not trying to hide her distress. 'What do you mean?' the boy said confused. 'I lost all my other crayons and the only one I have left is black.'

When professionals interpret a child's art, they use drawings to form a hypothesis that must then be proven. For example, when I handed nine-year-old Katie some paper and crayons and asked her to draw a picture of a person, she drew a tiny figure in the bottom corner of the paper. My training told me that this type of drawing could be a sign of low self-esteem or even of serious depression. But nothing I knew about Katie suggested that this would be true. She had no symptoms of depression, nor did she seem to lack any self-confidence. Her parents were going through a divorce, which was why she was seeing me, but she seemed to be adjusting remarkably well. Puzzled, I asked her why she drew such a small picture. 'Because I'm too tired to draw a big one,' she said with a shrug.

The point I am trying to make is that art can be an important aid in identifying early problems in a child, but only when we evaluate a child's art in the context of her development and other known facts about her life. Psychologists look for patterns and repetitive themes which seem to stand out considering the child's particular stage of development. If you see something about your child's art that is troubling you, then by all means check it out. Talk to other people who know your child and see if they have any similar concerns. Do not hesitate to seek professional guidance if you have any concern. When it comes to children's emotional well-being, it is always better to err on the side of caution.

When children show no interest in drawing

As I noted earlier, children show an interest in drawing about the time that they begin to speak, between twelve to twenty-four months old. Toddlers are very busy exploring their own world and they also learn about it by watching the significant people around them and by trying to imitate everything that they see. All day long they watch grown-ups pick up a pen or pencil and make markings on a paper. If there are older children in the home, toddlers want to have the same kind of fun that they are having, by drawing, painting and participating in other art activities. Toddlers readily perceive that writing and drawing are important activities and they are delighted the first time that they see how much fun it is to change the way that a piece of paper looks by going back and forth with a coloured crayon or marker. Most children begin scribbling between fourteen and sixteen months, just as soon as they can hold a crayon.

When children do not show any interest in drawing by the time that they are two or two-and-a-half, this can be an indication of a developmental delay. For example, at twenty-seven months Harry spoke only two words: mummy and 'fies' (for French fries). His parents were told by their doctor that some children are just slow in developing speech and that these skills would emerge. Harry could walk and run and sometimes he could even hop on one foot, which was advanced for his age. But Harry's nursery teacher seemed very concerned about his lack of interest in drawing. While the other children would sit at a table and draw or finger paint for five or ten minutes, Harry would get up from the table and go over to the block corner. This experienced teacher knew that many children, particularly boys, are slow to develop their fine motor skills and their early frustration will often make them prefer other activities. But she also thought it was strange that Harry would not even try to draw or finger paint. Her instincts were right. A comprehensive evaluation found that Harry did have significant developmental delays. His vocabulary, his ability to follow directions and his difficulty in understanding basic spatial concepts like 'up' and 'down' were all below age expectations. An intense stimulation programme was recommended with a speech and language therapist to help him with his language and cognitive development.

By the age of three, children typically have a good sense of spatial orientation in their drawings. Their images may be very crude but they are generally recognizable. Poor visual orientation along with poor fine motor development may be an early warning sign of a learning or reading disability.

When drawings are aggressive and violent

Children, boys in particular, often draw violent pictures. This is hardly surprising considering the number of aggressive images that they see every day. (One study found that children watching an hour of popular Saturday morning cartoon shows would witness an average of seventy aggressive acts.) I have known children who draw explosive battle scenes, flesh eating monsters and all sorts of gruesome and gory tortures. Most of the time, this is not an indication of a problem. As I mentioned in Chapter 13, drawing can be an appropriate way for children to sublimate their aggressive feelings and can actually be a sign of good coping skills. After many years of working with children, I can think of a dozen shy and gentle children who sometimes drew aggressive and even violent pictures to express flights of fantasy that they would never consider acting out.

But repetitive aggressive or violent drawings can also be a signal of distress and we must delve a little deeper to find out if there is a reason to be concerned.

For example, at age ten, Marcus constantly drew pictures of battle scenes. He particularly liked to draw scenes with enemy planes and tanks exploding into hundreds of pieces and body parts flying everywhere. His school notebook was filled with such pictures and they occasionally made their way on to Marcus's homework, much to the chagrin of his teachers.

I was treating Marcus at the request of his parents to help him cope with the problems he was having with his younger brother, Carl. Carl was the apple of his parents' eyes, while Marcus was more of a squashed grape. Carl was a handsome boy of seven, a good athlete and precocious in school. Marcus was overweight, clumsy and had a severe learning disability. Although ten years old, he could hardly read. Certainly Marcus had good reason to be angry about his lot in life, but I wondered if his drawings were simply an outlet for his anger or if they were a secret sign of emotional trouble.

I asked myself, and then answered, the following questions to help determine the answer.

Is this a common type of drawing for a 10-year-old boy?

Yes. Violence in stories and drawings and an interest in guns or war may make us uncomfortable, but they are not symptoms of psychopathology in this day and age. Many researchers feel that boys have an inborn predisposition to aggressive interests and play, which, from an evolutionary viewpoint, prepares them to take the adult role as a 'hunter' or 'protector'. Other researchers feel that boys and girls are simply following the role models that they see and this is the strongest influence on their behaviour.

Are the drawings unusually gory?

I looked over Marcus's drawings with this question in mind. Certainly there was enough carnage in any one of his drawings to make it clear that none of Marcus's enemies would survive his wrath. But as I looked closer this did not appear to be Marcus's main concern in his artwork. The drawings actually showed a preoccupation with the way things worked. The machines and munitions in Marcus's drawings were highly detailed and carefully drawn. The human effect of the destruction was drawn more quickly and without detail. When I had treated children who were aggressive in the real world, who had set fires and tortured their pets, their drawings focused on the suffering of the victims. They were 'blood and guts' drawings and seemed intended to upset the viewer. Marcus's drawings were not of this nature.

Did the drawings depict real people in Marcus's life?

The answer to this important question was 'No.' Marcus drew aggressive pictures about anonymous people and he did not depict aggression towards people that he knew. This is an important distinction. When a child draws an aggressive picture of real and recognizable people then the picture is no longer a symbolic expression of his feelings. In other words, the anger that a child feels is no longer a secret and the child recognizes this. Art which shows aggression towards real people in the child's life should always be considered a cry for help.

Did Marcus draw too many violent pictures?

The two things that concerned me most were the repetitiveness of Marcus's drawings and the fact that they 'spilled over' on to his homework where a child of this age would surely know they did not belong. Although they may not consciously think about it, children know the rules of the secret language just as they know the rules of the normal language of words. I would expect a 10-year-old to know that drawing the same thing over and over is like saying the same phrase over and over again. Someone will eventually notice. Similarly, drawing guns and other weapons on your homework would be like purposefully using poor grammar in school – it will not go unnoticed. With this in mind, I determined that Marcus's aggressive pictures, although they did not represent serious psychological symptoms, needed to be addressed.

After watching Marcus draw dozens of battlefield scenes, I said to him, 'I can see that you like to draw big battles with lots of cool machines. But I wonder if you can draw me an anti-war machine? You know in the real world, wars and battles hurt many people. The only reason that countries go to war is that they can't find a better way to solve their problems. An anti-war machine would be a great invention, wouldn't it? Why don't you draw me a picture of what you think it would look like?'

I watched Marcus hesitate a few moments, wondering if he would respond to my request. Then he picked up a marker and took a piece of paper out of the pad and said calmly, 'OK, I can do that.' He filled the page with a large box which had dozens of dials and levers and gauges. On one side was an opening for people to dump in guns and missiles and other weapons. On the other side of Marcus's machine was an opening where a dozen or more doves flew out.

By redirecting aggressive feelings through the language of art you can help children focus their imaginations and creative energies towards learning anger control and conflict resolution skills. If a child repeatedly draws angry and aggressive pictures, this should not be ignored, even though it is not necessarily a sign of a serious problem. Whether a child has a very obvious reason to be angry, like Marcus, or if his anger does not have an apparent cause, he still needs to learn how to cope with these feelings.

When drawings are too sexual

Sexual abuse in children is much more common than most people realize. Any type of sexual contact with children is considered abuse, whether it is done by adults, or as is often the case, by other children.

Sexual precociousness can also lead to serious problems, particularly for young girls. Sexual images on television and in teen magazines and rock videos have led to a climate where many preteen girls feel that their looks and 'sexual attractiveness' are the most important part of their self-image.

As I have said, adults should not jump to conclusions over a single drawing, but a series of drawings with sexual themes done by children over five or six should certainly raise concern. The most obvious concern is when children repeatedly draw explicit pictures showing genitals and breasts, but there can be more subtle signs as well. Some children who have secrets to hide draw pictures of themselves hiding or with part of their face or body obscured. Other children draw themselves as distorted figures or draw other people that way. Remember that even a trained professional cannot 'read' a child's art by looking at pictures alone, but must consider the images in the context of other things they know about a child.

If you are at all concerned about the sexual nature of your child's drawings, do not keep your feelings a secret! Talk to your child openly and frankly. Express your concerns and your values. Do not hesitate to look for help and guidance if you need it. There are unfortunately many negative influences that can affect your child's understanding of her sexuality and you must make sure that she has positive influences as well.

If you see something in your child's drawings that disturbs you, no matter what it may be, keep calm and avoid interrogating your child. Rather see your child's art as the start of a conversation, being ever mindful that your child is communicating through the secret language because that is the language he is most comfortable in. It is generally better to tell your child what you see rather than ask for an explanation.

For example, rather than ask, 'Why do you draw pictures where everyone is fighting?' just make a non-judgemental, but specific observation like, 'These pictures have a lot of fighting in them.' Just as in observing your child at play (see p. 90 on the techniques that make up Special Playtime) you will encourage your child to talk more about his feelings by making supportive comments rather than by asking leading questions.

If your child is experiencing problems, from a divorce, a trauma or from a physical or learning disability, and you see signs of emotional distress in his drawings, then you should know that art can also be a very unique way to help relieve your child from some of his suffering. We will explore ways to help troubled children through art in the next chapter.

Chapter 16

Art to the Rescue

Many counsellors use art techniques to help children communicate and explore their troubling feelings. Because they are so easy to use and so accessible, art techniques are used in a wide variety of settings to help children learn to communicate their emotions, cope with anxiety and heal emotional wounds. If you visit any place where people are concerned about children – from a shelter for homeless families to a paediatric unit at a hospital or a community counselling centre – you are likely to see adults talking to children in the secret language of art.

I believe that the home is also a place to help children through the secret language of art. You have bandages and all sorts of medicine at the ready for when your child is physically hurt or ill; should not you also have an emotional medicine kit ready for when your child suffers from psychological bumps and bruises?

In this chapter, I will discuss some of the many techniques that counsellors and other professionals use to help children with their problems, or to prevent problems from even occurring. Studies have shown us that when you help children accept their feelings and teach them coping skills to deal with problems you are increasing their resiliency by giving them the tools to deal with the inevitable problems that they will confront as they get older.

Art can help your child express his feelings

One of the reasons that art techniques are so useful for children is that they can help them express feelings and concepts for which children do not yet have words. Often we ask children, 'What is bothering you? What is making you feel this way?' But we forget that children do not have the cognitive development to have insight into their feelings, nor do they have the vocabulary to adequately describe them.

The Colour Your Day technique is a simple activity I recommend to parents to give their children an opportunity to share their feelings at the end of the day through a simple drawing.

Begin by explaining to your child that different colours represent different feelings. In our Western culture, certain colours are associated with certain feelings. For example, red often means angry, blue means sad, yellow means happy and so on. But over the years I have found that children have their own 'colour code' for feelings and we must respect their code even if it is different to ours. For example, one boy told me that the colour pink made him feel 'sad' because his father used to live in a pink house and he had moved away two years ago.

To begin the Colour Your Day technique, ask your child to pick five to eight different crayons to represent five to eight different feelings. Four- and five-year-olds know basic feelings like happy, sad, afraid, brave and mad. Between six and eight, children begin to understand at least a dozen more subtle feelings, including embarrassed, shy, joyful, guilty and so on.

Now give your child a sheet of paper and say, 'This piece of paper represents your day. Colour in this piece of paper to represent the different feelings that you had today.'

Some children make abstract drawings using the different colours to express their feelings. Sometimes the drawings are no more than a series of shapes and lines in different colours. Other children draw a more realistic picture, using different colours to represent their feelings about different people or situations.

For example, whenever I asked Anna, aged eleven, to 'colour her day', she drew pictures of the people she had encountered during the day. I was treating Anna for depression and this technique was particularly useful in helping her sort out and express her different feelings. Anna coloured the clothes of the people in her drawings according to the feelings that she had about them on that particular day. She frequently drew pictures of her social studies teacher, Mrs Penna, who Anna thought was very strict. On one day Anna drew a picture of Mrs Penna making a cross face and scolding the class full of pupils. Anna coloured her teacher's dress red, because she was angry at her for being so mean. On another day she drew a picture of Mrs Penna with red and yellow polka dots. Anna explained, 'Mrs Penna was half mean and half nice today so I made her dress half and half.' (Anna had decided that the colour red meant 'mad', and the colour yellow meant 'pleasant'.) On the surface, drawing her teacher with a polka-dot dress may not seem like an important event, but to me it was an emotional milestone for Anna and a turning point in her treatment. It is difficult for children to see that people can have two different feelings or character traits at the same time. They tend to characterize people as 'good' or 'bad' and they tend to think of their own behaviour in these absolute terms as well.

I recommend that you try using the Colour Your Day technique for a week to see if this is a way that your child can more readily communicate his feelings. This technique should make it much easier for your child to talk about his feelings and may bring a new dimension to your daily communication.

The feelings X-ray machine

When I met Stephen for the first time, I knew that I would have to dig deep into my bag of tricks to get him to open up. I had seen many children like Stephen before – sullen, distrustful, more apt to find the bad in any situation than the good. He was referred for counselling because he was considered an 'underachiever' at school. He only talked to a few other children when at school and he did not consider them his friends. He was often picked on and teased because he was overweight and clumsy. At home Stephen was considered to be the 'problem child'. His parents described him as always 'testy and wilful'.

When working with any child in therapy, a counsellor's first job is to establish a trusting relationship. This is not an easy task with a child who does not trust anyone, but it is a critical one. Art is almost always a good way to begin to establish a relationship, because children usually have pleasant associations with art activities.

After talking to Stephen for a few minutes about what to expect from our visits, I took a crayon and a piece of paper and drew a simple silhouette of a person. I explained, 'This is a feelings X-ray. When you colour it in, people will be able to see the feelings that you are holding inside and they may be able to help you with them.' For three weeks Stephen drew a 'feelings X-ray' for his parents everyday. Stephen filled one picture with teardrops. In another, he drew a cat that had died the year before. He drew a gravestone with his name on it in a third picture:

Stephen's parents were shocked that each picture depicted such sorrow in their son, whom they had just thought of as a 'difficult child'. But behavioural symptoms like hyperactivity and wilfulness can sometimes mask childhood depression. It is only through the secret language of emotions that we can understand the roots of many childhood problems. Fortunately, Stephen was able to communicate in this language and he got the help that he needed.

Family art

Do you sometimes feel like everyone in your family is going in a different direction? Dinners are rushed because everyone is too busy with their own activities? Weekends are so over-scheduled that they seem as stressed as week days? Here's an activity, called the Collaborative Family Drawing, that will literally get everyone in the family on the same page.

In this activity, the whole family draws a picture together. This type of activity helps children and teenagers develop a sense of belonging and importance in the family. It is a simple activity that only takes a few minutes, yet it encourages the family to communicate on an emotional level which rarely occurs in the day-to-day routine. All you will need is a large piece of paper and a box of crayons.

To begin, all the family members should sit in a circle around a table. The drawing paper and the box of crayons are placed in front of the youngest member of the family. Someone says 'go' and the youngest member of the family has thirty seconds to draw anything he wants. He then passes it to the family member on his right. Someone else says 'go' and the next person then has thirty seconds to work on the picture before she passes it to her right. The drawing continues to go around from one family member to another until it has been worked on five times. The sixth person who works on the picture must complete the picture and give it a name.

The Collaborative Family Drawing can tell you a lot about how each person in the family perceives his or her role. Some family members (usually the parents) are 'builders'. Builders draw houses, bridges, cars, gardens and so on. Other family members are people oriented. They draw themselves in the picture as well as other family members. They may also draw in friends, relatives or teachers. Still others might be action oriented. They draw in the cars, lawn mowers, hammers and other objects that provide motion and purpose to the family drawing.

Problems can also be revealed in a Collaborative Family Drawing. This is usually quickly evident in the picture for the 'collaboration' is missing. For example, I gave this assignment to one family I was counselling where the parents had remarried and the two stepsiblings constantly bickered and complained. In a series of pictures each of the step-children, Alice aged eleven and Connie aged fourteen, always undid each other's images. For example, if Alice drew flowers in the picture, Connie would draw a scorching sun to wilt them. If Connie drew a car in the picture, Alice would draw nails in the road to puncture the tyres.

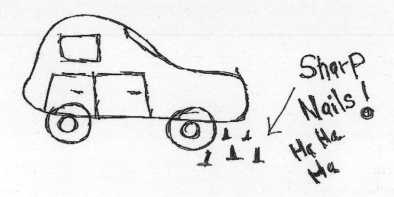

After watching these girls act out their animosity in their drawings, I decided to change the nature of this assignment and I asked them to draw a 'Getting Along Family Picture' where every family member must make a positive contribution to the picture. Not surprisingly they were reluctant to try this, but they acquiesced. This type of activity does not solve the problem. It took many months until Alice and Connie called a 'truce'. But it was a first step. The secret language of art can provide families with a new way to communicate and to look at their own behaviour. That is what you must build on.

Art and stress reduction

In nearly every meeting I have with parents, I emphasize the importance of teaching children how to calm themselves down when they are upset. When children are shy, angry, worried or afraid, learning relaxation techniques is a key to their treatment.

Learning to calm yourself down when you are upset is also an important part of preventing problems. Research tells us that when children learn how to 'self-calm' they are less susceptible to mental and physical health problems. Whatever reason a child might be under stress – taking a test, going to the doctor, standing up to a bully – keeping his emotions and physical reactions in check will be important. The next art technique I will describe, called the Calming Book, will be a useful way to help children find a reliable means to relax when they are stressed.

Before you begin this art technique you should first teach your child how to relax by breathing deeply and relaxing his muscles. Demonstrate to your child how you look when you are relaxed, showing him how your arms, legs, hands and feet look when they lose their tension. If your child is still tense, you can lightly massage his muscles until they are relaxed. Make sure that you do this at a quiet time, when the normal intrusions of day-to-day activities will not disturb you.

Now help your child make a list of sensory experiences that are pleasurable and relaxing, including sounds, tastes, scents, tactile sensations, scenes and images (e.g., clouds or sunsets), colours, people, experiences or events. Then look through magazines or family photographs for examples of the images that you have listed. Create pages for these images by gluing them on paper and placing them in a binder. On each page jot down some notes describing the feeling that each image evokes. Decorate a cover for your child's new Calming Book.

Have your child practise using his Calming Book the next time that he seems stressed or anxious. Sit down with your child and go through the book. Put on some quiet music. Try and relax yourself, particularly paying attention to your breathing, your own muscle tension and the tone of your voice. Remember that children learn most readily when imitating adults, so be a good role model. Talk to your youngster about the importance of handling problems by staying in control of his feelings and behaviour.

I advise families to keep the Calming Book in a place where a child will see it often. Just keeping the book around will be a continuous reminder of the importance of learning how to control his feelings when he is upset.

Creating a circle of hope

Circular forms in art are sometimes referred to as mandalas and are thought to have a particular psychological meaning to the people who draw them. In Sanskrit the word *mandala* means 'sacred circle'. In many ancient cultures circles are assumed to possess magical 'curative powers' and are used to aid in meditation, in healing ceremonies and as symbols for unity and wholeness. Carl Jung, a contemporary of Freud and the inspiration for many techniques in healing the psyche, is credited with introducing the concept of the mandala to Western psychology. Jung observed that his patients often spontaneously created circle drawings and he believed that mandalas expressed the desire of his patients to unify conflicting parts of their personalities and to seek transformation and wholeness.

Art therapist Cathy Malchiodi (*The Art Therapy Sourcebook*) notes that although mandalas often appear spontaneously in the work of people trying to understand their emotional problems, children and teenagers can also be directed to draw mandalas as a way of helping them contain their problems. She writes:

[In] my experience of working at a community drop-in center with homeless adolescents who had a variety of problems, including drug addiction, family problems, and a lack of security . . . creating mandalas seemed to have a calming effect on them, at least in the short-term. For most [of the teenagers], working within a circular form on paper provided a way to literally slow down and control or refocus often uncontrollable energies. While a mandala drawing will not magically reduce anxiety or troubling emotions, studies have shown that drawing within a circle format can have a calming physiological effect on the body in terms of heart rate and body temperature.

The technique is a simple one. When your child is worried or frightened or even angry about something that has happened, draw a large circle on a piece of paper and say: 'Draw something inside the circle which will make you feel better.' There is no wrong response. I treated a child for his anxiety about going in for surgery and he drew a picture of a big bowl of ice cream, which he told me he would eat after his operation. He hung the picture 'for good luck' on his hospital bed. A teenager I was treating whose parents were going through a bitter custody fight, drew a picture of himself in a circle frowning and with his eyes crossed. 'Will that picture make you feel better?' I inquired. 'Yes,' he said, 'because I'm going to show it to my parents and tell them "this is what you are doing to me with your constant fighting".' And that is just what he did.

Part summary

The secret language of art should be a part of the everyday experience of young children. Creating an art-friendly home and participating with your children in art projects can help you find a way to communicate with your children about everyday feelings as well as to help them through times of emotional distress. The secret language of art will be particularly helpful at times when children are anxious or afraid, or when they have to deal with a prolonged period of stress such as an illness or when mourning the loss of a loved one.

Looking at your child's spontaneous art can also give you clues about possible developmental delays, learning difficulties or emotional problems. It is particularly important for parents to understand that their child's art will go through different stages and that each stage serves its own purpose in a child's cognitive and emotional development.

Understanding what to look for in your child's art as he grows may help you see early warning signs of potential trouble. If you have concerns, you should always seek professional advice.

Art can enrich your relationship with your child in many ways, but unfortunately most adults are self-conscious about their lack of artistic talent and this prevents them from participating in the secret language of art. Rather than thinking of art as a product that someone creates for public display, think of it as just another healthy activity for you to enjoy with your child. Art activities can contribute to the emotional health of your whole family. Enjoy it.

Part V

The Secret Language
of the Face, Body
and Voice

Chapter 17

Speaking Without Words

Nine-year-old Lizzie opened the front door of her house and frantically ran into the kitchen. When she saw her mother, she threw herself into her arms, sobbing. She squeezed her mother around the neck and her mother responded by guiding her daughter to the couch, holding her tightly against her side, even while they were walking. She stroked the back of Lizzie's hair, patiently waiting until her daughter could tell her what was wrong. It took about five minutes, but then Lizzie's crying subsided and she slowly became calmer as her mother rocked her back and forth as she had done when Lizzie was an infant.

Consider all of the emotional messages that were communicated in this brief exchange – panic, anguish, sorrow, caring, nurturing, bonding – and yet not a word was spoken. Lizzie's mother knew that her 9-year-old was in deep pain yet something told her that she was not physically hurt and whatever emotional pain had happened could quickly be soothed. (Lizzie's mother was correct; her anguish was about not being included in her netball team.)

Like Lizzie and her mother, you also communicate with your child in the secret language of non-verbal communication on a daily basis. By watching her facial expression, gestures, voice tone, posture and more, you analyse your child's emotions and act instantaneously and intuitively according to her needs. You may respond in words, or like Lizzie's mother, you may respond non-verbally. Most of the time you probably use both words and non-verbal language.

Most parents are not consciously aware of the non-verbal

exchanges that they have with their children. They wrongly assume that their communication involves only what they say to their children and what their children say to them. But in a classic study of how people interact, it was found that only 7 per cent of emotional meaning is expressed in words. The majority of our emotional communication, over 50 per cent, is expressed through our body language. The other 30 to 40 per cent is expressed through voice tone, volume and inflection, what scientists refer to as our 'paralanguage'.

In this section of the book we will look at how paying attention to the secret language of non-verbal communication can help you feel closer to your child and can help you better guide her emotional and social development. I am convinced that parents who are more aware of the secret language of non-verbal communication are more competent parents and raise more confident children.

Few people would argue that business men and women who know the secret language of non-verbal communication have an important edge on their colleagues and others. They are better salespeople and they are better managers. They are better liked by their co-workers and are, therefore, usually more productive. Corporations spend tens of thousands of dollars each year training their employees to be able to communicate better with others, but these same skills are also important in our relationships with our friends, our spouses and most of all, our children. Genie Laborde, who has taught communication skills to major corporations like Coca-Cola, IBM and American Express, notes in her book *Influencing with Integrity* that while a great deal of attention has been paid to training people in the business community, 'the skills are useful anywhere people interact. The recognition and practice of these skills lead to better choices, better decisions and even better thinking processes.'

I can guarantee that as you become more skilled in speaking the secret language of non-verbal communication with your child, you will become effective at every aspect of parenting. I can also assure you that if you ignore the importance of this type of emotional communication you will be more likely to misunderstand your child and he will be more likely to misunderstand you.

Unfortunately, I see examples of poor non-verbal communication between parents and children almost every day. Recently I observed a scene in a bookshop where a mother quietly asked her 6-year-old to return a book that he was reading to the shelf so that they could go and do more errands. 'Honey, please put the book away,' she said sweetly, but her son just ignored her. 'We need to go now,' she said, with an absent-minded tone in her voice, as she picked up her own book off the shelf, doing exactly the opposite of what she had just told her son to do. 'I mean it,' she said, with a little more force in her voice, but still looking through her own book. 'I mean it,' she said again, but neither she nor her son moved a muscle. Then the mother looked at her watch and apparently realizing that she was late, loudly admonished her son. 'Did you hear what I said?' she asked angrily. And she pulled the book out of his hands and returned it to the shelf. Then she grabbed the stunned boy under the arm and led him out of the shop.

Does this scene sound familiar to you? Do you sometimes wonder why your children or teenagers do not respond to your requests or commands? If your answer is 'yes' then you should look at how you can improve non-verbal communication to get your child to be more cooperative and responsive.

Let us return to the example of the mother in the bookshop and see how she might have used more appropriate non-verbal communication to get her child to respect her request to put the book away and leave the shop.

What happened	How communication could be improved
The mother asked her son to put away the book in a sweet tone.	She could have made the same request in a firmer tone.
Her son ignored her request.	She could have made eye contact with her son by moving in front of him or asking him to look at her.
She made her request into a command ('We need to go now'),	Again, she could have used a firmer tone. She might have underscored *continued*

but she used an 'absent-minded' tone.	her verbal message with a gesture, like pointing to the door.
Even though she was saying that it was time to go, she picked another book off the shelf to look at.	She is doing the opposite of what she told her son to do. She could have just started to walk out of the shop and her son would have followed.
She said, 'I mean it' with a little more force.	When young children do not listen, you can guide their physical movements. To say 'I mean it' non-verbally, she could have taken her son's hands, closed the book he was looking at and guided his hands to put the book away.
She angrily asked, 'Did you hear what I said?' and pulled him out of the shop.	Her anger and aggressive behaviour is a result of her failure to communicate. Now she is giving her son the message, 'When all else fails, getting angry will get you what you want.' She would do better to simply look at her son directly and say, 'I have an important rule. When I ask you to do something, I want you to do it right away.'

When we analyse how the communication between this mother and her son could have been improved, we also reveal the major components of non-verbal communication: eye contact, facial expression, gestures, postures, touch, voice tone and volume.

An understanding of non-verbal communication is important for every parent, but it is particularly significant if you have children with behavioural problems or emotional conflicts. If your child is wilful and tests limits, then your knowledge of non-verbal communication can make her much more cooperative. If she seems sad or anxious or lonely, then knowing the secrets of non-verbal behaviour can be crucial in understanding the cause of these problems and in teaching your child how to overcome them. We will explore many techniques to help you better understand your child, and to help her with many types of problems, but first I would like you to consider the three key ingredients to effective non-verbal communication and how you already use them: expressing yourself non-verbally, reading non-verbal cues and synchronizing your words with your body language.

Expressing yourself non-verbally

Adults who have good rapport with children are very expressive in conveying their feelings. Take, for example, Nikki, comprehensive school teacher, who was beloved by her pupils and their parents. Every other parent with a child at Hawthorne Comprehensive School wanted their son or daughter to be in Nikki's class, because her pupils always seemed happier, more well-behaved and more studious than the other children at the school.

Any adult who observed Nikki's class was impressed by her enthusiasm, direct manner and the obvious affection that she had for her children, but these were not the things that made her a great teacher. To really understand the secret of her success, you would have to take a video of Nikki as she taught her twenty-seven pupils, and then watch it with the sound turned off. If you did this, as her supervisor had done when Nikki was a graduate student, you would see that her face was always animated when she spoke to her class. Whenever she spoke to an individual child, she made direct eye contact, yet through her peripheral vision she still made a connection with the other pupils in her class. If a pupil talked during silent reading, or passed a note, he got 'The Look' from Nikki and that was all the classroom discipline she needed. When Nikki's pupils got 'The Look', they stopped what they were doing immediately and waited for her to signal them what to do next. She might point to her ear to say 'It's time to listen.' She might mimic the act of opening a book to show a pupil what he should be doing. When she wanted to get the attention of her whole class, she would flick the lights or clap her hands three times.

Watching Nikki's silent videotape you would be most impressed by her commanding physical presence. I do not mean her physical stature: at five feet one inch and weighing only seven stone, she was not much bigger than some of her pupils. But rather, this young teacher seemed to exude a sense of purpose and control with her physical presence. She strode across the front of the room when explaining an assignment; she moved between two pupils who were starting to talk and immediately they went back to work; she kneeled down beside a pupil who looked like she was having difficulty and beamed at her and patted her hand when she solved the problem. After watching the videotape for half an hour, you might forget that there was supposed to be sound.

How do your non-verbal skills measure up to Nikki's? Of course, you do not have the same need for control in your home as the teacher of twenty-seven children and yet your children pay attention to your face, gestures, postures and so on in the same way as a classroom full of pupils.

TRY IT

Take a few moments after dinner tonight and concentrate on just one aspect of your non-verbal communication – your facial expression. Do you smile often? Is your expression tired and drawn after a long day of work? Do you make good eye contact when you talk or play with your child? Does your face express your feelings for your child to see when you are feeling affectionate or concerned or angry?

Look at yourself in front of the mirror and make faces at yourself. Concentrate on looking sad. Concentrate on looking afraid. Then make a happy face. Now make a face that shows you are surprised.

Experts in non-verbal behaviour tell us that there are actually three zones to the face.

- Zone 1 is the forehead and eyes.
- Zone 2 includes the nose and cheeks.
- Zone 3 includes the mouth.

Most facial expressions rely heavily on Zone 1, the forehead, eyebrows and eyes, while the mid part of the face conveys relatively little in terms of emotion.

Now go back to the mirror take a piece of paper and cover the lower two-thirds of your face, leaving only Zone 1 exposed. Can you show interest in your eyes? Can you show affection? How about pride or authority? See if you can be more aware of your facial expressions in your communication with your child. Your feelings are an important part of who you are. Let them show.

Reading your child's non-verbal cues

Every language, including the language of non-verbal communication, has two parts to it: the way we express ourselves and the way that we understand what other people are saying. Psychologists simply refer to these parts as expressive and receptive language. In the previous example, we looked at the expressive non-verbal language of a teacher as she conducted her class. We took it for granted that her receptive language, how she read her pupils' non-verbal communication, was also highly developed.

Exceptional teachers as well as exceptional parents are able to read the non-verbal cues of a child as a more reliable gauge of a child's emotional state than his words. One of the reasons that non-verbal communication is more important to communication than just words is that it is continuous. A child may stop talking, but he never stops communicating with his body and other aspects of non-verbal communication. As one researcher in this field noted, 'You cannot *not* communicate non-verbally.'

If you are only listening to your child's words then you are missing a great deal of his emotional communication. As we shall see in Chapter 18, when you pay more attention to your child's non-verbal communication you will be much more attuned to his needs. In Chapter 19, you will see how learning to read your child's non-verbal communication can help him learn to deal with bullies, develop better leadership skills and become socially adept. But for now, take a few moments to practise your ability to receive non-verbal messages. Turn on the television and see if you can find a channel with a movie or drama that you have never seen before. It is important to have not seen the programme because then you will have no preconceptions about how the characters are supposed to behave and feel. Now with the sound turned off, try and determine the mood of each character. What are they communicating to each other? Can you anticipate what will happen next? You will probably find this exercise easy to do. After all, you are receiving non-verbal messages from people all of the time and making assumptions about their meaning from what you see.

Now take this exercise to a higher level and think about how you are making your judgements about what you are seeing on the television. Are you paying more attention to the gestures, posture or the facial expressions of the actors? What about the environment or even the clothing that the actors are wearing? In the old silent movies about the Wild West, the 'bad guys' wore black hats and the 'good guys' wore white hats so that there would be no doubt who the audience was supposed to cheer for. Today, even though directors are usually more subtle, the wardrobes of actors are carefully chosen to reveal some aspect of each character's personality. They know, as should you, that we judge a person by how he chooses to look as well as by words and behaviour. It is important to remember that your older children also send out messages about how they want to be perceived by their choice of clothes, their hairstyles, their jewellery and, of course, their tattoos and body piercing. Paying attention to what they are trying to tell you is crucial to helping them with their awareness of themselves and others.

When words and body language do not match

The final key to improving your non-verbal communication with your child is to pay attention to how your non-verbal communication matches your words. Scientists who study non-verbal communication call this synchronicity. When your words and your non-verbal communication are in sync, then people, including your children, see you as 'believable' and feel connected to you. But when your words and non-verbal communication are out of sync, then your children may feel confused by your mixed message. They may feel unconnected and misunderstood and even unloved.

For example, Laura, aged twelve, came home with all Bs and Cs on her school report. For some children this would be fine, but Laura was used to getting As and Bs and had never received even a single 'average' mark before. 'These teachers are really hard markers,' Laura sheepishly explained to her mother. She was clearly disappointed in herself and worried about what her mother would think. Her mother wanted Laura to go to Cambridge like she had. 'Oh,' said her mother, after staring at the report for five minutes. 'Well, I'm sure you are trying your best,' her mother said in a cold monotone, 'and I want to help you if I can.' Laura's mother tucked the report under her arm and walked briskly out of the room. On seeing her mother leave, Laura dissolved into tears and ran to her bedroom weeping. Later that evening, Laura's mother told her husband, 'I don't know why Laura was so upset. I *said* that I wasn't disappointed in her.'

This mother's words said that she understood her daughter's falling grades, but her body language and voice tone gave Laura an entirely different message. Since actions always speak louder than words, Laura responded to her mother's non-verbal communication rather than the words themselves. It would have been preferable if Laura's mother had just stated her true feelings, saying something like: 'I'm disappointed in you. I want you to try harder.' Laura would still have felt badly, but this more direct communication would be less confusing. When you speak to your children openly and directly you create a dialogue. When you give them mixed messages, you are more likely to shut down the channels of communication.

TRY IT

Improving your non-verbal language takes practice, just like improving your vocabulary or your spelling or learning a foreign language. The next time that you have a meeting with someone to reach a decision, be aware of your non-verbal communication, including your gestures, your posture, where you stand or sit, your facial expression, your voice tone and volume. It does not matter whether you are at a business meeting to choose a new marketing strategy, or a family meeting to decide on where to go for your holiday, pay attention to the emotional communication that is going on as well as the intellectual process of trying to make a decision.

Try to use fewer words and more body language. Listen to the non-verbal messages of the people you are talking to and make sure that your words and your non-verbal messages are in sync. When you are done, think about what you learned about the decision-making process and how you felt about yourself and the people you were talking to.

Understanding the secret language of non-verbal communication as your child grows

Like other animal species, human babies are born with the capacity to communicate and learn without knowing a single word. From the time that they are a few days old, babies stare intently at the faces hovering above them, trying to figure out what is going on, even imitating simple facial expressions. Within a few weeks after birth, a newborn will start to learn the non-verbal language herself by imitating what the adults are doing around her. If you open your mouth or stick out your tongue in front of a baby she will try to do this too. Within a few months, she can copy an adult's lip protrusion, finger movements, brow movements and different facial expressions. By the time she is nine months old, her parents need only give her a 'look' to convey emotionally laden messages like: 'Be careful', 'Do you want to play?' or 'Stop that!' Babies may not respond by actually performing the behaviour that the parent wants, but they will always show that the message was seen and received through the changes in their own expressions and body movements. As we saw in Part I of this book, understanding the non-verbal communication of your infant will help you respond appropriately to her cries, provide the right kind of comfort to your baby when she is in pain, give her the right kind of stimulation and even talk to her through gestures months before you can talk to her with words.

Because infants can only express themselves through non-verbal communication, it is not surprising that as they learn words and develop more cognitive abilities their methods of non-verbal communication will change. In fact, in many ways the changes that your baby experiences in his non-verbal communication are a hallmark of his transition into toddlerhood.

Here are some examples of the differences between the ways that infants and toddlers communicate non-verbally.

Getting what they want: When an infant wants something, he might point his finger at that object and glance briefly at it, but then he establishes eye contact with his mother to see if she understood his desires. Toddlers will point at the object of their desire and then go to get it if possible. If this is not possible, they will continue to point and gaze at the object, without the need to check and see if their mother understands their wishes.

Greeting: Infants wave hello and goodbye or blow kisses at strangers. Toddlers know that different people get different greetings and they will normally be wary of signalling strangers unless they are being held or encouraged by their parents.

Anxiety: When babies are anxious they will look fretful and may rub their face or stroke their ears. Toddlers are more likely to tug at their clothing or rub their hands together. Thumb sucking for infants is a type of oral stimulation and contentment, but for toddlers it more likely indicates anxiety.

Frustration: When frustrated babies will cry, fling objects and flail. Toddlers are more deliberate in the ways they express frustration. They may pout and gaze at you unhappily. They may try to break the toy or object that is frustrating them. If there is something small that they can throw, you might want to duck.

Affection: Babies say 'I love you' with their face and particularly their eyes. Younger infants will 'flap' their hands and legs when they see their parents, siblings or a family pet. Toddlers are full of hugs and kisses. This is the age when children are most physical in expressing their affection. Enjoy it.

The non-verbal language of toddlers and pre-school children

Children rapidly increase their spoken language between the ages of eighteen months and four years, but when it comes to interacting with their peers non-verbal communication still takes precedence. When young children have difficulty interacting with their peers it is most likely a problem in non-verbal communication. Fortunately, because children learn so rapidly at this age, it is easy to teach them new non-verbal communication skills.

Consider Tommy, a 3-year-old who wanted to join two other boys playing in the block corner. Tommy walked up to the block corner, but stopped three feet away. He stood still, hunching his shoulders, his eyes cast downward, his hands in his pockets. The other boys ignored him. After a few minutes, Tommy went over to the teacher and complained, 'Ryan and William won't let me play.' Reacting from her years of experience, Ingrid, his nursery school teacher, told him just how to communicate in the secret language of non-verbal communication. She suggested, 'Just go over and build a big tower by yourself. Maybe they'll like to see what you are doing and then they'll want to play with you.'

Encouraged by his teacher, Tommy went back to the block corner and enthusiastically began to build a tower. William and Ryan took notice and turned towards him. Within a few minutes, they started passing Tommy blocks to help him build his tower higher and higher. All three boys laughed as it toppled down.

Through his teacher's simple suggestion, Tommy learned that the best way to join a group of children at play is to parallel or mirror their movements. Simply waiting for an invitation to play does not help.

Parents of young children are rightfully eager to help their children learn to increase their vocabulary, use longer and more complex sentences and improve their articulation. But this is also an important time to instruct children in non-verbal communication. If you have children of this age, you know that they soak up information like little sponges and even the most casual comment on how to use non-verbal behaviour, like the one Ingrid gave to Tommy, can make a significant impression. You may also want to take some time to give your young child more formal instruction in the language of non-verbal communication. Just as you might take a picture book to teach your child the names of zoo animals, or you might use a puzzle with cut-out letters to help him learn his alphabet, you can also use pictures, puzzles and other activities to help him learn about non-verbal communication.

TRY IT

Children as young as two or three can point to pictures of other children showing simple emotions. They have been reading facial expressions since they were infants and they are also surprisingly astute at reading body language. Go through several parenting magazines and cut out pictures of toddlers showing different emotions. Paste them on to index cards and play a simple naming game with your toddler. Say, 'Show me the little boy who is upset' or 'Show me the girl who is happy.' This activity will give your child a head start on learning to pair words with non-verbal communication. As your child gets older, add more pictures to your card set. By five your child can look through magazines and pick out the pictures himself. With older children, you can talk about the various aspects of non-verbal communication that reveal a person's feelings as you go through the cards. For example, try showing the three pictures below to your child. Ask your child to:

- Point to the child that is angry. What is there about his face that tells you that he is angry? What about his hands? How do you look when you are angry?

- Point to the child who is standing up for himself. What do you think he is saying? Do you think he will win this discussion? Why?

- Point to the child who looks tired. How can you tell when someone looks tired? How can you tell when someone looks very, very tired? What else do you think that this child is feeling?

The non-verbal language of the school-age child

By the time that children enter infant school, they should have very good conversational skills. You probably talk to your school-age child pretty much the way that you talk to another adult. But that does not mean that the secret language of non-verbal communication is any less important than when your child was younger. In fact, it may be more important than ever because effective non-verbal communication is crucial to your child's social and academic success. As an example, let us take a look at Alistair, an 8-year-old starting the second year of junior school. His family has just moved from Scotland and he does not know any of the teachers or pupils. Alistair is anxious about making friends and about succeeding in his new class, but he is shy and keeps to himself. In class he has trouble following what the teacher is saying. Her accent is different from the people he grew up with in Scotland and his teacher talks more quickly than he is used to. She seems nice, but Alistair thinks that she pays more attention to the children who sit up front and who are quick to raise their hands when she asks a question. (Alistair is probably right. Most teachers do pay more attention and give more positive feedback to pupils who 'look' like they are enthusiastic learners.) Alistair keeps to himself as much as possible. He does not want to be rejected or embarrassed, so he sits or stands alone and avoids eye contact with others. Even when someone sits next to him on the school bus, he folds his hands over his chest and scrunches himself down in his seat, staring out of the window. Every aspect of his non-verbal behaviour says, 'Leave me alone!' and that is exactly what the other children do.

Then there is Maggie, a pupil in the same classroom. She has been diagnosed with ADHD and even though she is receiving medication and getting help from her counsellor, she is not well liked by the other children. Maggie seems to always say the wrong thing at the wrong time. She has a difficult time 'reading' the non-verbal cues of others. She might start bragging about her new bike to a classmate and even though the other child rolls her eyes and turns away, Maggie does not realize that bragging turns people off. Most children would see that there is something wrong when a child turns away, but Maggie misses this and other non-verbal cues. Along with her ADHD she has what psychologists refer to as a non-verbal learning disability (NVLD). She simply does not make sense of the non-verbal messages that children and adults send her through their body language, much like children with a reading disability do not readily understand the meaning of letters and words.

Fortunately, children like Alistair who have trouble sending out appropriate non-verbal cues, and children like Maggie, who have trouble reading social cues, can be helped – as can your child. Take the ten question quiz below, and if you answer 'yes' to even one question then your child may be able to benefit from some instruction and coaching in the secret language of non-verbal communication.

TRY IT

Does your school-age child need help in learning the secret language of non-verbal communication? If you answer 'yes' to three or more of these questions then your child may benefit from specific instruction in the three key areas of non-verbal expression: expressing himself, reading the cues of others, synchronizing his words to his non-verbal behaviour.

Identifying problems in non-verbal communication

1. Your child has a poor sense of time and timing for his age.
2. Your child has difficulty following verbal directions, even though he is trying to be cooperative.
3. Your child does not seem to 'fit in' with other children of the

same age and prefers being alone or playing with younger children.

4. Your child has problems with personal space. He is often reprimanded for hanging on to another child.

5. Your child is extremely shy and is always alone.

6. Your child is frequently teased by other children for his appearance or mannerisms.

7. Your child's teacher describes him as having social problems at school.

8. Your child has difficulty playing with other children. Many games end in hurt feelings or arguments.

9. Your child is too aggressive with other children. He does not seem to learn from experience.

10. You feel that your child is too passive and is always trying to please other children.

If you have answered 'yes' to any one of these questions, then you will want to pay particular attention to Chapter 19, which will give you suggestions on how teaching your child about his non-verbal communication can help him if he is being teased or bullied, if he is socially isolated, if he is too passive with his peers or if he is too aggressive with other children.

Developing a better rapport with your teenagers

Adolescents are notorious for being less than forthcoming in their communication. They often complain about not being understood by their parents, yet they avoid talking to them. But do not let your teenager's recalcitrant attitude fool you. Surveys that ask teenagers, 'Who would you go to for help with a problem or for important advice?' always show that teenagers seek a parent's help and security when times get tough.

So how do you remain close and available to your teenager when his attitude and actions seem to push you away? This is the paradox that almost every parent of a teenager must face at some time. You can resolve it by a thorough understanding of the secret language of non-verbal communication.

Adolescence is a time when open communication is particularly important and at the same time very difficult for many families to achieve. I have lost count of the times that I have heard a parent of a teenager say to me: 'I just can't understand this kid', even though she feels that she has made many attempts to establish a more open and honest relationship.

A common complaint has to do with the way that teenagers dress. As I am sure you know, teenagers are very fashion conscious. When provocative attire is in fashion (as it is now), your daughter will probably tell you that her friends will think that she is 'weird' if she dresses differently. This is not just true of provocative clothes. What we wear or the things we put on our body (jewellery, tattoos, body piercing, hairstyles and so on) are an important part of our non-verbal communication. A teenager's dress will in part define her social standing in school; as an athlete, a serious student, a 'party person' and so on. Although it can be hard to do, it is important for you and the school to set limits on what kinds of attire are acceptable and what are not. Your teenager may rebel, but finding ways to resolve the conflict is part of the growing-up process for both of you.

When parents do not set limits, then teenagers do not have any structure to guide them and they will often become more and more outrageous in their dress to see how long it will take for you to say 'stop'.

It is also helpful to educate your teenager about the secret language of dress and to show her that what she wears or puts on her body also sends a message to others (people that study non-verbal language call this 'objectics' – the objects that we wear that send a message to others).

TRY IT

Find a seat in the shopping centre, park or other public place with your teenager and practise analysing people by what they wear. Do not be critical or 'catty' in criticizing others, but rather tell your teenager that this is a skill that she can learn to help her 'read' other people. Take a notebook along for each of you, pick a person and then write down everything that you see (try to be discreet in your observation). Then compare notes and talk about what each person is probably trying to say about himself and what he is really saying. This type of activity is designed to help teenagers see that everyone is always giving out messages about themselves, but these messages are not always the ones that they intend.

After concern about their teenagers' appearance, the second most common complaint that I hear from parents is that their children are trying to 'push them away'. Teenagers convey this message to their parents in many ways, the most obvious being that they maintain a much greater physical distance from their parents than when they were youngsters.

The study of physical distance in human relationships is referred to as proxemics and it is an important indicator of relationships. From a developmental standpoint, teenagers need to keep more physical distance between themselves and their parents to parallel their need for emotional independence, although at times of stress you may find that your teenager suddenly has a need to be closer.

You should respect your teenager's need for distance, but you can also send out your own non-verbal message that you are open to him when he needs you. The next time you invite your teenager to talk, create an optimal environment for open communication. Sit across from him, three or four feet away, at a slight angle (sitting directly across from someone may seem confrontational). Assume an 'open posture' by uncrossing your legs and arms. If you have something important to say to your teenager, even if it is something he may not want to hear, then say it directly.

Take note of whether your teenager's non-verbal behaviour changes or stays the same in response to your openness.

If you are unsure about the non-verbal messages that your teenager is sending to you, by all means consult a mental health professional for guidance. Your intuition is always your best guide to unlocking the secret language of your teenager. If you think that your teenager needs help, do not hesitate to get it.

Chapter 18

Read Your Child Like a Book

How well do you know your children? Most parents feel intimately connected to their infants and toddlers, anticipating their every need and every mood. They know what will make them happy and what will make them cranky or upset and they know what will soothe them. But as children grow older, particularly as they reach the age of seven or eight and become more emotionally invested in their peers, many parents start to feel that their children have entered a world of their own. They no longer feel that they have the same intuitive understanding of their children and the emotional life of them may seem like a mystery. As one mother of an 8-year-old told me: 'I feel like my child suddenly grew up when he turned eight. He used to chatter away constantly, but now he hardly talks at all. It seems more like he is eighteen, than eight.' Of course, 8-year-olds do not really act like teenagers. That stage of development has its own set of challenges for parents. But when their children are eight or nine, some parents may start to feel the loss of the intimate connection that they had to their children when they were young and they may wonder if they have done something wrong. Unfortunately, as children turn into teenagers, this does not get better.

Consider, for example, 15-year-old Samuel and his parents, Claire and Jacob, as they sat down for their Friday night traditional Sabbath meal. About halfway through dinner, Samuel announced that he wanted to change his name.

'I want you to call me, "Ten",' Samuel explained to his parents. 'That's what everyone calls me now.'

'What do you mean "Ten",' his father wanted to know. 'Ten what?'

'Just Ten,' Samuel explained derisively. 'Not ten anything, just Ten.'

'What kind of a name is Ten?' Samuel's mother inquired, treating her son's request matter-of-factly. 'A nickname?'

'No, it's not a nickname. It's a name!' Samuel exploded. 'It's my name, OK? Ten. Just Ten. Don't you understand English? Just call me Ten, not Samuel. OK? Can't you figure anything out for your-self?' And Samuel, or rather Ten, pushed himself back from the table and in a blur of motion stormed out of the room.

'I think he's on drugs,' Jacob said to his wife with grave concern.

'No, he's just rebelling,' Claire said nonchalantly. 'He'll forget about it in the morning.'

But Samuel's parents were both mistaken. Samuel was not on drugs and he did not forget about his request in the morning. When Samuel did not come to the breakfast table the next morning, his mother decided to check on him. Samuel's room was in complete disarray. His bed had not been slept in. He was gone. According to the note he left on his bed, Samuel did not intend to return.

This is an extreme example of how poor communication between parents and their children can lead to serious problems and yet scenes like this are really not that uncommon. In the UK more than 100,000 children and teenagers run away from their homes each year, the vast majority because, like Samuel, they feel they are 'misunderstood'.

This is also an example that shows how ignoring the secret lan-guage of children can lead to a breach of trust and eventual alien-ation between parents and their children. Long before the dinner conversation when Samuel announced he wanted to be called by a new name, he had tried to tell his parents that he no longer felt that he was a part of the family. He just did not do it with words. Months before, he had started to dress differently and he cut off almost all of his once long hair. When he sat with his parents, even at the dinner table, he rarely faced them, even when he talked. In retrospect, his parents described him as more distant and preoc-cupied than usual. They noted that they were surprised when their son had rearranged his room so that his desk faced the window, even though he had to almost climb over it to get to his wardrobe.

They said that Samuel would stare out of the window for hours at a time, as if he was a prisoner in his own home.

If Jacob and Claire had read these changes in Samuel as his attempts at communicating, rather than as just adolescent idiosyncrasies, then they would have known how unhappy he felt. Hopefully they would have opened up more direct channels of communication and avoided this tragic break in their relationship with him. (It took nearly a year before they found Samuel living in another part of the country and another year before he would agree to see his parents again.)

As you begin to pay more attention to the non-verbal communication of your child, you should also begin to see that this is just another way that he is trying to talk to you.

You may not feel as connected to your child as when he was very young, but I guarantee that if you learn the secrets of non-verbal communication then you will begin to feel more in tune with his emotional development.

The vocabulary of non-verbal communication

Just as in studying any new language, the best route to improving your knowledge of non-verbal communication is to break it down into its component parts. For the remainder of this chapter we will look at the most significant aspects of non-verbal communication and how they can be used to enhance your understanding of your child and the way that you communicate with him.

Posture

Jason, aged fifteen, sat slouched behind his desk in his algebra class. His head drooped on his left shoulder. His arms hung limply by his side. For the first few weeks of school his teacher, Mr Harrison, had hardly noticed Jason. He had seen many 'half-awake' looking pupils in his classes and he assumed that Jason was just another young man who would rather be anywhere else in the world than in an algebra class.

But Mr Harrison began to take notice when Jason got an 'A' on the first quiz and another 'A' on the second one. Two weeks later, Jason scored 100 per cent on the mid-term exam. In both his homework as well as his tests Jason wrote out his equations carefully and accurately, showing his concern that his work be easy to read and understand.

After reviewing the test scores and the homework assignments, Mr Harrison realized that Jason was clearly the most talented pupil in his class. Catching Jason as he was leaving the class one afternoon, Mr Harrison said, 'Jason, I wanted to talk to you for a moment. You seem to really have a gift for algebra.'

'Yeah,' Jason replied, shrugging his shoulders, hanging his head and speaking in an uncommitted voice. 'I love maths.'

'That's great!' Mr Harrison said. But he thought to himself, 'I never would have guessed.'

Jason became one of Mr Harrison's favourite pupils. He genuinely liked this bright young man with the disinterested demeanour. But Mr Harrison was an unusual teacher. Many teachers do not see past their pupils' poor posture and lackadaisical demeanour and treat students who do not look like they are interested with indifference, even when they are bright and motivated.

Like Jason, most teenagers do not think much about the way that they are perceived by others. They think that their posture, dress or mannerisms are a 'personal' part of who they are and not really anyone else's business. But they are incorrect.

Research tells us that good posture makes a significant difference in the way that children are treated. When pupils are taught to sit more erect, to lean forward slightly, to keep their hands in full view on their desk and to tilt their head slightly to one side when a teacher looks at them (a non-verbal sign of friendliness), they are rated as 'better pupils' by their teachers, regardless of their natural abilities or even their actual work. Not surprisingly, teachers pay less attention to pupils when they have poor posture and particularly when they look disinterested. When pupils get less attention they are more likely to do less well in school, even when they are intellectually gifted.

Your child's gait is also a part of his posture. We give off emotional messages when we walk just as when we are still. Children who are judged to be confident and competent typically walk more quickly and erectly than children who move in a slouched, more deliberate fashion. It is unfortunate, but nonetheless true, that when children walk with a strange gait, whether it is due to their walking style or it is the result of a physical handicap, they are often teased or rejected by their peers.

So what does this mean to parents? It means that when you tell your child to 'sit up straight' or 'walk with your head up', you are doing the right thing. But with older children and teenagers you need to go one step further. Without being critical, explain to your children that through their body language they are speaking in the language of non-verbal communication even though they are not uttering a word. Go through a book of photographs or through magazines and ask your children to pick out the pictures of people who they think are 'smart' and the ones who are 'dull'. Talk about the non-verbal reasons that they made these choices. Then take pictures of your child in different poses, letting them see how different postures convey different emotional impressions.

TRY IT

Take pictures of your child in the poses listed below. Then talk about each pose while you look at the pictures. Hang the pictures that show positive emotions on a wall or even tape them on to the bathroom mirror so that your child sees them every day. Showing your child positive pictures of himself is the non-verbal equivalent of teaching him to give himself a daily pep talk (what people sometimes call 'affirmations'). The more that children see positive images of themselves, the more likely they will be aware of their posture in their day-to-day life.

Take pictures of your child in the following poses:

- Pose like a super hero.
- Pose like someone who has not slept for three days.

- Pose like you have won a race and are getting a medal.
- Pose like you are afraid of something.
- Pose like you have just got a compliment from your teacher.
- Pose like someone has just made fun of you.
- Pose like you are being interviewed for a TV show.

As we shall see in the next chapter, teaching your children how to consciously use the various elements of non-verbal communication can help them be more successful in school as well as with their friends. This is surely one part of the secret language that you do not want to keep a secret.

Gestures

Gestures are the first 'words' that children speak. By eight or nine months infants use a dozen or more gestures, like waving 'bye bye', blowing a kiss or raising their arms to be picked up. They point to things that they want or that they are interested in.

As your children grow, even though they now have words to express themselves, gestures are still an important part of their emotional and social communication. By seven or eight years of age children use gestures much like adults do, both as a replacement for words, as when waving hello or goodbye from a distance, or as a way of adding emphasis to spoken words, like shrugging their shoulders when they say 'I don't know' or simply nodding when they say 'yes'.

In our culture people who use a lot of gestures are generally seen as enthusiastic and assertive. People who use few gestures are typically perceived as shy, anxious or even dull.

For example, Bruce was a 13-year-old boy who was known in his school as a 'bookworm'. Although Bruce was shy and introverted, he was well-liked by his classmates because of his intellectual gifts and the kind and considerate things that he did for people. But when Bruce changed schools, he was put in a class with pupils that did not know him and he soon became socially isolated because of his quiet ways. Like most shy youngsters, Bruce's gestures were minimal and his body language was stiff. He did very little to call attention to himself. Even when Bruce raised his hand in class to answer a question, he only raised it an inch or two above his shoulders, while more exuberant pupils waved their hands in the air, stretching themselves almost off their seats. It took Bruce nearly two years to find a group of friends who saw past his quiet manner and admired him for himself.

Gestures are important in developing relationships because they add to your child's ability to send and receive complete information about his feelings. When children do not use gestures to express themselves, or when they do not read the gestural cues of others, they are definitely at a social disadvantage.

TRY IT

How well does your child recognize and use gestures? If your child is seven or older, you can use the 'Gesture Test' as an informal way to assess his understanding of how gestures are used to communicate his needs and desires. There are ten questions. Give your child one point for each separate gesture he can show you in answering each question. If your child combines gestures, such as motioning someone to come over and then pulling out a chair for him to sit on, then count each part of the gesture as a separate point. I have added some examples to show you how children typically respond to this quiz.

1. How would you show that you want something? (examples: pointing, gazing at object)

2. How would you show your approval by using a gesture? (examples: 'thumbs up' sign, clapping, smile)

3. How would you show your disapproval of something? (examples: holding your nose, 'thumbs down' sign.

   Note: you may get a gestural 'curse word' in response to this question from children over ten. If this occurs, do not reprimand the child but rather ask him if he understands that this gesture is offensive.

4. How would you get someone to sit down where you wanted?

   (examples: pointing to a chair, pulling out a specific chair, taking someone by the arm and guiding them to a chair).

5. How would you get someone to stop what he was doing?

   (examples: hold your hands out palms up, make a fist and an angry face)

6. How would you signal to someone that you needed help?

   (examples: raise your hand, beckon someone towards you, wave both hands like you were flagging someone down)

7. How would you act if you wanted someone to leave you alone?

   (examples: turn your back to him, glance away, walk away swiftly)

8. What would you do if you wanted people to think you were self-confident?

   (examples: hold your head up, pull back your shoulders, make eye contact)

9. How would you show someone that you wanted her to be quiet?

   (examples: hold your finger to your lips, point to your ear, shake your index finger back and forth)

10. How would you show someone that you liked him?

    (examples: shake hands, pat him on the back, nod and smile)

You can encourage your child to use gestures to convey emotional meaning by making more gestures yourself.

Distance and touch

Different cultures have different rules about personal distance and touch. The United Kingdom and the United States are considered to be 'low-touch' countries and touching people in public is generally discouraged. For example, one study looked at couples sitting in cafés in four cities in four countries. In San Juan, Puerto Rico, couples touched each other an average of 180 times while they were sitting together drinking or having a meal. Couples in Paris touched each other 110 times. But couples in Gainesville, Florida, only touched each other an average of two times while together and in London, they did not touch at all. If you or your children have friends from different countries, it is always important to remember that different cultures can have vastly different rules for their non-verbal communication.

No matter what the country, children have different rules regarding touch and distance than adults and they typically use these parts of non-verbal language as a more deliberate way of defining their relationship with their peers. For example, the shy or awkward child will stand away from other children when teams are being picked for a game, conveying the message that he is a reluctant participant. The bully will stand just a few inches from another child in order to intimidate him (in our culture anyone within eighteen inches of us is considered to have invaded our personal space).

In today's atmosphere, physical touching between children who are not in the same family is considered inappropriate in any situation. This 'no touch' policy may be judicious, but it can be hard on some children who are naturally more physical than others.

For example, Eric was a good-natured and rambunctious 6-year-old who was constantly in trouble at his expensive private school. He would drape his arms over the next child in a queue, or teasingly push another child out of line. Nearly every day he was sent to the headteacher's office for wrestling in the playground, which was strictly forbidden by school rules. The headteacher suggested to Eric's mother that he might have an Attention Deficit Hyperactivity Disorder (ADHD). Eric's mother did not think that this was true. She had two other boys, now teenagers. She explained, 'They were also rough and tumble boys when they were Eric's age. But they calmed down at twelve or thirteen and they are now both well-behaved teenagers and good students.' Rather than put Eric on medication as the headteacher suggested, this wise mother found a new school, which was more tolerant of Eric's particular way of relating to others.

Just like other aspects of non-verbal communication, all children must eventually learn the adult rules of touching and distance, or they are likely to be misunderstood or even rejected by their peers.

Most children pick up the rules readily by just watching others, but some children do not. For these children it is helpful to make the rules very explicit, even writing them down. For example, here are the school rules that were given to 6-year-old Eric.

- Do not touch anyone at school unless you are playing a game that is supervised by adults.
- Do not stand closer to someone than the length of your arm.
- If other children touch you or stand too close, then move away from them.
- If they move closer to you again, tell a teacher.
- Never hit, kick or pinch anyone, even if you are just teasing.
- If anyone hits you, tell them to stop it. If they do not stop, tell a teacher.

Voice inflection and volume

As I have mentioned, non-verbal communication is not just seen, it is also heard. The meaning of our words can vary significantly, depending on our inflection, voice tone and voice volume. You can see this yourself by doing a little exercise that I sometimes give to children.

Say this sentence four times, conveying four different emotions: 'I left my bag in the car.' Say this same sentence like you are happy, sad, surprised and angry. As you can see, the meaning of the sentence completely changes as you emphasize different words, change the pitch and timbre of your voice or speak loudly or quietly. Now ask your child (seven or older) to do this same exercise. This will help him be more aware of how people use their voice to communicate different feelings to others.

If your child is having problems with other children or with his teacher, then this might be an area of his non-verbal communication that you want to investigate more thoroughly. Some children naturally speak very softly, giving others the message that they lack confidence. Other children have brash loud voices and it is not surprising that their teachers are always telling them to be quiet, even though they may be actually talking less than some other pupils. Give your child practice in changing his voice tone in different situations. Even if your child does not have a problem in school, this can still be a valuable part of his education in learning about non-verbal communication.

TRY IT

Take a video camera and, with your child, act out a conversation in the following places:

- Sitting in a house of worship.
- Reading in a library.
- Playing in the playground.
- Walking through a museum.
- Watching a sports event.

Now watch the video that you made with your child and comment on the different ways that your voices (and other aspects of non-verbal communication) change in each scene. As your child grows, his awareness of how to use his voice in different situations can become an invaluable asset in his social development.

Becoming a human lie detector

At twelve years old, Adam was a handsome and popular boy. He was a good pupil, but his mother also thought that he was a little 'wild'. That is why she was not too surprised when a neighbour called to say that she had seen Adam and his friends smoking cigarettes in an alley behind her house. Adam's mother, Rachel, told her son to sit down so that they could have an important talk.

'Are you smoking cigarettes?' Rachel asked her son sternly.

'No,' Adam replied in a firm voice, 'I'm not.' Adam sat with his hands folded in his lap. He looked his mother straight in the eyes for a moment and then looked away.

'Are you telling me the truth, young man?' Rachel continued, moving her face closer to her son and trying to be more intimidating.

'I said "no",' Adam repeated quietly, sitting straight and hardly moving. He did not budge an inch in response to his mother's attempts to intimidate.

'Well, I hope not,' Rachel said sternly, 'because smoking is one of the worst things that you can do for your body.'

'I know,' mumbled Adam, getting out of his chair and heading out of the door. 'I'm not stupid, you know.'

As her son left, Rachel wondered whether he was telling her the truth or not. Was he smoking cigarettes? He did not smell of smoke. She had not found any cigarettes in his room. But he seemed upset. She wondered if she was being overly concerned.

What do you think? Even from this brief description, would you conclude that Adam was lying or telling the truth? Can you tell from your own child's non-verbal behaviour whether he is being forthright or evasive?

Knowing whether your child is lying to you or telling you the truth may not be the most important use of the secret language of non-verbal behaviour, yet you may encounter times when knowing this information about your child is crucial. Parents of teenagers should certainly have confidence that they are obeying important rules and that they are not engaging in high-risk behaviours. They should be able to know when rules are being broken so that appropriate steps can be taken.

Of course, no one can really be a human lie detector. If that were possible, then we would not need judges or juries to decide whether people are guilty or not. But you can learn to read anyone's non-verbal signs more accurately, just the way that professional counsellors, negotiators or poker players do. Hopefully this knowledge will help you guide your child in his moral development and, more importantly, be aware if he or she is doing something which is unsafe.

But before we look at the non-verbal language that can indicate whether a person is being deceptive or being honest, let us take a moment to look at the nature of lying in childhood. First, we should consider when children really understand the difference between lying and telling the truth. Young children, those below the age of five, often blur the distinction between reality and fantasy. They may know that lying is wrong in a general sense, but they do not have the self-awareness to know that they are doing something wrong in specific instances. Nor do they really understand that different people have different views of the same thing. For example, I remember one morning when I came down to the kitchen for coffee around 7 a.m. to find my oldest daughter, Jessica, then four years old, with chocolate all over her face and hands. 'Have you been eating chocolate?' I asked, trying to look severe but really thinking she looked cute. 'No,' she replied a little sheepishly, because she knew full well that it was against the rules. 'Then what's on your hands?' I asked. Jessica looked down at her hands, then looked at me and said, 'How did that get there?'

By five or six years of age, however, children become very aware of the importance of being honest. Children at this age have a concrete way of thinking and most youngsters will tell you: 'You should never, ever, ever tell a lie.' Even though children at this age will sometimes hide the truth, they know full well that lying is wrong.

But by the time that children are eleven or twelve they have a very different view about truthfulness. For example, in one survey children were asked, 'Is it ever OK to tell a lie?' Ninety per cent of the 5-year-olds answered that it is never right to tell a lie. But 90 per cent of the 11-year-olds answered, 'Yes, it is OK to sometimes tell a lie.' The difference, of course, is that by eleven children understand that there are different kinds of lies. There are deceptive lies where you try to hide something, but there are also 'white lies' which are really not important (like telling someone that you like her new hairstyle even though you do not). There are even altruistic lies when you tell a lie to help someone out. For example, a teenager who says that a friend was at her house, when that friend was really at a party, is lying to keep her friend out of trouble. She is actually putting her own credibility at risk for her friend.

Understanding the developmental nature of lying, and its moral complexity, is important in judging how to respond if you believe that your child is lying. You may be 100 per cent convinced that your child is not telling the truth, but that does not mean that you should confront him or punish him. Instead you should emphasize the importance of honesty, just as you emphasize the importance of your other values. If you feel that your child or teenager is being deceptive with you, then you should use other aspects of the secret language to rebuild a relationship of trust between you and your child.

With this cautionary note, let us look back at Adam and his reaction when his mother confronted him about smoking cigarettes. As we shall see, his non-verbal language did suggest that he was being evasive and was probably not telling her the truth. These are some of the critical non-verbal signs to look for to determine if someone is lying.

Eye contact

Little or no direct eye contact is a classic sign of deception. Adam just glanced at his mother at the beginning of their conversation and then looked away. In a typical conversation most people make eye contact from 60 to 80 per cent of the time. Making too much eye contact can also be a sign that something is wrong. Because people know that looking away can mean that you have something to hide, they may overcompensate and look at you so much that it may seem like they are staring. Your comfort level is the best guide to help you judge whether eye contact is appropriate or not. The emotional part of your brain reads non-verbal signals much more quickly than you can consciously analyse another person's behaviour, so if you 'feel' that something is wrong, then it probably is.

Body position and gestures

If you remember the earlier description about Adam and his mother, you will recall that Adam sat quietly in his chair when being interrogated and that he hardly responded, even when his mother leaned closer to him in order to be more intimidating.

Psychologists that study lying (see Dr David Lieberman's book *Never Be Lied to Again* explain that when people are being deceptive, they typically make fewer gestures and sit more quietly than they normally would. In his normal conversations Adam was enthusiastic and even exuberant, but when his mother confronted him about smoking cigarettes he was quiet and reserved. If your children have something to hide they will want to draw less attention to themselves, so that they will probably gesture less, sit more quietly and speak in an even tone without much inflection.

It is important to remember that you can only judge a person's behaviour in comparison to the way he would normally react. Some children and, of course, some adults, do not reveal much emotion when they talk, so you cannot assume that their quiet attitude and restricted gestures indicate that they are being deceptive. Every person has their own style of non-verbal communication and you must look for a change in that style if you think you are being lied to.

Other mannerisms which can indicate deception

There are some other noteworthy non-verbal signs that can indicate that a person is being evasive or is lying outright to you. These include:

- The person puts his hands to his face and his mouth more than he normally does.
- The person seems stiff and unnatural in her movements, almost as if she is acting.
- The person sits with his body positioned away from you, possibly pointing towards a door or window. This may subconsciously indicate that he is anxious to leave.
- The person keeps her palms down or even sits on her hands. Holding your palms up is a nearly universal signal of openness and friendliness. It is a way of saying, 'I have nothing to hide.' Keeping your palms down or your hands hidden suggests the opposite.
- The person puts obstacles between himself and the listener and

has a 'closed' posture. When someone has something to hide, he often *looks* like he has something to hide. A teenager may curl up in his chair so that you cannot see him well or keep a bag on his lap. He may cross his legs, fold his arms over his chest and even hunch his chin down to his chest. The non-verbal message he is giving you is: 'The less you see of me, the better.'

Adam, who as you probably assumed was smoking cigarettes with his friends after school, did not show all of these signs while he was lying to his mother. Nobody shows all of the signs of deception, even when telling the most blatant lie. In fact, it is common for people to give you contradictory non-verbal messages when they are lying or telling the truth.

It is important to remember that you cannot judge your child's non-verbal communication by one or two characteristics, any more than you can ascertain the meaning of a paragraph just by picking out one or two words. You must evaluate what your child is telling you in the secret language of non-verbal communication using all of your powers of observation as well as your knowledge about his personality and past behaviour.

Getting practice in reading non-verbal behaviour playing 'feelings charades'

Now that you have had an opportunity to think about the importance of non-verbal communication, play a game of charades with your family. Begin by writing down on separate index cards the different emotions listed below. Now each family member should take a turn, pick a card and then, without words, try to convey the emotion. Now play a second time and try to convey the emotion adding your voice, but you can only say the sentence 'I'm glad to be here.'

This is a cooperative game where players earn points as a team. The whole family wins a point when an emotion is guessed within one minute. You can modify this game for younger children by making the emotions simpler (angry, sad, glad, afraid), or add more emotions for older children and teenagers.

The most important thing to remember in learning to read your

Confident	Apprehensive
Angry	Sincere
Bored	Proud
Relaxed	Awestruck
Defensive	Critical
Sad	Impatient
Reflective	Insecure
Rejected	Interested
Doubtful	Nervous
Frustrated	Indecisive

child (or anyone) like a book is to pay attention to what you see and hear beyond a person's words. Remember that your child's words convey only a small part of his emotional meaning. Make sure that you listen to the rest.

Chapter 19

Does Your Child Know the Secrets of Non-Verbal Communication?

Like most parents, you probably spend a significant amount of time encouraging your child's language skills: helping him to read; teaching him new words to increase his vocabulary; promoting the use of good grammar and correct spelling. But while all of these things are important, the language of words is not enough to bring children success. Ironically, some children who have exceptional verbal skills have poor non-verbal skills. While their intellectual gifts should bring them success, their poor non-verbal skills lead them to failure.

For example, Michael was a high school student that I counselled early in my career while working in a New York City private school for 'underachieving' students. Although he was fifteen years old, Michael constantly chattered away about whatever interested him at the moment, the way that 4- and 5-year-olds will sometimes do. With an IQ of over 150, Michael was knowledgeable about many subjects, but he was particularly interested in arcane New York City history. His chemistry teacher might have been lecturing about the Periodic Table, but Michael would somehow bring the topic around to the construction of the New York subway system in the early part of the century or how many bulbs it took to light up the Empire State Building.

Michael's verbal skills and energy made it hard for his teachers to get a word in once he started on one of his diatribes. Inevitably, most of his teachers would get angry at him and tell him to just be quiet. Then he would sulk and not speak to anyone for the rest of the day.

My counselling goal for Michael was to help him learn to anticipate the consequences of his behaviour. He made the same social mistakes over and over again and he was certainly bright enough to learn from the many obvious cues given by those around him. But Michael ignored the raised eyebrows, the exasperated sighs and the numerous attempts that people would make to change the subject. Once he started, Michael just kept talking as if everyone else was as interested in his ideas as he was.

For reasons that are not entirely clear, some children and teenagers have a great deal of difficulty learning the secret language of non-verbal communication which most of us take for granted. They misread or ignore the non-verbal cues of others and may not be able to tell whether someone is angry with them. They speak up at the wrong time in class or make inappropriate comments. They may be viewed as odd by their peers and even their teachers.

Psychologists Stephen Nowicki and Marshall Duke, who have pioneered the study and treatment of children with problems in non-verbal communication, believe that as many as 10 per cent of children may have a non-verbal learning disability and do not learn the rules of non-verbal communication as well as their peers. They write in their book, *Helping the Child Who Doesn't Fit In*:

> These children desperately want to fit in and have friends, but they usually fail to do so. They have been largely ignored or rejected, not only by their peers but also by well-meaning adults, who have not known the source of these children's troubles and therefore not known how to help . . . We believe that many children who don't fit in have trouble using non-verbal communication . . . They may stand too close to others, touch them inappropriately, or misunderstand and misinterpret friendly actions. These difficulties can lead to painful social rejection, especially when . . . the child has little or no idea that he or she is the source of the problem.

When a child has poor non-verbal skills it can affect any aspect of his social development. It can make him more vulnerable to teasing and bullying, more passive with his peer group and less likely to develop leadership skills. In extreme circumstances, poor non-verbal skills can lead to painful social rejection and isolation.

It is hard to say why some children do not learn the secret language of non-verbal communication the way that others do. Most professionals think that it is just a learning difference that makes it more difficult for some children to learn the rules of social communication. It is possible that their brains process information differently than those of other children, just the way that some children have difficulty learning to read or write because they see letters differently.

But the good news is that once we recognize that a problem exists, children can be taught the skills of non-verbal communication in a parallel fashion to the way we address other types of learning problems. In this chapter we will look at how to help your child with a range of social problems by teaching him the skills of non-verbal communication.

Teach your child a defence against teasing

Teasing is a common problem of childhood that will never go away. Every generation of children has its own brand of bullies and teasers as well as children who are more prone to be victims. As you might expect, children with poor non-verbal skills are more frequently the victims of teasing and bullying.

When children have unusual ways of expressing themselves, or when they do not read the non-verbal cues of others, they are quickly labelled by other children as being 'different'. And if you remember back when you were a child or a teenager, 'being different' was rarely considered to be a good thing.

Joshua, a 10-year-old who went to school in a Mid-Western suburb in the USA, was definitely a child who was 'different'. Although he was extremely bright, he did not seem to have very much self-awareness. A thin and angular boy, he wore thick glasses and mismatched clothes. His hair was rarely combed. He rushed from class to class, clutching his books to his chest, staring ahead as if he was a 'man on a mission'. When he was in class, Joshua avoided contact with the other pupils but vied for the attention of his teacher by wildly waving his hands in the air each time a question was asked.

Only a few pupils actively teased Joshua about his peculiar habits, but when they decided to pick on him they were unmerciful. Two boys in particular would trip him, poke him, grab his books or even take away his glasses.

Fortunately Joshua's school had an anti-bullying programme taught by the school counsellor, which included a defensive programme for potential victims of bullying and teasing. At the insistence of his English teacher, Joshua enrolled for the programme which met once a week after school. The programme emphasized dealing with bullies through non-verbal communication. The following are some of the skills taught in the programme. They might also be helpful for your child.

Avoid people who are mean

Avoiding bullies and teasers means that children must have an increased awareness of inter-personal distance. Most children naturally try to keep away from mean and aggressive children, but some children, like Joshua, are so unaware of their surroundings that they do not foresee when a situation could lead to a problem. In one of the activities in Joshua's anti-bullying group, each member of the group had to make a 'Beware of Bullies' map, showing their daily route both within the school and on their way to and from school, marking on it the places where potential trouble could occur.

The pupils were told to be aware that certain places, like the stairway in the school or the woods behind the playground, were particularly dangerous. They were told to avoid those areas if at all possible and, if it were not possible, to always walk by them with another person.

TRY IT

Make a 'Beware of Bullies' map for your child as a way to talk to him about avoiding bullies as well as other dangers. Do not worry about trying to draw an accurate, real map; this is a 'psychological' map which is used to make a point, not for finding directions. As you do this activity, try to see the world from your child's point of view. It is easy for an adult to say 'just avoid the kids who are teasing you', but children need to have concrete alternatives. Also children have peer pressure to consider. You might suggest that your child just sit in another area of the dining room to avoid a pupil who was bothering her. But that might mean that she would be sitting away from the table where her friends eat, making her feel socially isolated and even more vulnerable.

The most important goal of this exercise is to help your child to see that she has choices other than being victimized and that you and other adults will help her when she needs it.

Ignore the teasing

It is not easy to ignore someone who is making fun of you, but it is nonetheless an important non-verbal skill. The pupils in Joshua's anti-bullying class role-played how it would feel to walk by a group of pupils who were calling them names and making rude gestures. In this exercise the potential victim would practise keeping a neutral facial expression and ignoring what the teasers were saying and doing. The role-playing was videotaped so that pupils could see themselves in action. Videotaping children as they learn new non-verbal skills and then showing them what they look like is an important part of helping children learn new non-verbal behaviour.

Use confident body language

Most children are not consciously aware of their body language. But if you are a victim of teasing or bullying, then you have to be more self-aware and self-assured. Studies show that children are much less likely to be picked on when they have confident body language. Use the checklist below to help you determine whether your child has the kind of body language that says 'Give me respect,' or whether his body language says 'If you pick on me, it's OK.'

TRY IT

Observe your child and see how he rates in conveying confidence through his body language. Without being critical, make older children and teenagers aware that body language is an important part of how they are judged, both by adults as well as their peers. It is an indisputable fact that people with confident body language have more social success. Make sure that you are a good role model for your child. Practise your own confident body language and see if people react to you in a different way.

You might want to write down the list of non-verbal qualities that define confidence for your child and even have him carry this list with him. The more he can become consciously aware of his non-verbal messages the more confident he will act and feel.

Confidence Checklist

Confident body language	Uncertain body language
Stands straight	Slouches when standing
Sits straight	Sits with head down
Makes good eye contact in a conversation	Avoids eye contact, looks down or to the side
Walks upright	Slouches
Keeps hands out of pockets and in view	Hides hands
Has a pleasant facial expression	Looks unhappy or anxious
Uses gestures to emphasize a point	Does not use gestures effectively to get and keep attention

Speak in a neutral assertive voice and use the 'Repeat Technique'

Children who bully and tease are usually good at using their words and voice to intimidate others. The best thing for your child to do is to turn and walk away from a bully, but sometimes this is impossible. Rather than attempting to have a rational conversation with a bully or getting into a shouting match, I advise children to use the Repeat Technique, which is almost guaranteed to get someone to stop picking on you.

The Repeat Technique works because of its simplicity. The child being picked on just says the same few words, in a calm but firm voice, over and over again. The child never wavers from this simple phrase or sentence, no matter what is being said to her. For example, I once taught this technique to 7-year-old Daisy, who was constantly being teased by her 13-year-old brother, Mark. Whenever Mark made fun of her, I told Daisy to simply say, 'I don't like being picked on.' That is all she was to say, over and over again.

After Daisy had practised this technique with me, I invited Mark to attend a session with his sister so that she could practise it in a real-life situation. Mark was wary when I asked him to 'show me exactly how you tease your sister', but within a few minutes he enthusiastically took up the challenge.

'You're a little worm,' Mark started.

'I don't like being picked on,' Daisy replied.

'You really look ugly today, you know,' Mark tried again.

'I don't like being picked on,' Daisy said again without emotion.

'You're a little jerk and nobody likes you,' Mark said. But he was losing some of his enthusiasm.

'I don't like being picked on,' Daisy responded with a deadpan face and an even voice tone.

'You sound like an idiot parrot,' Mark said.

'I don't like being picked on,' Daisy said again, somehow making it clear that she could go on like this all day.

After about ten minutes Mark gave up. Deflated, he sat down in a chair and said, 'I get the point.'

At our next session Daisy reported that Mark had not teased her for the entire week. 'I'd just like to see him try it now,' she said to me with a mischievous smile.

Turning followers into leaders

I am sure that you have heard some children described as 'natural leaders'. But I bet that you have never heard of a child described as a 'natural follower'. To say this about a child would be an insult. No one likes to think of their child as passive and dependent on the whim of others. Yet some children behave in ways that would truly fit that description.

Children who are natural followers are more dependent on adults, are quicker to cry or show signs of anxiety and make more frequent appeasement gestures than other children (gestures designed exclusively to win the approval of others).

On the other hand, natural leaders are more assertive than other children. They are the first to suggest a new activity or a new way to solve a problem. Followers may have ideas that are just as good, or even better, but they hesitate to make suggestions or they may not make them at all. Natural leaders also make appeasement gestures (smiling, sharing toys or food, giving a compliment), but they do it for a different purpose. Followers use these non-verbal signals in order to be liked. Leaders use them in order to achieve a goal.

Aggressive children may have a high status in some groups of children, but they are not considered to be true leaders. Aggressive children dominate through fear and intimidation. When they cannot get their way by frightening other children they have no power and they typically become socially isolated.

Popular children typically have well developed leadership skills, although this is not always the case. Some children gain temporary popularity due to superficial qualities, such as physical attractiveness, athletic ability, or even the social status of their families. On the other hand, children who are popular throughout their development and into their adulthood have a variety of leadership skills, including an unwavering interest in the welfare of others.

For example, when aged fifteen, Linda was considered to have very plain looks. She was not unattractive, but her hairstyle and clothes were not particularly flattering and she did not seem to take any interest in make-up or other fashion trends. Linda was not 'popular', by conventional standards, but she was liked by everyone. Year after year Linda was voted to be a school prefect. She was also considered to be a leader in her church group and in her community.

Linda left secondary school with excellent grades to study nursing. Now in her thirties with her own small children, Linda is the sister in the paediatric ward of a major hospital. She is still active in her community and in her children's school programmes and her many friends are in awe of how she can do so many things so successfully.

While it is gratifying to have children who are popular and well-liked by their peers, it is the leadership qualities that you instil in your child which will help her fulfil her intellectual, emotional and social potentials as she grows. These qualities will not only contribute to her sense of self-worth, but they will also make her less susceptible to peer pressure and less likely to participate in high-risk behaviours like drinking or experimenting with drugs.

There are many character traits that contribute to making someone a leader (such as the desire to pursue excellence, having respect for others and the ability to persevere in the face of frustration). But for now we will just look at some of the behaviours that define leadership in children and teenagers, and how these behaviours can be taught if they do not come naturally to your child. It is worth noting that your child does not have to learn all of these skills. Some may be harder for your child than others. But even a small improvement in any one of these skills can make a difference in your child's social and emotional development.

Teach your child to initiate projects and activities

Children are much more likely to suggest new ideas when they are interested in a particular subject or activity. That is why it is important to help your child develop a passion for at least one thing that naturally interests him. For example, Zach is an American child who has been interested in geography since he was three years old. By five he would amaze his parents' friends by naming every one of the 50 US state capitals.

It will not surprise you that most of Zach's contemporaries did not share his love of maps or his interest in the effect of climate on world agriculture, but his parents encouraged him anyway. They took him to museums and lectures and planned their vacations to include tours of historical sites, nature walks and even archaeological digs. At least twice a month, they let Zach plan a field trip for the family. They would designate a whole day and a budget of $50 for the activity of Zach's choice.

Archaeology became Zach's primary passion by the time he was eleven, and his parents found a young archaeologists' camp for him to attend in the summer. It was there that his leadership ability became focused. The confidence and knowledge that had been fostered by his parents earned him the award of 'camper of the year'.

Teach your child 'refusal skills'

In the mid-1980s, when drug education for children first became a priority, the most popular slogan to motivate children to avoid experimenting with drugs was: 'Just say "No".' I remember thinking at the time that it was a naïve assumption to think that it was easy for children to do this.

If you will think back to your own childhood and teenage years, you know that it is hard to stand up to peer pressure. This is particularly true for children who are naturally prone to 'going along with the group' and trying to win the approval of others. Having children or teenagers practise how to react in different situations where peer pressure might induce them to participate in inappropriate or high-risk behaviour is the only way I know to protect them. It is often helpful to give children or teenagers a script to use while acting out a scene similar to one that they might encounter with their peers.

I tried this technique with Carrie, a 17-year-old girl who had been referred to me because her parents were concerned that her flirtatious manner and poor impulse control would soon get her into serious trouble. Carrie had been diagnosed with ADHD when she was seven years old. Ten years later she was certainly not as active or inattentive as when she was younger, but like many teenagers with ADHD, she still had poor judgement and poor social skills. A pretty girl, Carrie found it hard to resist the attentions of the many boys who wanted her to sneak up to their bedrooms or check into a nearby hotel.

To give Carrie practice in handling situations that would be true to her experience, I enlisted the aid of a peer counsellor in Carrie's secondary school. Patrick, also seventeen, had been trained to help other students with a variety of issues including counselling students who were engaging in high-risk behaviours. Peer counselling pro-grammes are increasingly being seen as the 'treatment of choice' for many teenagers who are reluctant to talk to adults about their per-sonal problems. I suggested that Patrick and Carrie write a script together where he would play an aggressively seductive boy and she would play herself. I suggested that the play consist of just a single scene and emphasized that it should include different ways for Carrie to successfully deal with this type of boy. I asked them to videotape themselves acting out the play so that we could all watch it together.

Having Carrie watch herself on video was also an important part of her learning. Getting a visual image of yourself performing a new skill, whether it is learning to serve a tennis ball or practising new social skills, is the quickest way I know to change your behaviour.

Another important technique we used was to have Carrie keep track of her newly acquired refusal skills. I asked her to keep a daily diary of her thoughts and feelings and in particular to note when she felt that she was using her new social skills appropriately. She shared this diary with Patrick on a weekly basis.

A few months later Carrie announced to me that she was a 'new woman' and that aggressive boys were no longer a problem. Although I knew that similar issues of peer pressure would cer-tainly affect Carrie in the future, as they do for most young women and young men, I felt that her new found social poise could form the basis for making more responsible decisions.

TRY IT

If you are concerned that your child is overly influenced by peer pressure, then write a Social Skills Script with her to practise more assertive behaviour. Keep the script short and make sure that your child thinks that it is realistic. Make it clear to your child that this is not about her, but about someone like her who might have similar problems with her peers. Videotape the play and watch it together. Switch roles and see how this looks on video. Emphasize to your child that peer pressure is not just a problem for children or teenagers but that it is a lifelong concern for many adults as well. Tell her that if you learn to practise new leadership skills, you can become the kind of person who makes decisions based on your beliefs and values rather than the desire to please others.

Helping children who are socially rejected

There are few things that are more painful to a child than being rejected by his peer group. Social rejection goes beyond teasing or bullying, which typically involves only one or two pupils. The socially rejected child cannot find even one other person he can talk to, play with or share common interests.

Even in this age when children are taught about the importance of understanding others and tolerating diversity, the primary reason for social rejection is that a child is perceived as different. This could be because of: physical differences, such as obesity, physical deformity or handicap; cultural differences, such as religion or accent; or psychological differences that make a particular child seem odd to others.

Michael, the 15-year-old I described at the beginning of this chapter, certainly fitted into the last category. His obsessive interest in arcane information about New York City and his inability to relate to others made other students as well as adults treat him like a pariah. When I worked with Michael, in the mid-1970s, I thought that he was 'one of a kind', an odd student who had some kind of psychological problem, although I did not know exactly what it was. Now, more than twenty-five years later, I know that Michael was not one of a kind, but probably one of thousands of children who are diagnosed with Asperger's Syndrome or high-functioning autism.

In the last ten years there has been a significant amount of attention paid to this diagnosis as professionals find more and more children who, like Michael, are very bright but socially inept. Although there is considerable debate as to the exact constellations of symptoms that define these disorders (children with similar symptoms are also sometimes diagnosed as having a pervasive development disorder, or PDD), these children share common problems of being unable to use non-verbal behaviour to regulate their social interaction. As a result they have few or no friends.

Although these children can have a wide variety of unusual behaviours, from obsessive interests to odd repetitive behaviours, it is their inability to learn the most basic skills of social interaction that is usually of most concern. Helping these children be aware of their problem in relating to others, and providing them with specialized help, can make the difference between whether these bright youngsters will go on to college and pursue a rewarding career, or whether they will continue to be rejected as they become adults, holding jobs beneath their ability and living a life devoid of friends and intimate relationships.

If your child has severe problems in relating to others, you must be patient and not expect quick improvement. On the other hand, once you help your child become aware of his need for better social skills, little things can make a difference. For example, Ed, a 10-year-old diagnosed with Asperger's Syndrome, was taught to give a quick wave to other pupils as he passed them in the school hallway. He told his counsellor, 'I didn't know you were supposed to do that! When I wave, people wave back at me and smile at me. That's a nice feeling.'

Or there is Paul, a 17-year-old who excelled in virtually every school subject, particularly the sciences. But he had never been invited to another pupil's home, never had a telephone conversation with another pupil and certainly had never been out on a date. In a social skills group, Paul was taught the importance of taking turns in a conversation, or what communication specialists call 'reciprocity'. In videotaped practise sessions, Paul was taught to:

- Listen to another person's conversation and wait for a pause before speaking.
- When speaking, every thirty seconds look for signs that the other person is still interested in what you are saying. These signs might include:
  - The other person breaks eye contact.
  - The other person turns his body away from you.
  - The expression on the other person's face seems bored or disinterested.
  - The other person takes a step back or shifts his chair away from you.
- When wanting to say something while someone else is talking, raise his index finger in an upward motion.
- If the other person gestures to 'stop' (hand up, palm forward) or 'wait' (raised index finger), then wait until they finish their thought, pausing in their conversation.

TRY IT

Reciprocity is a critical social skill for children to learn in order to make and keep friends. If you think that your child interrupts others too much, or he does not listen to what is being said, you might want to play the 'Conversation Game' to help teach him better social interaction skills.

Make about ten conversation cards like those listed below. Shuffle the cards and choose the top card to start. Set a timer for ten minutes and, sitting across from your child, engage him in a conversation with the goal that each person should talk an equal amount of time. Remind your child of the non-verbal cues that indicate when a person wants to say something or when they are not listening to what is being said (see the list made for Paul above). You may want to write out this list on a piece of paper to act as a reminder to your child. At the end of the conversation each person should try to paraphrase what the other person has said. This will clearly indicate that each person has had a chance to express his opinions and that the other person has listened.

Conversation cards

- Talk about your favourite holiday.
- Talk about your hobby or another interest.
- Talk about your favourite movie.
- Talk about something that was mentioned in today's newspaper.
- Talk about something that happened at school or work.
- Talk about an upcoming sports or community event.
- Talk about the 'best day' you ever had.
- Talk about something that happened recently that made you laugh.
- Talk about your favourite restaurant and why you like it.
- Talk about someone you admire.

If you believe that your child has severe problems in his social skills, then you should certainly seek an expert's advice. Children with social skill problems will certainly benefit from specialized groups, but this will rarely be enough. Just as with other aspects of the secret language, improving a child's social communication takes constant practice, every day if possible. Here are some basic guidelines in teaching your child social skills:

Decide which are the most important skills for your child to learn (see the social skills checklist below).

Teach concrete skills and break them down into small steps. For example, if you want your child to invite a friend over, first he must learn how to make a simple short phone call. Then he must learn how to select an activity that he and another child would enjoy. Then he must decide on another child who would be likely to accept his invitation.

Motivate your child by setting a concrete goal and then rewarding him for achieving that goal. A social goal might be: 'Playing a board game with another child for fifteen minutes without arguing.' If your child does this, then perhaps both children could get a treat.

Provide opportunities for your child to practise new social skills. Certainly you can encourage your child to practise social skills at home, particularly in family meetings or in conversations that you have with your child. Also find social situations that your whole family can participate in. It is important that children see their parents in social situations to understand the importance of developing their social skills and to also see them as role models. I usually recommend that families seek community service activities, or projects sponsored by a church or synagogue or other place of worship. Groups that are organized for the purpose of helping others are naturally more inclined to be patient with children or teenagers who have social skill problems.

Finally, encourage your child to join groups of children with similar interests. It may be a junior football league, a stamp collectors' club, even a group that swaps trading cards. It will be much easier for your child to practise skills with children who share common interests than with children with whom he has little or nothing in common.

TRY IT

The following social skills checklist is based on the social body language skills suggested by Sally Ozonoff, Geraldine Dawson and James McPartland in their book *A Parent's Guide to Asperger Syndrome and High-Functioning Autism*. They note that these are the major skills taught in social skills groups, but add that for children to be effective in using them, they must also be practised in the home. You can use this list as an informal way to assess your child's social skills and to see in which areas he is strongest or weakest.

Rate each skill on the social skills checklist on a 1 to 5 scale, with 1 equal to poor and 5 equal to excellent. You may want to make a second copy of this checklist and give it to your child's teacher or to your spouse to fill in as it is often helpful to see if different adults have a different perspective on your child.

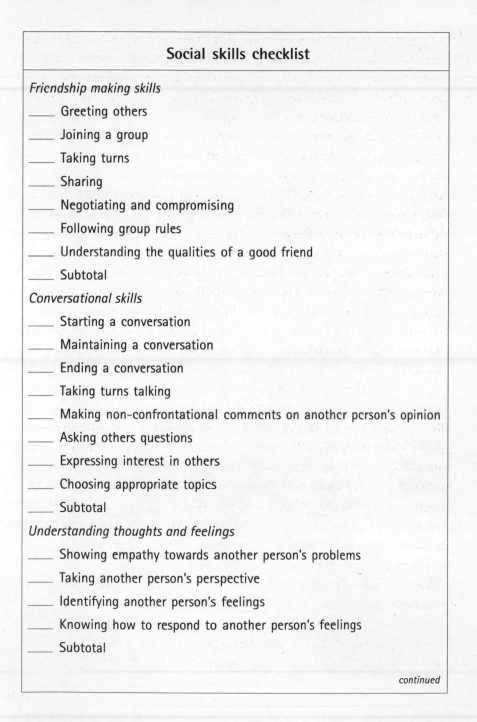

Social skills checklist

Friendship making skills

_____ Greeting others

_____ Joining a group

_____ Taking turns

_____ Sharing

_____ Negotiating and compromising

_____ Following group rules

_____ Understanding the qualities of a good friend

_____ Subtotal

Conversational skills

_____ Starting a conversation

_____ Maintaining a conversation

_____ Ending a conversation

_____ Taking turns talking

_____ Making non-confrontational comments on another person's opinion

_____ Asking others questions

_____ Expressing interest in others

_____ Choosing appropriate topics

_____ Subtotal

Understanding thoughts and feelings

_____ Showing empathy towards another person's problems

_____ Taking another person's perspective

_____ Identifying another person's feelings

_____ Knowing how to respond to another person's feelings

_____ Subtotal

continued

Social problem solving

_____ Coping with being told 'no'

_____ Handling teasing or bullying

_____ Coping with being left out

_____ Handling anger in others

_____ Subtotal

Self-awareness

_____ Knowing your personal strengths

_____ Knowing your unique differences

_____ Accepting your self

_____ Subtotal

_____ Grand total (add all the subtotals together)

If your child has social problems, whether he is three or fifteen, then you should certainly pay attention to his non-verbal skills and how he uses them with his peers. Social success is such an important part of a child's self-image, do not let your child suffer longer than he has to. Many parents are not aware that they can teach their children social skills in much the same way that they help with academic or even athletic skills. All it takes is for you to patiently break down the skills that your child is missing into small steps, and then practise them over and over again. I guarantee that the time you invest in helping your child with his social development will pay lifelong dividends.

Chapter 20

Connecting with and Directing Your Child Using the Secret Language of the Body and Voice

How well do you connect with other people? Would you describe yourself as warm, friendly, sympathetic and an understanding person? Most of us like to think of ourselves as possessing these and similar qualities. But, in fact, some of us have more of these 'people skills' than others and this can make a difference in our effectiveness as parents.

Let us take, for example, Veronica, a 13-year-old who felt that her mother was out of touch with her needs. Veronica wanted to wear make-up to school, but her mother said that she was too young. She thought that she should be allowed to go out on dates, but her mother would not allow this either. She had pierced ears, but she said that her friends were also getting their navel pierced and she wanted a belly button ring too.

When Veronica's mother, Liz, found marijuana hidden in her daughter's room, she felt that she needed some help in dealing with her daughter's precociousness before things got out of hand. So she made an appointment with the school counsellor.

'I try to talk to her all of the time,' the single mother explained, 'but she doesn't want to hear what I have to say. Take last night. I was cleaning up after dinner, washing and rinsing the dishes and Veronica was right there. So I said, "How was your day, dear?" Instead of answering, she just turned and stalked out of the kitchen and screamed, "As if you really care!" Now what did I do to deserve that? I was trying to be interested.'

'Tell me more,' said the counsellor, but as Liz continued to talk the counsellor took out her appointment calendar and began to write. Then the counsellor started to search through her desk for something, pulling out scraps of paper and notes. Liz stopped talking and the counsellor looked up. 'Go ahead,' the counsellor said to the increasingly distraught parent, 'I'm listening.' And the counsellor opened a drawer busily searching for something.

'No, you're not listening!' said Liz with indignation in her voice. Then she said, 'Oh', suddenly mollified, 'I see what you mean. I was listening to Veronica but also doing the dishes, so she felt as if I wasn't listening. You were just making me feel like Veronica must have.'

'That's right,' the counsellor agreed, but shaking her head 'no', trying to make the point again non-verbally. 'When you give your child mixed messages, when your words say one thing and your body says another, children are bound to get angry.'

Many well-meaning parents make mistakes that are similar to Liz's. It is not that they do not care about their children, but rather their non-verbal behaviour is not consistent with their verbal messages. When this happens, children can get the feeling that their parents are not sincere and that their words are not believable. They may get angry, like Veronica, or they may just withdraw and isolate themselves. Whatever their immediate reaction, the long-term result is that they will feel misunderstood by their parents and resentment is likely to follow.

Mixed messages can affect the relationship between parents and their children at any age. Recently I overheard Clarissa, the mother of 4-year-old Justine, complain: 'Justine just doesn't listen me or seem to even care about what I want! Every morning we fight over what she will wear to school. Every evening we fight about what she will eat for dinner. She talks back to me and doesn't seem to care at all about my feelings. Today I turned around and Justine was sticking her tongue out at me for no reason at all!' Clarissa wanted to know how to discipline her daughter so that she would be more respectful and compliant.

Now you might be thinking to yourself that 4-year-olds have a reputation for being difficult and this might explain Clarissa's problem in getting her child to listen. But the natural desire of a 4-year-old to be more independent and to assert her will should not permeate her relationship with her parents. Being strong-willed at four, or any age for that matter, is a character trait, not a lifestyle. The problem that Clarissa is having with her daughter is not about discipline, it is about her relationship with her child, the basic connection of affection and mutual respect that is supposed to make parenting a joy. But the mutual frustration and misunderstanding between Clarissa and her daughter makes every day seem more difficult than the next and sets the stage for years of self-doubt and unhappiness for both mother and daughter.

Fortunately there is a solution for this mother and the tens of thousands of other parents who feel that they are disconnected from their children or teenagers. Better communication skills – particularly non-verbal skills – can be effective in rebuilding relationships at any age. The skills I will discuss in this chapter can help you in developing a better relationship with your child, as well as your spouse, or friends, or boss, or colleagues. Everyone responds to the secret language of non-verbal communication.

The building blocks of connecting to children

When a child is referred for counselling, whether it is for shyness, a behavioural problem or adjustment to a divorce, the first thing that a therapist must do is build a relationship based on trust. This is also true if you are trying to help your child with a problem at home. Having an open and trusting relationship with your child will give you a foundation to help him through any kind of emotional difficulty, at any age.

Researchers also tell us that having a positive connection to your child is the best way to prevent emotional and behavioural problems. When we survey teenagers who are high achievers, who have an active social life and positive values, we almost always find that they describe their relationship with their parents as closer than the relationships their friends have with their parents.

You can begin increasing your positive connection to your child by simply paying more attention to your non-verbal language. Whether you are playing a board game, reading a story or just having a conversation over dinner, pay attention to your body language and voice tone as well as your words. Here are some things to keep in mind.

Use a calm and warm voice tone to convey your interest

When we refer to someone as 'warm', we are often picking up on their voice tone and quality. Generally speaking we associate voice 'warmth' with a lower register, a slower and more deliberate way of speaking and a calm though slightly animated tone. Some people are born with a naturally warm voice tone. Listen to the news on television or the radio and you will probably hear people who are born with a natural voice quality that makes them seem trustworthy and likable.

Whatever your natural way of speaking, you probably have much more control of your voice tone than you realize. When you want to connect with your child or teenager you should speak in a relaxed, but naturally animated voice. Think about trying to convey warmth and your brain will know what to do.

This is particularly important to do if your child seems distressed about something. Your calm and reassuring tone will make it easier for him to open up.

TRY IT

Tape record a conversation that you have with your child for at least five or ten minutes. Listen to your voice tone and to his. Be objective in analysing your voice. Do you express your emotion in your voice? Does your voice change in its pitch and volume as you discuss different topics? Does your child respond differently to changes in your voice tone? If you are not happy with what you hear, try and exaggerate your voice in your next conversation. If you speak quickly, consciously try to speak more slowly. If your voice sounds high pitched, try to lower it. Tape another conversation with your child and see if you hear a difference and if your child reacts to you in a different way.

Remove barriers between yourself and your child. Create an 'intimate' space

When you are trying to make a connection with your child, it is important to give him your full and undivided attention. Many people do not realize that even when they are trying to be open, available and interested, they still give off the impression of being guarded and defensive. This is because they put barriers between themselves and the person they are talking to.

A barrier can be any physical object that is placed between you and your child: a book or newspaper, your sewing, the kitchen table, the laundry that you are folding on your lap. Barriers also include the common disruptions that occur in every household like the phone ringing, loud music from another room or even the comings and goings of another family member. If you are serious about connecting with your child, then you must try to eliminate all of these interruptions.

Even better than just removing barriers, you can create an intimate space for you and your child which will encourage closeness and warmth. Perhaps you have comfortable cushions that you can put on the floor to define a physical space separating you and your child from the rest of the room. Or maybe you are lucky enough to live near a park where you can find a grassy spot that will be a special place for you and your child to go to connect. Your child is likely to respond to your non-verbal efforts without really being able to define what is different about you. But believe me, you will feel the difference in your relationship immediately.

Use an 'open' posture and gestures. Be on the same eye level as your child.

When I am working with a parent and child in counselling, I frequently invite them to play together. I will ask the child to select a toy or game from my bookshelf and bring it over to the centre of the room. Then I wait to see what happens. At least half of the time the child takes a seat on the carpet and the parent remains in the chair, even though they are supposedly playing together.

Your posture and eye level say a lot about your desire to be with your child and it is something that your child immediately picks up on. Facing away from your child, or sitting with closed body language, with your legs crossed or your arms folded across your lap, will give your child the non-verbal message that you are only half-present. To give your child your full attention, sit facing him at the same eye level and make sure that your posture conveys a relaxed and attentive attitude. Ask your child to do the same by saying something like, 'Let's face each other when we talk. That way we can see as well as hear what the other person is saying.'

Find a comfortable distance that is right for you and your child

Physical distance is an important issue in all emotional communication. Most young children want to be close to their parents and would rather sit on your lap than sit next to you. A typical teenager, on the other hand, would just as soon be on the other side of the room. Researchers tell us that a good distance for a personal conversation is between eighteen inches and four feet. Closer than this is considered a person's intimate space and is fine for hugs and cuddles or good natured rough-and-tumble, but it is not good for a conversation. One reason is that when we get too close to another person it is more difficult to make prolonged eye contact and eye contact is probably the most important aspect of feeling emotionally connected.

Pay attention to what you and your child say to each other using eye contact

Joel, an ex-marine who considered himself a strict but loving father, demanded that his two boys, aged twelve and fourteen, look at him when he talked. Even if they were eating a meal, he expected them to put down their knives and forks and make eye contact with him when he was speaking. Joel believed that making eye contact with someone was a sign of respect and that avoiding eye contact was a sign of disrespect and weakness.

But Joel was oversimplifying this aspect of emotional communication. While it is true that you need to look at someone to take in the subtle forms of non-verbal communication, sustained eye contact is not natural to the way that people converse. Making and breaking eye contact is necessary for a fluid give and take conversation. People normally break eye contact when they stop to think about something and look back when they want to express their thoughts or hear the thoughts of the other person. You and your child also use eye contact to establish the rhythm of your conversation. A speaker makes eye contact less than a listener, but then signals that he is ready to listen when he glances at the speaker and waits for a response.

Paying attention to your eye contact as you talk or play with your child can be a good way to gauge your relationship. As you look at your child and he looks at you, you should also pay attention to other aspects of his facial expression. When his eyes are open wide and his eyebrows are raised, he is showing interest. When he is covering part of his face with his hands or giving you a forced smile, he may be only giving you half of his attention. If you do not feel connected to your child during a conversation, then trust your intuition. Try changing the subject or telling a joke. Try doing an activity together that you both enjoy, like cooking or playing a game of catch. Making an effort to connect with your child or teenager will give him the most important message: 'I will find a way to show you how I care for you.'

Pay attention to your child's need for touch and physical comfort

Parents are constantly in physical contact with their infants and toddlers, but by the age of three, after the child has been toilet trained, learned to dress herself and is too heavy to pick up and carry, physical contact between parents and their children begins to decline. By the time the child is six or seven there is a noticeable drop in physical contact, as children shift their interests and energies towards their peers.

Yet even as your child gets older, touch remains an important part of the way you communicate your emotions to him. You convey affection by a kiss on the cheek, by stroking your child's arm or simply by holding his hand. You can also convey many other important emotions through touch such as sympathy (holding firmly, patting), security (holding hands, linking arms, arm around shoulders), nurturing (brushing hair, adjusting clothing) and much more.

Your physical contact with your older child or teenager will largely depend on your own comfort level with touch. As I mentioned in Chapter 18, the UK is considered a 'low-touch' culture and many parents, particularly fathers, feel awkward making physical contact with their older children.

Although this is certainly understandable, it is also important to remember that touch is a way of expressing affection and caring. The most important thing to remember is that your physical contact must feel comfortable for you and your child and support your emotional connection.

TRY IT

How much physical contact does your child need or desire? Use the checklist below to see how much touching you do with your child in a given day and whether your child seems to want more or less physical contact. Put a tick by each type of physical contact that you make with your child, noting his reaction. Then decide if your child needs more or less physical contact to stay connected with you.

___ Patting	Your child's reaction _____
___ Stroking	Your child's reaction _____
___ Kissing	Your child's reaction _____
___ Holding	Your child's reaction _____
___ Guiding	Your child's reaction _____
___ Embracing	Your child's reaction _____
___ Linking arms	Your child's reaction _____
___ Grooming	Your child's reaction _____
___ Tickling	Your child's reaction _____

It goes without saying that I am only talking about appropriate touch between parents and children. Erotic touch is never appropriate between parents and children at any age or in any circumstance. I am not just referring to the inappropriateness of touching erogenous zones of the body; even a simple shoulder massage can be erotic if sexual feelings are present.

If you are concerned for even a moment that physical contact between you and your child is inappropriate, then assume that it is. We are faced with a paradox because humans naturally use touch to express positive emotions to those we care for and yet our heightened awareness of the frequency of child abuse in the family and its devastating effects on children must make parents always err on the side of caution.

Mirror your child's movements to build rapport

In her book *Influencing with Integrity*, business consultant Genie Laborde notes that although it may feel strange, one of the most successful ways to build rapport with someone is to mirror their non-verbal language. She notes that when you mirror another person's voice tone and volume, their postures and gestures, and even their breathing, people feel more in tune with you and become more agreeable.

Ms Laborde admits that no one knows exactly why this happens, but she suggests that the laws of nature and physics seem to want everything to be synchronized. She notes that, 'Different sized clocks with the same sized pendulums, when placed together on a wall, will gradually synchronize their swings.' Students of body language have pointed out that when adults are engaged in an intimate conversation, they typically fall into their own natural rhythm. When one leans forward, the other moves back. When one person scratches his nose with his left hand, the other might pull on her ear with her right hand.

Although this type of mirroring may occur naturally, if you consciously try it with your child it may not feel natural at all. Do not worry about trying to mimic your child, just try to get in the same rhythm. If he swings his leg back and forth while you are talking, you might try tapping a pencil on the table to the same beat. If he sighs or takes a deep breath, just slow your breathing down a little bit, exhaling in a steady stream of air.

If nothing else, this conscious awareness of your body language and that of your child will make you more attuned to your non-verbal communication and this is a key factor in fostering a positive emotional connection with your child.

Directing your child using the secret language of non-verbal communication

Ten years ago I rarely heard about young children with serious behavioural problems. Of course, I got referrals for young children who had too many tantrums, or were overactive and hard to manage at their nursery school, but these were relatively infrequent. Today it seems that hardly a week goes by that I do not hear about a 3- or 4-year-old in trouble at his nursery school and in danger of being expelled. Expelled! I shake my head and wonder, 'How can a child's behaviour get to be so bad so early in his life that the only solution is to get rid of him?'

But as I talk to other psychologists and to groups of teachers and parents I am faced with the inevitable fact that this is a trend. Children are having more serious behavioural problems than ever before and they are having them significantly earlier in their lives. Perhaps even more disturbing is the fact that parents and teachers do not seem to know what to do. Too often, drastic measures happen too quickly.

For example, Owen was a 4-year-old at a private nursery school where he was known by all the teachers as 'the holy terror'. On an average day he was sent to the headteacher's office three times, which was his punishment for his most serious offences, hitting and biting other children. The head would reprimand Owen and put him in the time-out chair for three minutes. She would usually keep him with her for another fifteen or twenty minutes, just to give his nursery teacher a break.

Owen's less serious offences included screaming, knocking down blocks, throwing toys and running out of the room. One of the adults in the classroom always had an eye on Owen, but he still managed to create an atmosphere of constant havoc. After three months at his school, the school staff gave up. Owen was referred to social services and was soon put on medication.

There are many young children like Owen who are given medication at four or five when this was almost unheard of even a decade ago. I have to believe that we can come up with better alternatives for most of these children if we take the time to discover the secrets behind their emotional and behavioural problems.

Many people believe that we need to pay more attention to the lifestyle of children with behavioural problems. They argue that their behaviour will improve when they watch less television, have a better diet and get more sleep and exercise. I could not agree more.

But I also believe that these children will benefit from the adults in their lives improving their skills in emotional communication. There is no question that some adults, both teachers and parents, are simply better than others at managing the behaviour of children. Through their non-verbal communication they command respect and they get it.

Everyone, adults as well as children, responds differently to recognized authority figures. Consider the images that you get when you think about people in the following professions: a sergeant-major, a headteacher, a policeman and a judge. When I close my eyes, here is what I see:

- *Sergeant-major*: 'In your face' posture. Hands on hips. Loud, commanding voice.
- *Headteacher*: A neatly dressed person, sitting with erect posture at a desk, a countenance showing a mixture of warmth and sternness.
- *Policeman*: Black uniform, full of impressive equipment, shoulders squared back, hands folded on his chest or resting on his hips.

- *Judge*: A long red robe, a wig, a sombre expression, an elevated position that commands authority.

The images that define an authority figure are all aspects of the secret language of non-verbal communication: posture, facial expression, clothing, gesture and so on. Authority figures use their non-verbal communication to convey their power much more than the words that they speak. Their message is seldom misunderstood.

Now I am not suggesting that you act like a drill sergeant, a policeman or any other of these recognized authority figures with your children. But I am suggesting that you can learn to be an authoritative parent with your children (or an authoritative teacher with your pupils) to help youngsters learn to better control their behaviour. Children should be cooperative. Children should follow adult requests and directions without talking back. Children should be respectful and considerate and concerned about others. Learning how to better use your body and voice to convey authority will help your children develop the behavioural control that is so important to their emotional and social development as well as their academic success.

Start with a gesture

Gestures are the most important part of the secret code that we use to convey authority. We typically think of gestures as only involving our hands, but they can also involve our head and overall posture as well. Although we rarely stop to analyse it, we have many ways to convey directions to our children using gestures. We can point to something that is important. We can shake our fingers or our heads to signal 'no'. We can point to our own eyes when we want to say 'look at me as I'm talking.' Body language experts call these 'speech independent' gestures because their meaning is clear without uttering a single word.

Although we must remember that a particular gesture may vary in meaning from culture to culture, here are some gestures that we commonly use to direct children:

Sit down.	Motioning downwards with your index finger, pointing to where the child should sit.
Be quiet.	Raising your index finger to your lips.
Come here.	Curling your index finger towards you and pointing to yourself.
I'm warning you.	A raised index finger, usually held in front of your face, and sometimes shaken.
Pay attention.	Usually done with a gaze, such as raising one's eyebrows and widening one's eyes. Also can include a tilting of one's head downwards or to the side.
Follow me.	Motioning with one's whole arm in an arc, starting by pointing at the child and ending by pointing in the direction that you are going in.
Time to go.	Pointing to your watch or wrist.
Look!	Excited pointing towards an object, usually combined with a widening of the eyes.
Go.	Pointing away from you, or flicking your hand and wrist in a 'shooing' motion.

To get your child to be more cooperative, try being more aware of how you use gestures, particularly as a way to underscore the meaning of your words. For example, when you want your child to get off the swing say 'Come here' firmly and also motion with your index finger towards the spot that you want your child to come. Using directional gestures with your words is equivalent to underlining a word when you are writing. When you use gestures to underscore your words, your child knows that this request or directive is more important than other things being said.

You should also use gestures to give positive reinforcement to your child when he is behaving in accordance with your requests or directions. Verbal praise can be a powerful way to shape a child's behaviour, but non-verbal reinforcement can be even more effective.

TRY IT

As the parent of a sometimes stubborn preschool child myself, I am always trying to shape my daughter's behaviour so that she will use good table manners, pick up her toys and be cooperative and respectful to others. When she does what I want, I try to use gestures to go along with my words of praise. See how many gestures you can use in showing your approval for the good behaviour of your child and take note if he or she acts more cooperatively. Here are some examples of gestures in our culture that indicate your approval:

• Thumbs up.

• Index finger and thumb making a circle with other three fingers extended ('A OK!')

• A brief clap of your hands.

• Both hands raised high in the air with fists clenched (as athletes often do after scoring a goal or winning a race).

Naturally, if you have a young child like I do, you will want to make sure that your child understands the meaning of a gesture before you use it. When she was an infant my daughter learned that clapping is a sign of approval, but until recently she did not know that a 'thumbs up' sign was also a way to say 'good job'. But after only a few times combining a praise with this gesture (along with a smile of appreciation) she learned that this was one of my common signs of pleasure at her cooperative behaviour.

Using non-verbal cues

Another way to use gestures to get your child to be more cooperative is by using them as cues. Most classroom teachers use non-verbal cues to get the attention of their children. They may flick the lights on and off, or stand in front of the board and tap on it. I knew one parent (a former teacher) who rang a bell to signal to her children that it was time to wash their hands before dinner, and another who played a rousing march on her tape recorder to signal to her children that they should 'march up and get ready for bed'.

Thomas Phelan, the author of a popular book on discipline, *1–2–3 Magic*, suggests that you can use finger counting to make your children understand that they have three chances to stop a particular misbehaviour. Your raised index finger is the first warning. Your raised middle finger is the second warning. Your raised ring finger means, 'You haven't stopped misbehaving, now you will get a time-out.' One of the many parents I have met who is an enthusiastic advocate of this technique told me: 'You can't believe how quickly children learn to respond to these cues when they see that you mean business. One or two times I have had to put my child in time-out when he didn't respond to the cues, but that was it. Now I never get past the count of "one". When I raise my index finger, he immediately stops what he is doing, because he knows that if he continues he will get into trouble.'

Talk like you mean it

Effective communicators use their voice to keep their listener's attention. Ineffective communicators have little or no awareness of their voice quality. They may speak in a monotone or mumble their words. They may be so quiet that their listener can hardly hear them, or so loud that they annoyingly dominate a conversation. How good are you at controlling your voice tone to convey your authority? If you have young children, you should remember that they are much more sensitive to voice tone and volume than older children and you should vary your voice to go along with the importance of your message.

You should also be aware that yelling at your child is not an effective way to get cooperation. Yelling is a verbal assault and as such must be defended against by the person being yelled at. One mother constantly yells at her 5-year-old when he does not do what she wants – which is frequently. He predictably dissolves into tears when his mother raises her voice and it takes her nearly half an hour to calm him down again. But this does nothing to stop his misbehaviour. He has learned that crying will stop his mother's verbal assault, but he has not learned anything about being more cooperative. Another young boy I know assumes a karate stance when his father yells at him and he yells back, 'You can't yell at me, I'll tell Mummy on you.' My point is that yelling will only make your child be more defensive, it will not make him more compliant.

Virtually every book on disciplining your child emphasizes that you should use a firm but calm voice tone when dealing with your child's misbehaviour. Consequences for misbehaviour, whatever they may be, should also be given in a neutral tone. In their book *Backtalk: 4 Steps to Ending Rude Behavior in Your Kids*, Audrey Ricker and Carolyn Crowder note that after an appropriate consequence is given for rude behaviour, you must immediately disengage from the struggle and calmly go on with life. The authors insist that to effectively change your child's behaviour you must avoid a battle of wills with your child, explaining: 'After enacting the consequence [do not] show any response to the child in your body language or your voice and facial expressions. The child will soon quit, because the action is no longer getting the negative-attention responses from you he wants – hurt, anger, helplessness and irritation.'

Finding different ways to relate to your child using non-verbal communication should not be a difficult task. After all, you are already adept at modifying your non-verbal communication to suit many different situations. You are certainly very conscious of your non-verbal behaviour if you are pulled over by a policeman, if you go for a job interview or if you are trying to make an impression at a social gathering. Probably no one has told you how to behave in these circumstances. You just follow your instincts. In these situations and in countless others, you not only pay attention to what you say, but how you say it, through your voice tone, gestures, posture and so on. You know that paying attention to your non-verbal communication will more readily get you the results that you want.

This is also true of parenting. Paying attention to your non-verbal communication with your children will more readily get you the results that you want. Of course, you do not want to be self-conscious about your behaviour all of the time, but as you think more frequently about how your non-verbal behaviour affects your relationship with your child, this powerful way of enhancing your communication will soon become second nature.

The Importance of Emotional Education

Most parents readily accept their role in helping their children with traditional education. They encourage early reading skills, go over their children's homework and guide them in selecting courses which will aid them in the career of their choice. But today's children need more from their parents. They need them to take an active role in their emotional education as well.

Helping children with their emotional development is not a parenting skill that was required of past generations. It was assumed that children would go through the normal stages of emotional and social development without any special guidance from their parents. It was assumed that they would just learn about their own feelings and the feelings of others and would act according to conventional values. This was the natural order of things.

But the natural order of things has changed for children. There are now influences on the emotional and social development of children that no one could have anticipated even ten years ago, and parents, too, must change with the times. By 2010, there will be more children living with separated parents than with their two natural parents. An increase in sedentary lifestyles and changes in family eating habits have made childhood obesity a real problem. Nearly twice as many children are diagnosed with depression as twenty years ago and they are showing symptoms at a much earlier age. In spite of a decade of drug prevention awareness programmes, drug and alcohol abuse can be found at virtually every British secondary school and there are no signs of an imminent reduction in this problem. An unprecedented number of our children are diagnosed with behavioural problems like ADHD and an unprecedented number of these youngsters are being treated with powerful drugs. Parents must take heed.

Certainly the media must share the responsibility for the increase in the emotional problems of children. Child advocate James Steyer reports in his book, *The Other Parent: The Inside Story of the Media's Effect on Our Children*, on the appalling exposure of today's children to sex and violence. One study carried out in 2001 found that the average child in the United States, who watches nearly twenty hours of TV a week, is exposed to over 14,000 sexual references each year. Another study estimated that by the time that American children enter middle school, they have seen eight thousand killings and a hundred thousand acts of violence on broadcast television. Neither of these studies included the influence of video games, movies, music or satellite or cable TV. With the current trends in British television programming, and its high American content, the situation in the United Kingdom cannot be that different.

Obviously parents can limit the risk factors that can so drastically affect their child's emotional development. Nearly any parenting book you pick up will advise you to go back to the basics: watch your child's diet, do not spoil him, make sure that he gets plenty of exercise and sleep and drastically curtail his use of television and video games. But given the pervasive changes in our culture over the last twenty years, I believe that parents need to go one step more. They need to be proactive in shaping the emotional lives of their children, just as they are proactive in guiding their children's intellectual growth.

As you have found out in this book there are many ways to support your child's emotional growth – through play, through art, through stories and by increasing your awareness of his non-verbal communication and social development. I hope that you will take some time in your busy day to try out some of these techniques. The increasing emotional and behavioural problems of children should no longer be a secret and it should not be a secret that parents can play a significant part in helping children solve these problems. I will be very gratified if any of the thoughts and ideas in this book have helped you in raising happy, healthy and successful children.

References & Further Reading

Barkley, Russel. *Taking Charge of ADHD*. New York: Guilford Press, 2000.

Bennet, William J. *Book of Virtues*. New York, NY: Simon & Schuster, 1995.

Bodiford-McNeil, Cheryl and Eyeberg, Sheila M. *Short Term Therapy for Disruptive Children*. Plainview, NY: Childswork/Childsplay, 1996.

Brown, Marc and Laurene. *Dinosaur's Divorce*. New York: Little, Brown, 1988.

Devine, Monica. *Baby Talk: The Art of Communicating with Infants and Toddlers*. New York: Insight Books, 1991.

Duke, Marshall, Nowicki, Stephen, and Martin, Elisabeth. *Teaching Your Child the Language of Social Success*. Atlanta, GA: Peachtree Publishing, 1996.

Elmore, Tim. *Nurturing the Leader Within Your Child*. Nashville, TN: Nelson Publishers, 2001.

Garcia, Joseph. *Sign with Your Baby*. Seattle, WA: Northlight Communications, 1999.

Gardner, Richard A., *Dr Gardner's Stories About the Real World*, vol. 2, Cresskill, NJ: Creative Therapeutics, 1983.

Gardner, Richard A. *The Boys and Girls Book About Divorce*. New York: Bantam Young Readers, 1985.

Goleman, Daniel. *Emotional Intelligence*. New York: Bantam Books, 1995.

Gross, Ruth Belov. *You Don't Need Words*. New York: Scholastic, Inc. 1991.

Hogg, Tracy. *Secrets of the Baby Whisperer: How to Calm, Connect, and Communicate with Your Baby*. New York, NY: Ballantine Publishing, 2001.

Kincher, Jonni. *Dreams Can Help*. Minneapolis, MN: Free Spirit Press, 1988.

Jones, Sandy. *Crying Baby, Sleepless Nights*. Boston, MA: The Harvard Common Press, 1992.

Laborde, Genie. *Influencing with Integrity: Management Skills for Communication & Negotiation*. Palo Alto, CA: Syntony Publishing, 1983.

Lefevre, Dale. *Best New Games: 77 Games and 7 Trust Activities for All Ages and Abilities*. Champaign, IL: Human Kinetics Publishers, 2001.

Levick, Myra. *See What I'm Saying: What Children Tell Us Through Their Art*. Dubuque, IA: 1998.

Lewis, David. *The Body Language of Children*. London: Souvenir Press, 1978.

Lewis, David. *How to Get Your Message Across*. London: Souvenir Press, 1996.

Lieberman, David J. *Get Anyone to Do Anything and Never Feel Powerless Again*. New York: St Martin's Press, 2000.

Lieberman, David. *Never Be Lied to Again*. New York: St Martin's Press, 2000.

Malchiodi, Cathy. *The Art Therapy Sourcebook*. Lincolnwood, IL: Contemporary Books, 1998.

Marano, Hara Estroff. *'Why Doesn't Anybody Like Me' A Guide to Raising Socially Confident Kids*. New York, NY: Quill, 1998.

Masi, Wendy and Leiderman, Roni Cohen (eds). *Baby Play*. San Francisco, CA: Creative Publishing International, 2001.

Medhus, Elisa. *Raising Children Who Think for Themselves*. Hillsboro, OR: Beyond Words Publishing, 2001.

Nowicki, Stephen Jr. and Duke, Marshall. *Helping the Child Who Doesn't Fit In*. Atlanta, GA.: Peachtree Publishers, 1992.

Oppenheim, Joanne. *Kids and Play*. New York: Ballantine Books, 1984.

Orlick, Terry. *The Second Cooperative Sports and Games Book*. New York, NY: Pantheon Books, 1982.

Ozonoff, Sally, Dawson, Geraldine and McPartland, James. *A Parent's Guide to Asperger's Syndrome & High-Functioning Autism*. New York: The Guilford Press, 2002.

Phelan, Thomas W. *1–2–3 Magic: Effective Discipline for Children 2–12*. Glen Ellyn, IL: Child Management, 1995.

Ricker, Audrey and Crowder, Carolyn. *Backtalk: Four Steps to Ending Rude Behavior in Your Kids*. New York: Simon & Schuster, 1998.

Sammons, William. *The Self-Calmed Baby*. New York: St Martin's Press, 1991.

Seligman, Martin. *The Optimistic Child*. New York, NY: HarperPerennial, 1995.

Shapiro, Lawrence E. *How to Raise A Child with a High EQ: A Parents' Guide to Emotional Intelligence*. New York: HarperPerennial, 1997.

Shapiro, Lawrence E. *An Ounce of Prevention: How Parents Can Stop Childhood Behavioral and Emotional Problems Before They Start*. New York: HarperCollins, 2000.

Shapiro, Lawrence. *The Very Angry Day That Amy Didn't Have*. Plainview, NY: Childswork/Childsplay, 1997.

Shure, Myrna. *Raising a Thinking Child*. New York: Pocket Books, 1996.

Silberg, Jackie. *Games to Play with Toddlers*. Beltsville, Md.: Gyphon House, 1993.

Steyer, James. *The Other Parent: The Inside Story of the Media's Effect on Our Children*. San Francisco, CA: Atria Press, 2002.

Thompson, Michael and Grace, Catherine. *Best Friends Worst Enemies*. New York: Ballantine Books, 2001.

Webb, Nancy Boyd (ed.). *Play Therapy with Children in Crisis*. New York: Guilford Press, 1991.

Weston, Denise Chapman and Weston, Mark. *Playful Parenting*. New York: Tarcher/Putnam, 1993.

White, Michael and Epston, David, *Narrative Means to Therapeutic Ends*. New York, NY: W. W. Norton & Co., 1990.

Zinna, Kelly. *After Columbine*. Silverthorne, CO: Spectra Publishing, 1999.

Index